# MENACE
# IN THE
# WEST_____

Recent Titles in
**Contributions in American Studies**
*Series Editor*: Robert H. Walker

In the Driver's Seat: The Automobile in American
Literature and Popular Culture
*Cynthia Golomb Dettelbach*

The United States in Norwegian History
*Sigmund Skard*

Milestones in American Literary History
*Robert E. Spiller*

A Divided People
*Kenneth S. Lynn*

The American Dream in the Great Depression
*Charles R. Hearn*

Several More Lives to Live: Thoreau's Political
Reputation in America
*Michael Meyer*

The Indians and Their Captives
*James Levernier and Hennig Cohen, editors and compilers*

Concerned About the Planet: *The Reporter* Magazine and
American Liberalism, 1949-1968
*Martin K. Doudna*

New World Journeys: Contemporary Italian Writers and
the Experience of America
*Angela M. Jeannet and Louise K. Barnett, editors and translators*

Family, Drama, and American Dreams
*Tom Scanlan*

"Ezra Pound Speaking": Radio Speeches of World War II
*Leonard W. Doob, editor*

The Supreme Court: Myth and Reality
*Arthur Selwyn Miller*

# MENACE IN THE WEST

## The Rise of French Anti-Americanism in Modern Times

DAVID STRAUSS

*Contributions in American Studies, Number 40*

GREENWOOD PRESS

WESTPORT, CONNECTICUT.LONDON, ENGLAND

E
183.8
F8
S83

Library of Congress Cataloging in Publication Data

Strauss, David, 1937-
   Menace in the West.

   (Contributions in American studies; no. 40
ISSN 0084-9227)
   Bibliography: p.
   Includes index.
   1.  United States—Foreign relations—France.
2.  France—Foreign relations—United States.
3.  United States—Foreign opinion, French.
4.  Public opinion—France.  I.  Title.
E183.8.F8S83        301.29′73′044        77-94748
ISBN 0-313-20316-4

Library of Congress Catalog Card Number: 77-94748
ISBN: 0-313-20316-4
ISSN: 0084-9227

First published in 1978

Greenwood Press, Inc.
51 Riverside Avenue, Westport, Connecticut 06880

Printed in the United States of America

10 9 8 7 6 5 4 3 2 1

To my parents

# Contents

# Acknowledgments

A number of organizations and individuals have facilitated the completion of this study through their support, both financial and intellectual. I am grateful to the Fulbright Commission, Columbia University, the Colgate University Research Council, and the Kalamazoo College Faculty Development Committee for grants to pursue my research in France and prepare the manuscript for publication. The following libraries have helped in tracking down the source material for this study: the Bibliothèque Nationale in Paris; the Bibliothèque Municipale and the Bibliothèque Universitaire in Lyon, France; Columbia University; Colgate University and Kalamazoo College. I have also used the Wallace Collection at the American Embassy in Paris, which contains a number of French travel reports on the United States.

At an early stage, this study was read and criticized by Professors Richard Hofstadter, Orest Ranum, Henry Graff, Mark Kesselmann, and Serge Gavronsky. I have benefited from their advice. Parts of the present manuscript have been read by Professors Simon Copans, Simon Jeune, Denise Artaud, and Howard Mumford Jones. Their suggestions have been most helpful. Numerous conversations with Kalamazoo faculty colleagues David Barclay, Robert Stauffer, and David Collins, who share my interest in cross-national studies, have sharpened my grasp of a difficult subject. I am especially grateful to Paul Gagnon and Durand Echeverria, two specialists in the field of Franco-American relations, whose careful scrutiny of the manuscript has helped me to avoid some of the pitfalls of studying images. It goes without saying that I bear the exclusive responsibility for the judgments which appear in this work.

My wife, Anne Strauss, has contributed her proofreading skills and compiled a bibliography of modern French travelers. Her support has been felt in less direct, but more important ways. Lastly, I want to thank four efficient and long-suffering typists: Dorothy Dudley, Helen Richardson, Patricia Ryan, and Dodie Harley.

David Strauss
July 1977
Kalamazoo, Michigan

# MENACE
# IN THE
# WEST_____

# Introduction

It is fashionable for the intelligentsia
to detest America.

—Paul Morand, 1931

In recent years, American intellectuals and policy makers have been particularly sensitive to the views of foreign critics of the American scene. In part, the study of foreign images of America is a case of criticism breeding analysis of criticism, but more deep-seated factors are also at work. As early as 1831, Alexis de Tocqueville noted the thin-skinned American response to criticism of any aspect of the national life.[1] No doubt, this sensitivity has been inherited by modern Americans; however, the preoccupation with outsiders' criticism of the United States since 1945 may be explained by more practical considerations. The views of foreign intellectuals about America do, in fact, affect their countries' relations with the United States, most clearly when intellectuals occupy positions of power or when they instruct the minds of those who do. The American government has acknowledged the importance of and has attempted to influence foreign opinion by creating such agencies as the Peace Corps, the United States Information Agency, and the Fulbright program. These institutions operate on the assumption that foreign elites' unfavorable images of the United States are the product of ignorance or incorrect information and that these impressions will be modified if intellectuals are exposed to more—and more accurate—information about the United States.

The study of foreign observers' images of America is one way of testing the claim that ignorance of and hostility toward America are correlated, but this does not exhaust the potential contributions of such studies. It has long been recognized that citizens of one country, even intellectuals, frequently fail to perceive or analyze the commonplace assumptions, values, and habits which are integral to their everyday life. In this respect, the foreign observer, with an outsider's perspective, may serve a useful function. He may help the native to understand what is frequently taken for granted in the home country.

The interest of foreign intellectuals in American culture, however, cannot be explained entirely by the abstract desire to serve the interests of science in revealing the characteristics of the New World experience. It is the product, as well, of a concrete concern for the future of their own countries. Frequently the foreign observer of the United States undertakes his voyage when old institutions are beginning to fail at home. Projecting his hopes and fears for the future onto the United States, his voyage is a way of testing that future. In this sense, observers of America reveal not only the cultural realities of the New World, but their own concerns and values of the moment. To assess the American scene, descriptions of it and the same elements of French life are juxtaposed. The national identity is reaffirmed in contrast to a foreign experience.

For a variety of reasons, French critics over the years have provided some of the most interesting and useful commentary on the United States. Two factors which have stimulated their interest are the large contribution of Frenchmen to the establishment of the United States and their great hopes for the American future. In addition, the existence of a well-established intellectual community in France during the whole of this two-hundred-year period has provided a continuing source of potential travelers.

For students of anti-Americanism, moreover, the French image of America is of particular interest. French intellectuals have acquired a well-deserved reputation for their skill in articulating hostile views of the United States, a reputation which is particularly baffling in view of the alliance of the two countries in three wars and more recently during the cold war. Sigmund Skard is surely correct in maintaining that "even more than in the case of other nations, the French concepts of American civilization have, right up to the present, been apt to fall into standardized patterns of piecemeal verification of preconceived ideas that are often harshly negative."[2] This study will attempt to shed light on some aspects of the question of French anti-Americanism.

Both the interest of Frenchmen in the United States and the quality of their images of America have varied substantially over time. Certain periods such as the 1770s and the 1830s have been particularly fruitful. In those years, the image of the United States as a model republic and then a conformist democracy took shape in France. To advance the study of recent Franco-American cultural relations it is essential to find a period which has had a comparable effect in shaping the contemporary French image of America. The temptation is strong to stress the years following World War II; however, French commentators on America from that era point us back to the 1920s as the period in which their own views were formed. Jean-Paul Sartre remarked during his visit to the United States in 1945:

When we were twenty, around 1925, we heard about the skyscrapers. They symbolized for us the fabulous American prosperity. We were dazzled by their appearance in the films. They were the architecture of the future, just as the cinema was the art and jazz the music of the future.

He added that "to the eyes of a Frenchman of my generation, New York possesses the melancholy of the past."[3] In view of the formative role which the 1920s played, it is important to review the whole process by which French intellectuals discovered and reacted to American culture in that period.

What makes the 1920s a special decade for Frenchmen is the discovery of an unprecedented volume of cultural influences reaching France, which originated in the United States. American tourists, multinational corporations, jazz bands, American films, and the assembly line were among the most notable of these cultural influences. Taken together, they constituted the first evidence of what we now call "mass culture." Their penetration was observed in the context of increasingly acrimonious disputes over debts, disarmament, security, and reparations which led to the widespread belief among French intellectuals in the decline of France as a world power. Increasingly anxious about their future, they came to America to reflect on the implications of cultural change.

In considering French intellectuals' response to America in the 1920s, several observations about methodology are in order. These concern the principal terms of the inquiry, namely, "anti-Americanism" and "intellectuals." The former has been used in recent years to denote sharp criticism of American policies, frequently resulting in violent demonstrations against the symbols of American power abroad. In its original meaning, however, the word "Americanism" referred to a set of values, practices, and institutions which had their origin in the United States and were far more permanent than official policies. Hence, anti-Americanism was a philosophy, ideology, or institutional framework based on assumptions and principles which ran counter to the Americanist position. In this sense, neither Americanism nor anti-Americanism were confined to the United States, although the Americanist position usually originated in the New World. Indeed, controversy between supporters and opponents of Americanism frequently took place in Europe in the nineteenth century.[4] In this book, the words will again be used in their original sense. They will refer, not to the debate over a particular policy issue, but rather to the views of advocates and critics of the system: that is, the cultural values and institutions which were believed by Frenchmen to be an integral part of American civilization.

While the focus of this study is on the intellectuals who were hostile to America in the 1920s, this should not imply that pro-Americanism was nonexistent in France. It was clearly fashionable by 1930 to attack the United States, but a number of intellectuals either defended the American system as a whole, including some policies of the American government, or expressed a keen interest in aspects of American culture. American technology had its supporters in the French business classes, while artists, musicians, and writers were keenly interested in American films, skyscrapers, and jazz.

The spread of anti-American views was also limited by the capacity of the average French citizen. Most of the works considered here presuppose a certain sophistication about the range of values and institutions upon which a social order might be built. The articulation of such views has traditionally been the function of intellectuals, both in France and elsewhere, although educated members of the public may achieve a greater or lesser understanding of these formulations. It also follows from the complexity of the task that the format for the study of America as a civilization was most likely to be a book or a long essay. Frequently, the occasion for such a study was provided by a trip to the United States: hence, the emphasis here on travel volumes.

While the accounts of travelers comprise a high proportion of the book-length works which deal with America as a civilization, similar books and articles by critics who remained in France have also been included. Indeed, the distinction between travelers and other French authors seems by and large naive. After all, Frenchmen in the twenties who remained in France were fully exposed to American culture and power, which was no longer restricted to the New World. Moreover, the observer who did experience directly the landscape of America could not escape his French predispositions and concerns. The traveler "carries on his shoulders all the time his imagined reader. The perception of every experience is colored by the expectation of telling it and by a fantasy of what the reactions to the story will be."[5]

America and Americans were also important subjects for writers of fiction in France. Poets, dramatists, and novelists portrayed American characters and the American scene as a greater or lesser part of their fictional works in this period. The images which emerge from this literature are an important source of information about the French view of America. Unfortunately, a systematic study of this material is a project as large as the one I have already undertaken. A selective reading of the most important novels and of secondary accounts of fictional works, nonetheless, provides a supplement to the analysis of non-fictional studies of America.

Of course, French periodical literature also dealt extensively with the United States in the 1920s. However, much of this literature reported news, that is, events of the moment. Only rarely were these events analyzed in terms of the enduring values and institutions of the country as occurred in book-length works. Nonetheless, it is also true that the travel literature was influenced by and responded to recent events and the reporting of events in periodicals. Values and institutions in one nation do not change quickly, but they do change and the assessment of them may be influenced by events, particularly momentous ones such as World War I. How, then, can their impact be assessed?

Two means of determining the relationship of events to the French conception of the American system have been employed. First, French studies of America have been scrutinized for the connection of events with the assessment of American culture which was made by the authors themselves. Second, certain leading periodicals in which the work of anti-American intellectuals was frequently serialized have been read for the years 1917-1932. The evolution of the views expressed toward American foreign policy and cultural developments has been correlated with French travelers' assessments of American civilization.

While the attitudes of leading French spokesmen on American civilization to discreet developments in American foreign and domestic policy have been presented, there is no intention to provide an exhaustive account of the nuances of French opinion on Prohibition, immigration restriction, the debt affair, or the security problem. Such a study would be interesting but is not essential to understanding the development of French intellectuals' image of America as a civilization.

In the sixteen-year period which is the primary focus of this study, approximately 175 book-length travel volumes were published in France. The student of this literature is confronted with the problem of discovering whether or not a particular work is either influential or representative. The solution which has been adopted here is to search for acknowledgment of influence from the travelers themselves and to check periodical reviews to determine the receptivity of other intellectuals to a given work. In the process, it becomes clear that a relatively small number of the travel volumes carried an inordinate amount of influence both with other travelers and also with reviewers in periodicals. Hence, the understanding of French views of the American system can be facilitated by examining with special care the works of these individuals and coming to terms with their authors' role in the political and intellectual life of France.

The interpretation of the rise of anti-Americanism in France depends in large measure on the relative importance which is given to the two terms of the problem, namely, the French intellectual and

American civilization.[6] Students of national images have been sharply divided on this question. Some have emphasized the role of the predispositions and concerns of the viewer or subject. Such a conception of the problem is suggested by the question which Hippolyte Taine is reputed to have asked a student of his about to embark on a visit to England. "Young man, what preconceived ideas are you going to verify?"[7] Other scholars have treated national images as representations of actual forces at work in the nation. According to this approach, the cultural distance of the observer from the life of a foreign country makes him a more dispassionate and perceptive analyst than the native critic. Stressing the scientific character of foreigners' observations, one scholar has called travelers "amateur anthropologists."[8]

The inadequacy of both of these approaches for a study of the French image of America in the twenties derives from their assumption of a clear distinction between the observer and the foreign nation. In some cases, the distinction may be valid. In this instance, it is inaccurate. The problems and concerns of the French observer were in no small measure the product of the rising influence of American culture and power in Europe. The aspects of America which the observer chose to represent were usually those which he had actually encountered in Europe. It is clear, then, that the image of America is a representation of actual forces in American life, but a selective or partial one. This interaction between the concerns of the French observer and the dynamic aspects of American experience was neatly expressed by Paul Bourget, the French novelist who visited the United States in 1894:

What draws me to America is not America, but Europe and France; it is the disquietude of the problems in which the future of Europe and France is hidden. Race, democracy, and science all threaten Europe, but in America they seem to have succeeded.[9]

In this formulation, the cultural development of Europe is considered the product of external forces which have their origin in America. It is therefore necessary for the European who wishes to understand his own culture to study the development of the United States.

This assertion of the formative influence of American life, which surfaced briefly in the 1890s, was widely accepted among French intellectuals in the 1920s.

The organization of this study has been largely determined by a desire to clarify the interaction between the concerns of the French observer and the dynamic aspects of American life. Part I describes two different conceptions of American life which held sway among French observers in the prewar and wartime eras. These approaches, combined with the ideological orientation of the observers discussed in Part II, chapter 4, comprise the initial perspective against which French observers judged the events of the twenties. Their reactions to the broad pattern of events set in motion by the war, including the decline of Europe and the rise of American civilization, are presented in the last two chapters of Part II. Parts III and IV detail the attitudes of the intellectuals to the major new developments in American foreign policy and American society during the twenties. These reactions forced Frenchmen to reformulate their image both of the United States and of Franco-American relations as shown in Part V. The final section demonstrates that the new conceptions of the twenties proved to be surprisingly durable despite the upheaval of the Great Depression and World War II.

## NOTES

1. *Democracy in America*, ed. by Phillips Bradley (New York, 1955), II, 183.

2. *American Studies in Europe* (Philadelphia, 1958), I, 33.

3. *Situations III* (Paris, 1949), 122. The French fascination with America in the 1920s may be confirmed in a comparative way as well. Theodore Zeldin has suggested that leading French authors lost interest in England at this time and turned increasingly to a consideration of America, Russia, or Germany. *France, 1848-1945*: Vol, 2. *Intellect, Taste and Anxiety* (Oxford, 1977), 111-113. The decisive impact of her crowd's encounter with American culture in the late twenties is described by Simone de Beauvoir in her autobiography. She recalls evenings spent with Sartre, Paul Nizan, and André Herbaud during which Sartre would sing American popular songs such as "Old Man River" and listen to recordings of Negro spirituals. *Mémoires d'une jeune fille rangée* (Paris, 1958), 335. The same crowd was partial to American cocktails (martinis, side-cars, and bronxes) and American films. Simone de Beauvoir recalls that Sartre wept while listening to

Al Jolson sing "Sonny Boy." *La Force de l'âge* (Paris, 1960), 21, 54.

4. In the 1890s, a split occurred within the French Catholic church between those who favored traditional practices and reformers who wished the church to accept the concept of religious liberty. The latter, taking their inspiration from American Catholics, were called "Americanists."

5. Ithiel de Sola Pool, "Effects of Cross-National Contact on National and International Images," *International Behavior*, ed. by Herbert Kelman (New York, 1965), 108.

6. The most detailed discussion of the methodological problems involved in the study of images is offered in *International Behavior*.

7. Quoted in André Maurois, *Etudes américaines* (New York, 1945), 222.

8. Richard Rapson, *Britons View America: Travel Commentary, 1860-1935* (Seattle, 1971), 195-212.

9. *Outre Mer* (New York, 1895), 4.

# PART I

# The Roots of Anti-Americanism: Entente and Opposition, 1776–1925

# chapter 1

# Days of Entente _____

> For most Europeans, America did not exist until 1917; a few would
> trace her origins back to the Civil War. Almost everyone forgets
> that for both the New World and the Old the period of the late
> eighteenth century marks the high point of the critical spirit.
> —Jean Canu, 1934

On November 1, 1918, Emile Boutroux, the philosopher and friend
of William James, proclaimed in the prestigious *Revue des Deux
Mondes*, "If there were ever two peoples in this world who feel an
instinctive attraction toward each other, they are the French and the
American people."[1] Just two months later, in the *Revue de Paris*, the
literary critic, Jean Guehenno, adopted essentially the same view.
"There is a spiritual bond which unites France and America. The two
countries are in the forefront of the human adventure. They are both
motivated by the same divine rage for liberty."[2] These two declara-
tions of Franco-American friendship, representative of many such
statements on both sides of the Atlantic in this period, reflect, of
course, the euphoria of wartime collaboration. They view the entente
as the logical extension of an historical agreement on values between
citizens of the two countries.

The entente conception of 1917 was not exclusively a product of
the collaboration of France and America in World War I. As its
advocates frequently asserted, the two countries had been joined on
the battlefield on the momentous occasion of America's revolt against
England. This collaboration, whose effects reverberated through the
nineteenth century and were still felt in the twentieth, arose out of

the international political struggles of the late eighteenth century.[3] However, the political and diplomatic aspects of Franco-American relations were inseparable from the French philosophes' identification of America as a model republic. For a brief period of time after 1776 Frenchmen were not only fighting side by side with Americans but had identified their allies as a model which France could follow in reforming the *ancien régime*.

The diplomatic and political features of the collaboration were simple in their outlines. The French found the occasion of Anglo-American conflict an excellent opportunity to avenge themselves for the losses of 1763. At the very least, French aid would bring about the destruction of the British empire in the New World. Viewed more optimistically, the support of the American colonies might lead to the reconquest of New World territory for France. Frenchmen of whatever political persuasion, including supporters of the monarchy, could unite behind a policy designed to combat the traditional national enemy from across the English Channel.

While the collaboration with America produced a favorable climate for the creation of a positive image of the United States, the climate alone cannot fully account for the wave of enthusiasm for the United States which developed in 1770 and lasted for almost a quarter of a century.[4] French pro-Americanism, while it had some vague support among the common people, was an intellectual rather than a popular phenomenon. Moreover, its partisans, in certain respects, clashed with the architects of the Franco-American alliance. After all, the alliance was designed by the monarchy to defend France's traditional interests, while the model republic was promoted by the monarchy's critics who were searching for an alternative to the *ancien régime*. French support for the American cause had the effect of legitimating the celebration of American institutions. By supporting American independence, the monarchy was giving aid and sustenance to its political rivals in France.

To attract supporters to their cause, it was essential for the philosophes to portray America in most attractive terms, and to argue for the existence of a community of ideals between the two countries. This they accomplished by drawing first on Voltaire's portrait of the Pennsylvania Quaker. The simplicity of the Quaker's life, his quiet prosperity, provided an excellent contrast with the supposed luxury and corruption of the *ancien régime* in France. As the American Revolution drew nearer, the image of the good Quaker was generalized and applied to the other colonies. Increasing attention was also paid to the political institutions of America, thereby providing another opportunity to contrast American liberty with French autocracy.

To finish this portrait of a utopian society, the philosophes claimed that prosperity and liberty were not incompatible with a flourishing culture. Benjamin Franklin's visits to France in 1767 and 1770 called attention to his contributions to science and suggested that America was not a cultural wasteland. Moreover, Franklin's collaboration with French intellectuals helped to create an intellectual community between France and America based on common values. Franklin's participation in the salons of Mme Helvétius and Mme d'Houdetot, and his invitations to French intellectuals to join the American Philosophical Society, lent credence to his impression of an intellectual community extending across the Atlantic. The cosmopolitan atmosphere of the eighteenth century helped to encourage the view that Americans were important contributing members of an international community of enlightened citizens.

The sense of collaboration was, of course, reinforced by the war itself which brought French soldiers into a successful military campaign. Meanwhile, the emergence of an independent United States helped to justify the claims of the monarchy's critics that a liberal system of government was a workable alternative to the French system. This was particularly true in the late 1780s and the early 1790s as the Americans wrote a new federal Constitution and elected their first national government. Frenchmen were also familiar with the elaboration of state constitutions during the revolutionary period. The impact of the American experiment was particularly strong on such moderate critics of the *ancien régime* as Lafayette and Condorcet.

The revolutionary period, then, created a special place for America in the hearts and minds of Frenchmen for two reasons. First, it was France which served as the midwife to American independence. The French could never forget that they had a large role in the creation of the American nation. The memory of this event would have been less vivid if America had been just another nation. However, in the

French (and European) view, America had been identified as a utopia. The French association with America was therefore especially significant because it was linked to the search for a more perfect social order in the future. The alliance awakened memories of universal values as well as the idea of the generosity of the French nation sacrificing its own material welfare in a noble cause. No wonder that Frenchmen should take offense in later years when the United States failed to achieve these utopian visions.

The entente of 1917, like the alliance of 1778, was preceded by a period of preparation in which relations between the two countries grew increasingly cordial. While there was no mania for America before 1917, as there had been at the end of the eighteenth century, relations between the two countries began to warm early in the twentieth century. More precisely, the preparation for wartime association grew out of the Anglo-French entente of 1904. In the preceding year the Quai d'Orsay had appointed Jules Jusserand to represent France in America. The new ambassador, who was to occupy his post almost continuously until 1925, became synonymous with the opening of a new era in Franco-American relations. Not only was Jusserand fluent in English, but he was an enthusiastic spokesman for Anglo-American culture. He soon became a close friend and confidant of President Roosevelt, who consulted him on a wide range of issues, some of which were unrelated to Franco-American affairs. The Jusserand-Roosevelt friendship was, of course, taken as a symbol of improved relations between the two countries. In 1912, Jusserand organized the celebration of the 300th anniversary of Lake Champlain's discovery, an occasion which brought to the United States a number of French dignitaries and revived memories of Franco-American collaboration during the revolutionary war.[5]

The improvement in formal relations was complemented by a growing exchange of ideas and information between scholars in the two countries. The work of William James received serious attention in France, particularly among the followers of Henri Bergson. The Bergson-James correspondence is testimony to this development. At the same time, a movement of exchange between universities provided an opportunity for Frenchmen to teach in the United States and vice versa.[6] In the course of the first decade of the twentieth century Jean Giraudoux and André Tardieu became instructors at

Harvard. The impact of this experience was evident in 1917 when Tardieu was appointed to head the High Commission, an organization which facilitated wartime collaboration between the two countries; a year later, Giraudoux was chosen by the same commission to address various American groups.[7] These intellectual exchanges, while less dramatic than Franklin's contributions during the revolutionary years, helped to create a similar sense of community between individuals in both countries.

The support for Americanism stemmed from two groups which were motivated by substantially different considerations. Almost all Frenchmen could agree that the Franco-American entente was a p,ditical necessity given the struggle against Germany, the national enemy. Many French defenders of America were motivated by such political considerations. Aside from Jules Jusserand, the chief spokesmen for Franco-American friendship were drawn largely from the academic world. Prominent among them were Gilbert Chinard, Henri Hauser, and Firmin Roz. Chinard, a leading specialist on Franco-American cultural relations in the eighteenth century, taught at Johns Hopkins and Princeton. Hauser was visiting professor at Harvard in 1923 while Roz was selected in 1917 to offer a course on American Civilization at the University of Paris.[8]

However, a small coterie of Frenchmen were primarily motivated to join the pro-American ranks by a passionate attachment to American technology. Like their counterparts, the eighteenth-century philosophes, they saw the American system, at least in its economic aspects, as a model for France. Naturally, they found the entente a propitious moment for defending their cause. Among their vocal supporters were Roz's successor at the Sorbonne, Charles Cestre, the first Frenchman to complete his graduate work at an American university. In addition to supporting the entente, Cestre was also an early spokesman for the assembly line.[9] Other disciples of American factory methods were Victor Cambon, a member of the Society of Civil Engineers; Emile Schreiber, editor of the French business daily, *Les Echoes*;[10] the future prime minister of France, Edouard Herriot and the author Jean Gontard.[11]

The image of America which emerged in this period was a product of the two forces drawing Frenchmen to America: the need to defend the entente and the desire to borrow American methods of production. The relationship of the spokesmen of the two positions to each other resembled, in some ways, the interactions of the two sources of support for America in the eighteenth century, monarchists and their critics. The supporters of entente, like the pro-government elements of the eighteenth century, were primarily concerned with cultivating American friendship for reasons of state. While the entente supporters were less wary of endorsing American institutions and values than their monarchist counterparts of the eighteenth century, their primary concern was not to change France but to defend her. The advocates of Ford and Taylor methods, on the contrary, were interested in America largely because she might become a model for a new social and economic system in France. In this respect they resembled the philosophes who had also urged France to adopt American ways. Moreover, as in the eighteenth century, so in the twentieth, the defenders of American ways in France were blessed with an excellent opportunity by the collaboration of the two countries on the battlefield. The military and diplomatic context provided ideal conditions in which to press the claim that American values and institutions were compatible with French ways.

In one respect, the requirements of the two groups opposed each other. Advocates of the assembly line needed to portray the United States as an industrial nation, devoted to the production of large quantities of goods by modern methods. Such an image, however, raised the specter of materialism, and as such, ran counter to the need to picture the United States as an idealistic country. The solution to this dilemma, however unconvincing, was to argue that if production was only a means to further the growth of a democratic society and free men for humanistic pursuits, America could still be viewed as a basically idealistic civilization. This strategy enabled the advocates of mass production to reconcile their picture of America with the position adopted by the defenders of entente.

The positive image of America which developed in this period was largely the result of the emphasis on Franco-American friendship and the consequent implication that the two nations adhered to similar values. This theme was thoroughly explored in Jules Jusserand's *With Americans of Past and Present Days*, originally published in 1916, before American entry into the war, and then translated into French in 1918. The purpose of the book was evident in the dedication:

. . . it cannot but be of advantage to themselves and to the liberal world that the two Republics . . . should ever live on terms of amity, not to say intimacy, comparing experiences, of help to one another whenever circumstances allow.[12]

The dedication, which amounted to an invitation to America to enter the war with the Allies, was the prelude to a book which argued that Franco-American friendship had been the unique feature of relations between the two countries. Jusserand chose key events of the past, particularly French aid to the United States during the Revolution, to illustrate his point. The cultural compatibility of the two peoples was evident as early as 1778, when, despite the prejudice of Americans against French mores, the behavior of Rochambeau and his troops won the general acclaim of the American people. Compatibility was also apparent in the relations of leading citizens from each country. Jusserand pointed to the friendships between Jefferson and Chastellux, Ezra Styles and Rochambeau, and Washington and Lafayette, as evidence of the mutual attraction of the two peoples.[13]

While the war of 1776 was a promising example of Franco-American amity, it threatened to cast doubt on the depth of Anglo-French friendship. Jusserand scrupulously avoided any such suggestion by assuring his readers that France entered the war only to promote American independence, not to destroy British power. Far from exulting in the British defeat at Yorktown, the French soldiers positively rejoiced that American independence was achieved without further loss of British lives. Jusserand thus tried to win the favor of the Americans without offending the sensibility of the British. In conclusion, he claimed that "there is, perhaps, no case in which, with the unavoidable mixture of human interest, a war has been more undoubtedly waged for an idea."[14]

If the American Revolution was an awkward illustration of Franco-American friendship, because it suggested Anglo-French enmity, it was quite useful for casting aspersions on the German character.

Victor Cambon pointed out that, while Lafayette was fighting for the American cause in behalf of France, the Hessians were supporting the British. "Already, Germany contributed her forces to the service of tyranny, while France brought aid to liberty."[15]

Jusserand's book can be understood as the product of a wartime diplomat anxious to engage the United States as an ally of France, but it is evident that French travelers continued to invoke the revolutionary alliance as evidence of the abiding friendship of the two countries even after 1918. Gilbert Chinard, referring to the treaty of 1778, suggested that "in spite of minor and temporary difficulties, France and the United States have maintained and strengthened the ties of a friendship which were primed by common memories and solidly based on true sympathies."[16] The tendency of Frenchmen to underestimate the strength of the American memory was deplored by Henri Hauser. "We no longer realize how fresh are the memories of the Revolution in this young country. We suppose that Lafayette and Rochambeau are only themes for official propaganda, whereas, in fact, they are a living reality."[17] As late as 1927, one year after the signature of the debt accord between France and the United States, Charles Cestre launched his magisterial volume on America by explaining the significance of the Statue of Liberty, fashioned by his compatriot Bartholdi in celebration of the 100th anniversary of the Franco-American alliance of 1778. Cestre brought his study to a close by proclaiming the enduring character of American sympathy for France.[18]

The reality of Franco-American friendship for these Frenchmen was not simply based on a consideration of past events; it was evident in their assumptions about the future. They continued to feel that the prospects of Franco-American collaboration were excellent. In the event of another European war, Henri Hauser expected the tradition of Yorktown, Saratoga, and Bois-Belleau to be decisive in drawing America into the conflict on the side of the French.[19] Herriot was equally optimistic; he felt that the memory of American sacrifices in World War I would outweigh the isolationist impulse of the American people.[20]

The spirit of the entente was even reflected in a variety of current developments. While Hauser recalled the playing of the *Marseillaise* during the 1923 Memorial Day parade in New York by American veterans of the war,[21] Charles Cestre pointed to the creation of a course in American literature and civilization at the Sorbonne:

It would have been unthinkable for the University of Paris, the center of French thought and the grand master of the University, whose actions confirm the leading currents of national thought, not to commemorate the spiritual alliance of the two sister republics while the identical heroism of their soldiers on the same battlefields had confirmed the similarity of the idealism which animates their hearts.[22]

On American soil the establishment of the Franco-American Board of Commerce and Industry in 1919 to promote the sale of French products was also evidence of the vitality of the entente.[23]

Businessmen and engineers joined the diplomats and scholars in supporting the entente. By invoking Franco-American friendship they hoped to quiet the fear of American industrial methods in France. After all, if idealistic America had adopted these methods without destroying her own values, France might safely follow suit.

French advocates of mass production adopted several strategies to convince their readers that the new methods were benign in their effect on human beings. Charles Cestre tried to show that mass production was a logical extension of the industrial revolution which had its roots in the European past; the new system applied the machine to work which would otherwise have been done by hand.[24] Emile Schreiber adopted a different tactic. He introduced the entente conception to assure his readers that no harm would come from the assembly line.

The American people are very close to us in their profoundly democratic political institutions, their liberalism, and their persistent manifestations in favor of oppressed races. . . . In addition, the already historic proclamation of President Wilson, exposing the reasons which pushed the United States into the War, prove that our hearts beat in unison and that we envisage in identical fashion the solution to the most serious problems of humanity.

The American entry into the war, only the latest evidence of agreement in values between France and America, would be "the prelude to a fruitful collaboration which, let us hope, will shift some day from military affairs to become economic and intellectual."[25] For Schreiber, the entente was only a model of the relationship which must be established between the French and American economic systems. In each case, America would supply key resources to change the status quo.

The fact that American ideals were in accord with French values was not simply incidental to Schreiber. It served to counteract the belief of some Frenchmen that there was a connection between modernization in German industry and the authoritarian German government. Schreiber was scrupulous in denying this connection. "Germany, no doubt, has acquired a formidable power by means of processes whose value must not be discounted, but because she is imperialistic and militaristic, brutal and tyrannical, she turns the individual into a machine, thus distorting the goal. Her conceptions should not be confused with ours."[26] The Franco-American entente was a strong argument to support the view that the new methods in industry were consistent with a democratic regime.

We should not assume too readily that the image of American life in the travel volumes of the Taylorites was focused exclusively on American industry. Such an emphasis, by implying a society given over entirely to mass production, would have made the new methods less appealing to French readers. Nonetheless, it was necessary for advocates of the assembly line to visit factories and report on their application of the new methods. Most travelers preferred to select plants which had been recently modernized. Especially popular was the new United States Steel plant in Gary, Indiana. Not only did it feature efficient processes, but in the vicinity, Frenchmen could observe the workers' housing and the progressive school system which added a special dimension to their view of the new industrial society.[27] Hazelton, Pennsylvania, was another popular spot for French travelers. Here J-L Duplan, an immigrant from Lyon, had established a silk factory. Duplan's plant, noteworthy for its success in electrifying the silk-making process and encouraging a competitive spirit among the workers, was especially interesting to French visitors because it offered evidence that Frenchmen could compete successfully in the American business world.[28] Without question, however, the mecca for all advocates of mass production was the Ford factory in Detroit. The assembly line was described, photographed, and praised by Herriot, Gontard, Cestre, and others in the period before 1927.

An essential part of the task for the Taylorites was not only to praise modern methods, but to show that the industrial environment was tolerable for workers. The favorable reports on housing and schools helped to make this point. The travelers' impression that workers were spirited and competitive, but not overworked, also suggested that the new conditions were desirable. As for the factory itself, travelers shared the enthusiasm of Jean Gontard, although few factories were as idyllic as the one he described:

[It] is located . . . in the middle of a park. Its large windows sparkle in the beautiful sunlight of late July. How far we are from the drab factories painted by Jean-Paul Laurens from which exhausted workers go forth with pale faces and dull clothes amidst heaps of silks. Here, in these green surroundings, I see happy faces everywhere. They never close the windows. They never fear that the workers might be distracted by the brilliant sun outside or the park full of flowers and butterflies. On the windows, I see none of the iron bars which so often make the factories like old cloisters and prisons.[29]

The argument for adopting American methods would be strengthened if the atmosphere of the factories was matched by the human environment in the rest of the country. In fact, for the most part, the advocates of mass production succeeded in describing America and Americans in appealing terms, although they retained their differences from France and Frenchmen. The judgment of Edouard Herriot, adopted as a conclusion by Jean Gontard, makes this point clear: "The United States is the land of joy, the country of the free and natural life. It is slanderous to picture [Americans] as captives of a mechanized civilization, who are ground by the gears of the machine."[30] It is apparent that Herriot and Gontard, by characterizing the Americans as free and happy, anticipated the fears of the critics who argued that the new methods would destroy the independence of the individual and his enjoyment of life. They had succeeded, moreover, in reformulating the eighteenth-century philosophes' image of a happy, prosperous America.

Joy and freedom were occasionally mentioned as American traits, but they received less attention than energy. Already in the prewar period, Frenchmen had emphasized this aspect of the American character; indeed, Firmin Roz had entitled his first book on the United States, *L'énergie américaine*. The writers of the early twenties accepted their predecessor's views. "Energy and character," concluded Victor Cambon, were "the two most appreciated virtues in America."[31] Charles Cestre maintained that "the spirit of American life" was characterized "by vigorous effort."[32] Once again, the successful businessman, who was able to channel his energy into productive enterprises, was seen as the typical American. Charles Cestre contrasted the businessman with the French peasant.

[The latter] returns to his land to finish his days under his fig tree. An American would have used his capital to buy a ranch on the plains and would have tried to multiply his revenues by ten like a big farmer. This is the difference between the French character, solid but timid, and the American character, enterprising and bold.

The difference, however, never developed into hostility. In fact, Cestre protested that the American understood French prudence very well, and respected the Frenchman for his ways.[33]

If the typical American was a businessman who directed his energy toward increasing his profits, then the American character might appear to be tainted with materialism. Most critics, however, avoided such an accusation by emphasizing the adventurous qualities of the businessman and pointing out, as Cestre did, that he was less interested in accumulating money and goods than in action. Another alternative was to argue that the businessman used his profits for basically nonmaterial purposes. Firmin Roz cited Herbert Croly's *The Promise of American Life* as evidence that the increase in productivity was useful in achieving a more democratic society.[34] In similar fashion, Victor Cambon found no reason to apologize for the large fortunes amassed by businessmen in the United States. Andrew Carnegie illustrated the benefits of individual wealth to the society by financing the construction of libraries and subsidizing peace organizations.

Even after attempting to quiet the fears of Frenchmen with regard to new factory methods, it is clear that the authors were uneasy about the prospect of recommending to their own countrymen the adoption of aspects of a foreign civilization. Such a one-way influence, even voluntarily accepted in France, suggested a kind of imperialism, whereas a true entente entailed a mutual receptivity to cultural influences. The charge of imperialism might be rebutted, if, in addition to the adoption of American methods in France, it could be shown that the United States was receptive to some aspects of French culture.[35]

Victor Cambon articulated one such version of cultural exchange. Despite his admission that "without striking a blow, world hegemony henceforth belongs to the United States of America," Cambon was not alarmed about American power. On the contrary, he welcomed America's help and intended to "demonstrate in which areas their initiatives can be profitable." Cambon's calm reflected his confidence in French culture as a counterweight to American methods. After all, "when one is an old nation of artists—and none since Pericles was more so than France—one has both a duty and an interest in initiating younger nations to one's tastes."[36] An equilibrium existed between American industrial power and French cultural hegemony. This complementary situation enabled Cambon to justify French imitation of America without feeling a sense of national disgrace.

Charles Cestre was more explicit than Cambon about the balance between France and the United States. He argued that France could learn order and efficiency from America, while teaching Gallic taste to Americans.[37] A similar formula was adopted by Emile Schreiber as he sailed toward France. He prayed that his ship would become a symbol of exchange. "Let her bring to hard-working America a bit of our gentle artistic France, and fill us with their sense of reality and practical spirit." Schreiber, like Cambon, was well aware of the charge that France might lose her national identity by accepting American ways. He claimed, however, that "a great nation can, without declining, borrow and adopt new ideas from a young people, while conserving the respect for its own tradition and past."[38]

The travel volumes provided an excellent medium for reporting on American industrial life, because the visits to factories and the discussions of new methods could be interspersed with descriptions of the American countryside and other nonindustrial aspects of American life. As in the prewar period, and despite the desire to spread factory methods, French travelers left a dominant impression in the minds of their readers of a continent which was diverse in both human and natural resources. "The spirit of American life," according to Charles Cestre, was based in no small part on "the inexhaustible resources, the vast, generous and splendid nature of the New World."[39] Cestre's volume, which treated each region separately, was ideally organized to convey this impression of wealth and diversity.

Natural diversity had its counterpart in the realm of human landscape. Here variety was the result of both ethnic and regional differences. As Henri Hauser maintained:

The longer I am here, the clearer it becomes that there is no American opinion. There are, in this country—which is, in reality, a continent—as many opinions as there are regions and groups. When we speak of the United States in Europe, we always forget that to go from New York to San Francisco, one must turn the big hand of the clock back four full hours. [ sic. ] . . . We also forget the moral distance which separates an old New England family of pure Anglo-Saxon origin, or mixed with elements of Dutch, Canadian or Scandinavian blood, from some group of Slavs, Orientals, Italians, or Syrians, who are superficially Americanized.[40]

By emphasizing that America was a continent rather than a country, Hauser made it clear that there was no such thing as a uniform way of life to which all Americans adhered. The United States had not yet become a system in the eyes of early postwar travelers.

The emphasis on diversity made it possible for travelers to identify with attractive aspects of American life. Certain areas, certain institutions, and certain individuals exerted a profound appeal for French observers. Boston remained a clear favorite among American cities for several reasons. Edouard Herriot's preference for the city was based on Bostonians' love for France.[41] Charles Cestre explained why he felt at home in Boston. There,

in the intelligent middle class whose judgment and knowledge have been broadened by reading and travel; in university circles valued for their erudition as much as their breadth of vision, in the literary world remarkable for its refined taste and its sympathy for the old and beautiful traditions of Europe—and especially France—one meets the freest and most enlightened minds, a true intellectual elite, which, except for certain religious and moral peculiarities, is the equal of the European "intelligentsia."[42]

Other travelers joined Cestre in praising the American university and its achievements. Herriot devoted a chapter of his volume to "La culture spirituelle" in the United States. Firmin Roz remarked that American students led a happy life in their universities, although their curriculum was somewhat less demanding than the rigorous regime of study in a French university.[43]

Aside from the universities, there remained ethnic enclaves to which Frenchmen were drawn. In Quebec, Herriot found a warm welcome from the population of French origin, and concluded that this area was "a piece of France."[44] Other Frenchmen were reassured by evidence of the French presence in the American past. Jean Gontard was reminded of Lafayette's reception in 1824 at Battery Park on the southern tip of Manhattan during his own visit there a century later.[45] Charles Cestre found considerable evidence of the hospitality of the American continent to French inhabitants, past and present. He pointed to the French population in Louisiana, San Francisco, and New England. He recalled Achille Murat's stay in Florida during the Restoration period, and was reminded of Chateaubriand's adventures at Niagara Falls during a visit there. In Baltimore, he remembered the descendants of the Bonaparte family still living in the city. America, although a distant and exotic continent, had its friendly and familiar aspects for Frenchmen.[46]

The benign image of America and the conception of a Franco-American entente served a useful purpose during the war as they had during the years of the Revolution; in the postwar period, however, they constituted an unnecessary and undesirable burden for citizens and policy makers alike. The idyllic view of America and Franco-American relations which survived the war created expectations which could not be met. Once the wartime collaboration ended, the gap between the realities of diplomatic and cultural relations and the image of entente would accentuate the disillusionment of both Frenchmen and Americans. Moreover, the necessity of repudiating the entente image rendered more intense the anti-American reaction in France which would have developed in any case.

Equally unfortunate was the effort to link the entente with the advocacy of the assembly line in France. The two separate sources of pro-Americanism of the World War I period, while they broadened its base of support, rendered the entente as unstable as it had been at the time of the Revolution. Then, the philosophes had exploited the good feeling which proceeded from Franco-American collaboration against the English. Once that cooperation was over, however, the climate for advocating the model republic became far less favorable. Similarly, justifying the spread of American methods on the grounds that France and America shared common values was advantageous in the early postwar years. However, the disintegration of the entente then raised questions about the assembly line which had nothing to do with its intrinsic character. Conversely, the doubts about the materialistic aspects of mass culture suggested to Frenchmen that the entente was an inaccurate representation of Franco-American relations. American methods and the entente conception would have proven controversial in any event during the twenties. Their linkage helps to explain the extreme reaction against both.

In addition to the events of the twenties, the cultural heritage of Frenchmen also contributed to the perilous position of the entente. As early as the revolutionary era, Frenchmen had conceived of the United States and France as antithetical cultures. Whereas the entente portrayed the national experiences of the two countries as continuous, the antithesis emphasized the cultural and diplomatic distance between France and America. This tradition had played an important role in the mutual conception of relations between 1776 and 1914. Since most French observers of the twenties had been educated in the prewar period, they were familiar with the older conception. It was therefore available to them when the events of the twenties cast serious doubts on entente.

NOTES

1. "Le Président Wilson, historien du peuple américain," 5.
2. "Whitman, Wilson et l'esprit modern" (January 1, 1919), 124.
3. The continued interest among French liberals in the American political system as late as the mid-nineteenth century is discussed in Henry Blumenthal, *France and the United States: Their Diplomatic Relations, 1789-1914*

(Chapel Hill, 1970), 76, and at much greater length in Simon J. Copans, "French Opinion of American Democracy" (unpublished Ph.D. dissertation, Brown University, 1942).

4. In the ensuing discussion of the positive French image of America in late eighteenth-century France, I have relied heavily on Durand Echeverria, *Mirage in the West: A History of the French Image of American Society to 1815* (Princeton, 1957).

5. Jusserand's activities are discussed in some detail by Simone Jeune, *De F. T. Graindorge à A. O. Barnabooth* (Paris, 1963), 335. The dignitaries who came to America in 1912 included Gabriel Hanotaux, former Minister of Foreign Affairs, and René Bazin, noted author of the period.

6. *Ibid.*, 330, 337.

7. The High Commission itself was a particularly rich source for reports on the American experience during the war. In addition to Tardieu's published collection of speeches, his successor, Edouard de Billy, put out a volume of his speeches, and Jean Giraudoux wrote a brief account, *Amica America* (Paris, 1918), describing his experiences in the United States.

8. In the prewar decade Hauser was author of a study entitled *L'impérialisme américain* (Paris, 1905).

9. Cestre wrote two studies of American industrial methods: *L'usine et l'habitation ouvrière aux Etats-Unis* (Paris, 1921) and *Production industrielle et justice sociale en Amérique* (Paris, 1921). Monaghan, *French Travellers*, 23.

10. Schreiber wrote under the pseudonym of Emile Servan in 1917. His second book on the United States, written in 1934, was signed "Emile Schreiber." Schreiber was the father of Jean-Jacques Servan-Schreiber, the founder of the French weekly, *L'Express*.

11. Before completing his general study of American methods, Gontard had written two books on California: *A travers la Californie* (Paris, 1922), and *Dans les sierras de Californie* (Paris, 1923).

12. P. viii.

13. *Ibid.*, 106.

14. *Ibid.*, 90, 132.

15. *Etats-Unis-France* (Paris, 1917), 4.

16. *Le doctrine de l'Américanisme* (Paris, 1919), 1.

17. *L'Amérique vivante* (Paris, 1923), 14.

18. *Les Etats-Unis* (Paris, 1927), 1, 338.

19. *L'Amérique vivante*, 157.

20. *Impressions d'Amérique* (Lyon, 1923), 124.

21. *L'Amérique vivante*, 156-157.

22. "Coup d'oeil sur la civilisation américaine," *Revue Internationale de*

l'Enseignement (July 15 and August 15, 1919), 247. The increased interest in America on the part of French academics was also reflected in the lectures on aspects of American society and history delivered at the Collège de France by André Siegfried and Bernard Faÿ. In the field of comparative literature, Fernand Baldensperger at the Sorbonne specialized in the study of Franco-American relations like his counterpart in the United States, Gilbert Chinard.

23. Jean Gontard relied on the Franco-American Board for his letters of introduction to American managers of factories.

24. *Les Etats-Unis*, 93.

25. *L'exemple américain* (Paris, 1917), xxii-xxiii.

26. *Ibid.*, xxi-xxii.

27. Cestre, *Les Etats-Unis*, 196. Cambon, *Etats-Unis-France*, 209-215.

28. Cestre, *Les Etats-Unis*, 89. Cambon, *Etats-Unis-France*, 230-242. Duplan himself testified to the effectiveness of new industrial methods in his *Lettres d'un vieil Américain à un Français* (Paris, 1917).

29. *Au pays des gratte-ciel* (Paris, 1925), 130. Jean-Paul Laurens, 1838-1921, was a painter best known for his scenes from church history.

30. Quoted in *ibid.*, 267.

31. *Etats-Unis-France*, 97.

32. *Les Etats-Unis*, 2.

33. *Ibid.*, 178, 24.

34. *L'Amérique nouvelle* (Paris, 1923), 19.

35. *Etats-Unis-France*, 13.

36. *Ibid.*, vii, 2, 41.

37. *Les Etats-Unis*, 128.

38. *L'exemple américain* , 262, 264.

39. *Les Etats-Unis*, 2.

40. *L'Amérique vivante*, 110.

41. *Impressions d'Amérique*, 106.

42. *Les Etats-Unis*, 42.

43. *L'Amérique nouvelle*, 44.

44. *Impressions d'Amérique*, 112.

45. *Au pays des gratte-ciel* , 26.

46. *Les Etats-Unis*, 26, 156, 300, 154, 99, 95.

# chapter 2

# Old World Versus New World _____

> Between the two continents there is utter
> disproportion, ascension here, depression there;
> two communities the flow of whose life blood,
> the measure of whose breath, the possibilities
> of whose growth are all at opposite poles—
> positive and increasing for the one, negative
> and decreasing for the other.
> —André Tardieu, 1927

"I love antitheses," remarked Jules Huret, correspondent for *Le Figaro* and a friend of Mallarmé. "The sensations which they produce are strong, and when it is not a question of delicate matters, the effects which one obtains, though accurate, are more striking."[1] Huret's taste for antithesis as a way of defining relations between America and Europe has been shared by both American students of the Old World and European critics of America. "Almost from the beginning the new world has repudiated the old, defining its own virtues as the precise antithesis of the supposed vices of Europe."[2]

As both Huret and Cunliffe suggest, the use of antithesis has been governed far more by moral and aesthetic considerations than it has by a desire to identify accurately the two terms which are contrasted. Almost invariably, the antithesis sets off entities which are invested with a different moral weight and thus encourages the reader to identify with one and oppose the other. For example, Americans who contrasted the Old World and the New World wished to dramatize the superiority of the United States.[3]

The antithesis can also be a convenient device for criticizing one's

own country or for achieving a metaphorical escape from the supposed horrors of a particular situation. The first European traveler in the New World, Christopher Columbus, adopted the second strategy. With scant empirical knowledge of their inhabitants, he portrayed the Caribbean Islands in the poetic language of the day. The islands thus became a mythical paradise in contrast to the European inferno, which, in the fifteenth century, had been buffeted by death and disease.[4]

The French philosophes of the eighteenth century, while identifying themselves with the American republic, were using the same strategy as Columbus. The virtues of the American system they celebrated stood in direct contrast to the vices of the monarchy which they wished to repudiate. However, even in the eighteenth century, the philosophes' response was not the only French view of America. The antithesis could serve just as well for other elements in France who embraced the French system and found it useful to identify America as a threat to France or Europe. This anti-American position was derived from a variety of sources—natural, social, political, and diplomatic.

As early as 1768, even before the mania for America had developed in France, a widespread opposition to the New World arose in France and throughout Europe based largely on geographical and climatic factors. The work of De Pauw, the Dutch naturalist, which was translated into French in 1768, maintained that life in the New World was adversely affected by the climate. In his view, species of all kinds, plants, animals, and human beings, whether Indians or Europeans, degenerated because of the unhealthy soil and air. Such degeneration affected both the size and the quality of the species, and was, of course, in contrast to the vigor of organisms in Europe. De Pauw's view, adopted by French intellectuals including Buffon and Raynal, was, in turn, repudiated by them under the influence of Franklin, but De Pauw continued even during the Revolution to espouse his view of degeneracy and to perceive Europe as the center of the universe.[5]

Numerous other factors threatened the philosophes' perception of America as a perfect society. Underlying that view was the general tolerance and receptivity of the Enlightenment to foreign manners and customs, based on the belief that common values and institutions could exist under the veneer of exotic habits. This view was easier to maintain from a distance; Frenchmen, even those under the influence of the philosophes, who actually visited America, experienced a feeling of distance and sometimes distaste for American mores despite a theoretical attachment to American institutions. Thus, the French officers in America at the time of the Revolution noted certain American habits, such as indolence and disorganization, which irritated them and served to balance their enthusiasm for the revolutionary cause. Of particular importance was the opinion of the Marquis de Chastellux, a friend of Jefferson and an officer in the French army, who denied that a refined cultural life was possible in America. Chastellux, observing with distaste the banality and crudeness of American life, and despite his enthusiasm for republican institutions, concluded that the new country would always lack cultural refinement.[6] In this opinion, he anticipated twentieth-century French critics of the United States who also focused on the vulgarity of American life as justification for rejecting the New World experience.

Also contributing to the rejection of America were the poor experiences of Frenchmen who went to live in the New World. The Scioto affair, in which Frenchmen thought they were purchasing large amounts of property in Ohio, served to discourage many. Not only were the Gallic immigrants deceived, but they found the wilderness to be anything but the paradise they had imagined. Shortly thereafter, the exiles from the French Revolution, many of whom settled in and around Philadelphia, also confirmed the uncivilized character of the American experience. Their opinions helped to convince Frenchmen that the American social environment was incompatible with French ways.

These negative perceptions were reinforced by the trends in economic and diplomatic relations between the two countries following the Revolution. There was considerable disappointment when Frenchmen discovered that their expectations of a shift in trade relations, which would make France the major trading partner of the United States, did not develop. Despite the Franco-American alliance, England retained her trade position with the United States. This fact worked to undermine the picture of France and America as good partners. So did the erosion of diplomatic relations between the two countries during the years following the outbreak of the French Revolution. When the United States refused to come to France's aid in the naval war against England and went so far as to sign the Jay treaty, the Directory waged war on American ships and only the patience of John Adams and Napoleon's interest in negotiations prevented the outbreak of a full-scale war between the former allies.

Moreover, the political scene both in France and the United States also undermined the alliance. In the United States, as reports from England clearly established, the new political institutions were showing signs of instability in the 1780s. Despite the strengthening of the system under the new Constitution, American institutions became irrelevant to the French situation following the Revolution of 1789. For Frenchmen who looked to a unicameral system and concentration of power, the bicameral system and separation of powers were not adequate.

Finally, a few Frenchmen, even from 1776, had foreseen the possible long-range consequences of the American Revolution. It had, after all, created an independent locus of power which might eventually challenge European predominance. This perception, which rejected the cosmopolitan view of the philosophes and upheld the nation-state as the primary unit of power, foreshadowed the fears of the American system which would emerge periodically in the nineteenth century and become the main concern of twentiethcentury Frenchmen. Simone Linguet, for one, predicted increased immigration from Europe to America, the consequent development of American resources, and her rise to a position of world predominance. This, in turn, would tempt America to send her forces across the Atlantic and subjugate Europe. Linguet was persuaded that such an American conquest would mark the end of civilization because Americans possessed "no elevation of soul."[7]

These anti-American sentiments emerged briefly at the end of the eighteenth century, but the cosmopolitan atmosphere and the strong sense of identification with the American experiment held them in check. It is evident, however, that even at the height of the FrancoAmerican alliance, the roots of anti-Americanism were well established in French soil. The friendship between France and America was a reality, but it was also fragile. Moreover, the high level of expectations created by the alliance of 1778 could be counterproductive. It would always be difficult for either country to live up to the disinterested standards which had supposedly characterized the behavior of each in 1778.[8] With the rising nationalism of the nineteenth century, anti-Americanism, expressed in the form of the antithesis between French and American experiences, would come to the fore. A few French liberals continued to see America as a model republic, but they remained without much influence except during the revolutions of 1830 and 1848.[9]

As befits an age of nationalism, the antithesis was used by travelers to reassure their fellow countrymen that the native land was indeed superior to the particular foreign country in question. Jules Huret recognized this function when he explained that Frenchmen, while in France, were likely to be critical of the mother country. Once in a foreign land, however, French travelers acted according to the dictum of Balzac. The novelist maintained that even a Parisian atheist would die for the church in Constantinople. Patriotism, according to Huret, was a basic element in the psychology of all individuals; in this regard, travelers were no exception. As they came into contact with a foreign civilization, travelers experienced "an instinctive need for security and self defense." This need was gratified by an unfavorable view of the foreign country which "restores our belief that the land we have just left is the best on the entire globe, that the sky is softer there, that the inhabitants are the only tolerable ones."[10] Given such a state of mind, criticism of foreign countries and enthusiasm for France were the inevitable product of foreign travel particularly in an age of nationalism.

The major French observers of America from 1860 to 1914 expressed their nationalism by assuming an aristocratic posture toward American society. This reactionary stance did not always correspond with their own position in France. After all, Jean-Jacques Ampère[11] and Ernest Duvergier de Hauranne[12] were liberal disciples of Tocqueville and critics of Napoleon III. Nonetheless, their disdain for American manners was similar to that of the conservative novelist Xavier Marmier[13] and Ferri-Pisani, the aide-de-camp of Napoleon III's cousin.[14] Later observers of America including novelist Paul Bourget and Professor of Political Science Paul de Rousiers responded in similar fashion.[15] De Rousiers's colleague André Siegfried, who was a republican witness of Progressive America, adopted a perspective which was similar to that of traditionalist Edouard Rod, a novelist.[16] Both Paul Adam, the chronicler of American business, and Jules Huret also employed the contrast theme to good advantage.[17]

The change in the terms of antithesis between 1860 and 1914, as revealed in the above works, is a good indication of changing cultural relations between France and America in the same period. In the mid-nineteenth century, travelers conceived of America as a democratic society with commercial habits, and, as such, it was by definition uncivilized. At the end of the century, America was portrayed by French observers as a rising industrial power in contrast to the refined civilizations of Europe. By the early twentieth century, America, in the eyes of some travelers, had achieved the status of a civilization. This new position in no way reflected a recognition of American literature or painting. The United States was still presumed to be culturally undernourished, but her achievements in the economic and political realm gave her a new standing in the opinion of French observers.

The conviction of mid-nineteenth-century Frenchmen that America could be adequately described as a democratic society with commerical manners was clearly set forth by Jean-Jacques Ampère: "In the United States, society is democratic but civilization is European."[18] By defining democracy as antithetical to civilization, Ampère and other travelers narrowed substantially their concept of life in America. If they encountered civilized behavior in the United States, it was described as "European," while uncivilized actions were considered typically American. This scheme provided a useful device for organizing observations about American life by travelers in the period from 1860 to 1890. Each time they encountered individuals and places of a refined character they were claimed for Europe.

One of the consequences of adopting this scheme was that it eliminated the possibility of the development of a specifically American culture, or American literature. Since true literature was the product of a civilization, America could produce no literature. American prose, consistent with the character of American society, would be "uncultivated, violent, and neglected," and this was not literature in the classic sense of the word.[19] Any evidence of civilization in the United States was also defined as "European." Ampère, for example, spoke of an encounter with "a Virginia planter whose

manners are completely European." After reading Longfellow's
*Evangeline*, Ampère concluded that "*Europe has passed this way.*"
Further contacts in Boston with the New England aristocracy and a
visit with Senator Sumner produced the reaction that "I am not
entirely in a barbarous land. This European streak which penetrates
the United States is worthy of attention."[20]

Duvergier had an equally pleasant experience in Boston. At the
Atlantic Club, he lunched with Emerson and Agassiz; later, he
visited Wendell Phillips and Longfellow in their homes. As a result of
these contacts, he had "only nice things to say about the city and its
inhabitants." Indeed, such a civilized atmosphere was incompatible
with Duvergier's conception of American life. He explained that, "in
truth, this is no longer America; it is England, and the country is
correctly named New England."[21]

While enclaves of European culture were more frequent on the
East Coast, they appeared occasionally in other areas as well. Cincinnati, for instance, which had acquired a reputation as one of the least
civilized of American cities, was described by Duvergier as "a rich
and gracious ensemble which recalls our most beautiful European
cities." When he crossed the Ohio River to attend a political rally in
Louisville, Kentucky, Duvergier observed sharp differences between two speakers at the meeting. The more vulgar of the two was
considered typically American, while the other candidate, described
as "literate" and "restrained," was therefore "European."[22] In this
manner, the antithesis served to remove from America places and
persons of a civilized character and prevented them from moderating
the picture of a North American cultural desert.

It is not surprising, then, that once the exceptions to the rule of
vulgarity were declared "un-American," the remaining inhabitants
could be described as materialistic and conformist. From his observations, Duvergier concluded that "the American is at bottom nothing
but a big, robust, child who is astonished and amused by everything."
The simplicity of the American character was consistent with the
uniform focus of American men on business affairs. In Duvergier's
view, they were "machines for making money."[23] More distressing to
him than American materialism was the rampant conformity which
characterized the society. Duvergier denounced the "life of the
herd" which he observed in Washington, D.C.[24] He discovered "a

uniform model on which 99 percent of the men are molded. Compounded of a Methodist minister and a schoolmaster, they [the Americans] repeat like parrots the banalities which their minister or newspaper teaches them." While this behavior disgusted Duvergier, he was prepared to admit its social utility. "The intellectual myopia of the great masses, which goes by the name of common sense, guarantees republican liberty from easy excess."[25]

It is evident from the remarks of Duvergier and Ampère that the antithesis was more than a device for ordering the observations of travelers. In addition, it provided a means for travelers to express their allegiance to a particular way of life. The contrast between democratic society and European civilization was at once a way of understanding the society and of condemning it. At the same time, it asserted the superiority of France and Europe. Sometimes the rejection of American ways was implicit. Xavier Marmier, however, wished to permit his readers no uncertainty. Just a few days after his arrival in New York, he expressed his fervent desire to leave "this tumultuous republican zone, immersed in business, whose virtues inspire no attachment and whose vices are revolting."[26] Duvergier, while more attached to republican institutions and less given to rhetoric than Marmier, confessed that "the farther I advanced into the land of democracy, the more I felt like an aristocrat without being aware of it."[27] This statement suggests that Duvergier's republican sentiments were not sufficiently strong to outweigh his preference for the customs of his class and country. Indeed, his remarks recall the similar reaction of Chastellux to eighteenth-century America. The latter's admiration for the model republic could not overcome his distaste for American culture.

The promotion of republican institutions, a characteristic activity of liberal travelers before 1870, was no longer necessary after the rise of a republic in France; between 1870 and 1890 travelers turned from American politics to the exotic aspects of American life, particularly the West. Not until the nineties did French observers begin to introduce their countrymen to industrial America. In this transitional decade, travelers recognized the economic and social raw materials which, in the twentieth century, would make the United States a civilization, but they were not yet prepared to view America as a unique culture independent of Europe. Nor was the new industrial society immune from the vulgarity of the democratic republic of 1860. A new social structure was developing, but it was substantially different from European society.

The typical approach of French observers to American life in the nineties was to single out the industrial aspects of American life and set them off against the aesthetic qualities of Europe. Paul de Rousiers, for example, condemned Chicago for permitting its center to be overrun with railroads; in contrast, Paris, which de Rousiers regarded as "above all an elegant city," kept its industry and railroads out of the center. For de Rousiers, the essence of American life was the factory and its methods which were "brutal, rapid, unpolished and enormously profitable."[28] Paul Bourget put the same point in somewhat different terms. "I love best the cities of old Europe, but I admire most the businessmen of the New World."[29] Again the contrast pitted New World industrialism against Old World elegance.

It was in the early twentieth century that the United States emerged for many French critics, not merely as a region with distinct manners, but as a civilization whose institutions and values formed a coherent system in contrast to the European way of life. The existence of a distinct civilization, and its opposition to European ways, was evident in the remarks of André Siegfried. "The charm of the United States lies in its exotism. Superficially the country seems English; in reality, this is truly a New World, having only a distant kinship with the old continent." A few pages later, Siegfried doubted even this small area of agreement between the two continents. "The New World is truly another world," he argued, and pointed out that American newspapers rarely printed news of Europe, because Americans had so little interest in the affairs of the Old World.[30]

While Siegfried implied the existence of an independent civilization, Jules Huret was far more explicit. His trip to the United States led him not only to confirm the existence of American civilization but to assure his readers that they were part of a broader European way of life:

European civilization exists not only in confrontation with Asian or African barbarity, but also in opposition to American civilization. America is a new and abundant vine with a still unknown fruit. The wine must be put in bottles for several years before deciding what class it belongs to. If one drinks it now, it is a little sour and acid.[31]

It is evident that America's new status as a civilization was recognized just as the United States was emerging as a world power. The coincidence of these two developments indicates that French travelers' perception of an independent American civilization was related to their realization that the United States was an economic and political threat. Already, in 1893, Paul de Rousiers had wondered, in connection with American wheat producers' control of the European market, whether "the old nations of the old continent must allow barbarians to serve as their models."[32] In 1899, the year after America's war for empire, the *Correspondant* published an article entitled "The American Peril."[33] In the early years of the Progressive period, this theme would appear frequently in the travel literature. Edouard Rod spoke of the increasing "rivalry of the Old and New Worlds." The element of threat involved in this rivalry was evident from his admonition to Americans not "to crush us under your machines, nor strike us with your electricity, nor smother us in your steam."[34]

The rivalry observed by Rod was defined by Jules Huret as "this gigantic battle between old Europe and young America." The outcome of this clash was now certain; it was "no longer a combat, but a massacre."[35] Among the French industries under threat, according to Huret, were automobile and steel companies trying to compete with their more efficient American rivals. However, France could more readily accept these economic setbacks than it could "the secret thoughts," of some "imperialists" who "not only use the Old World as a dumping ground for their excess industrial production, but also dream of making it a vacation land. It is doubtful whether Europe will allow this to happen."[36] Clearly, the recognition of America as a civilization by French observers coincided with their perception of the nation as an economic threat to Europe.

The rise of a civilization in the New World caused little change in the behavior of its inhabitants, according to travelers. Americans were still perceived as conformist and materialistic. Special emphasis was now placed on American energy. It is not surprising that as the contrast between Europe and America became more systematic after

1900 the distinction between the behavior of their inhabitants was sharpened. Jules Huret denounced factory methods in the United States as "not a matter of an occidental propensity, but an organic and constitutional characteristic of the [American] race." As a spectator at a football game, he was dismayed by the players' propensity for violence. "These young people are entirely different from ours; their understanding of life could not possibly resemble ours. The difference in values was reflected in their character and their habits."[37]

American energy did not necessarily produce violence. Put to constructive use, it could have positive effects. Paul Adam discovered

with my poor morbid eyes . . . a nation of athletes and their olympic glories, a nation of magicians and the multitude of its miracles, an uprooted and adventurous people, rich, proud, valiant, smitten with their bold illusions, daring them and realizing them in the sun.

After this exalting experience, he "returned to a hospital of individuals rooted in their gardens, soon to be their cemeteries, who are put to sleep by the musty odor there."[38] Adam, unlike Huret, hoped that American dynamism might infuse France with energy, without, at the same time, destroying the unique qualities of French life.

The obvious material achievements of American civilization, the foundation of America's new power, in no way diminished the travelers' esteem for European culture. On the contrary, the recognition of American power led to the expression of renewed, if not increased, loyalty to Europe. Jules Huret remarked that "I have too often noticed our material inferiority relative to the Americans, not to rejoice over the facts which reestablish a balance in other areas."[39] In effect, European cultural achievements were sufficient to compensate for her material decline in the travelers' view. For Rod, the threat from the machine had increased "the filial attachment which I retain for our old civilization,"[40] while André Siegfried insisted that Europe "remains in spite of everything the heart of world civilization."[41] The antithesis, which had become more comprehensive with the recognition of America as a civilization, also enabled the travelers to demonstrate their fundamental loyalty to France and Europe.

Correlated with the rise of American power was a tendency on the part of many travelers to identify themselves with all of Europe rather than just France. The enormous gap which they experienced between American life and their own values rendered the differences between particular European countries almost trivial by comparison. Huret made this discovery in a Colorado hotel when he was accosted by a strange waiter who exclaimed,

Ah, sir, how happy I am to see a European! I am an Englishman from Manchester and I don't like this country at all. Life here is too rough and brutal. Thus, on the rare occasions when I see a European, I am happy for several days.

Huret greeted this outburst in a sympathetic fashion:

I made common cause with this English waiter. I understood him like a brother. And I remarked to myself that a thousand leagues from their native lands, an Englishman and a Frenchman, who in Europe would feel only their hostility toward each other, found strong enough affinities to like each other without being acquainted.[42]

The distaste for American habits led travelers to minimize cultural differences, which ordinarily they believed were serious obstacles to friendship.

It is evident that as American power increased in the late nineteenth century, the role of antithesis became more central for the French traveler in America. Opposition between the New and Old Worlds had been perceived in the eighteenth century by biologists like De Pauw and social critics like Chastellux. In the mid-nineteenth century, the antithesis had served primarily to distinguish democratic materialism from the civilized behavior of an aristocratic France; by the early twentieth century, it pointed to a conflict between a rising American power and an older European civilization which could still hold its own, but was suffering in some areas from economic competition. While the United States remained a distant and exotic continent, which was only occasionally threatening to Europe, the travelers had developed a useful way of representing relations between the two worlds, which would prove increasingly serviceable in the years after World War I.

NOTES

1. *En Amérique* (Paris, 1904), I, II.

2. Marcus Cunliffe, "Europe and America," *Encounter* (December 1961) 27.

3. *Ibid.*

4. Howard Mumford Jones, *O Strange New World* (New York, 1964), 13.

5. Durand Echeverria, *Mirage in the West* (Princeton, 1957). Chapter 1 contains an interesting account of the controversy over New World degeneracy.

6. *Ibid.*, 151. Theodore Zeldin has noted a similar tendency among French Anglophiles in their relations with England. Even such a fervent defender of English political institutions as Emily Boutmy, one of the founders of the École Libre des Sciences Politiques, proclaimed his preference for Gallic culture. *France, 1848-1945*: Vol. 2. *Intellect, Taste and Anxiety* (Oxford, 1977), 108.

7. Echeverria, *Mirage in the West*, 64.

8. Henry Blumenthal, *France and the United States: Their Diplomatic Relations, 1789-1914* (Chapel Hill, 1970), 4.

9. René Rémond, *Les Etats-Unis devant l'opinion francaise, 1815-1852*, 2 vols. (Paris, 1962).

10. *En Amérique*, II, 410.

11. Ampère, son of the French physicist and professor of literature at the Collège de France, published his work on the United States in 1855. It is included as representative of the period after 1860, because three new editions were published in 1860, 1867, and 1874, suggesting that Ampère continued to be read long after 1855.

12. Duvergier de Hauranne was a liberal journalist whose detailed articles on American life during the Civil War were published in *Revue des Deux Mondes*.

13. Marmier, a member of the French Academy and one of the most popular writers of travel literature in the nineteenth century, published his study of America in 1851. Like Ampère, he is included as a representative traveler because versions of the original work were reissued in 1860 and 1874. Monaghan, *French Travellers in the United States, 1765-1932* (New York, 1961), 66.

14. Ferri-Pisani was a career army officer who joined Prince Napoleon for his tour of the American battlefields during the Civil War.

15. Both Bourget, a friend of Henry James, and de Rousiers were disciples of Hippolyte Taine and referred to his fictional portrait of the Cincinnati pork

merchant F. T. Graindorge, which had been created in 1867. *Outre Mer* (New York, 1895), 174. *La vie américaine* (Paris, 1892), 71.

16. Although of Swiss origin, Rod is included here because he spent most of his life in Paris and was read primarily by the French public.

17. Huret was the most widely read French traveler of the prewar period (Monaghan, *French Travellers*, 51) and obviously exerted an influence on Adam among others. The latter called Huret's study "an admirable collection of articles." *Vues d'Amérique* (Paris, 1906), 221.

18. *Promenade en Amérique* (Paris, 1855), I, 74.

19. *Ibid.*, I, 75.

20. *Ibid.*, I, 9, 74, 36.

21. *Huit mois en Amérique* (Paris, 1866), I, 357. Ferri-Pisani was also convinced of the virtues of Boston, and especially Harvard. "The superiority of this small world of literature and sciences, over that of business and politics, was incontestable." *Prince Napoléon in America, 1861*, trans. Georges Joyaux (Bloomington, 1959), 276.

22. *Ibid.*, I, 322, 292.

23. *Ibid.*, I, 53, 268.

24. *Ibid.*, II, 276.

25. *Ibid.*, I, 164.

26. *Les Etats-Unis et le Canada* (Tours, 1874), 31.

27. *Huit mois en Amérique*, II, 233.

28. *La vie américaine*, 75, 93.

29. *Outre Mer*, 158.

30. *Deux mois en Amérique du Nord* (Paris, 1916), 1, 5, 80.

31. *En Amérique*, II, 209.

32. *La vie américaine*, 2.

33. The article, written by Octave Noël, appeared in the issue of April 10, 1899, and pointed out the originality of American imperialism, which stressed economic rather than political control by the mother country. Cited in Pierre Laurent, *L'impérialisme économique américain* (Paris, 1931), 109.

34. *Reflets d'Amérique* (Paris, 1905), 90, 46. Jules Cambon, then French Minister to the United States, feared that the Spanish-American War might give the American government an excuse to attack Spanish territory in the Old World. In this sense, he saw the war as a turning point in world history which would lead ultimately to an American conquest of Europe. Blumenthal, *France and the United States*, 199.

35. *En Amérique*, I, 107.

36. *Ibid.*, II, 139.

37. *Ibid.*, I, 292, 141.

38. *Vues d'Amérique*, 7.
39. *Ibid.*, I, 353.
40. *Reflets d'Amérique*, 6.
41. *Deux mois en Amérique du Nord*, 83.
42. *En Amérique*, II, 209.

# chapter 3

# Anglo-Saxons Versus Latins _____

Let us have no illusions; the first reflex of
the Methodist or Baptist preacher is to condemn
French immorality.
—André Siegfried, 1927

"Among the truest and most indestructible facts," declared Paul
Bourget, "the most fundamental is that of race." Bourget's conviction
of the centrality of race was not only shared by his compatriots, but it
became for him and others a device for organizing their observations
on American life. All travelers were deeply aware of America's
Anglo-Saxon origins and of the recent influx of immigrants from
other countries. This multiplicity of racial stocks, they agreed, was
likely to pose serious problems for the United States. As Bourget
noted, "On one point, my visit to the United States has not modified
my ideas: I am speaking of the concept which I brought with me of
the irreconcilable antagonism of the races."[1]

The problem of race, as travelers recognized, was not confined to
the United States. Racial conflict in Europe, however, usually took
the form of a confrontation between nations, while in the United
States, where different nationalities lived within the same community, conflict between races was a daily matter. In Bourget's view, the
absence of serious class conflict in the United States was related to
the virulence of the race problem. Europeans suffered from the
threat of a revolt by the poor against the rich, whereas, in America,
the poor were divided along racial lines. Native American workers

and their bosses were likely to establish a common front against the new immigrant workers. Most travelers agreed with Bourget that racial divisions in America were a more serious problem than class conflict. Almost all were persuaded that the melting pot was not effective, but few were prepared to predict an eruption of racial conflict, as Bourget did.[2]

The Anglo-Saxon origins of the United States were, in the eyes of travelers who accepted the primacy of race, a key to understanding life in the New World. American institutions, manners, customs, and a substantial part of the population, according to this view, were basically English in character. The clash between Anglo-Saxons and foreigners, which resulted from the demographic development of the country, was, however, relatively marginal for French observers compared to the conflict which arose by virtue of their own presence in an Anglo-Saxon world. In this sense, the Frenchman's tour of the United States was an occasion for renewing a struggle already hundreds of years old: the confrontation between the Latin and the Anglo-Saxon. Moreover, the New World was a choice environment in which to consider the ramifications of this clash. In addition to the predominant Anglo-Saxon elements on the continent, there were important enclaves of Latins, notably in Quebec, New Orleans, and Cuba, with whose values and life styles the travelers identified.

The belief in the fundamental importance of race was certainly a useful device for ordering observations of life in the New World. However, it was incompatible with the environmental assumptions which underlay the acceptance of the antithesis between the New and Old Worlds. That scheme posited the existence of a set of principles and institutions in America in radical opposition to those values of the past which guided the development of European societies. The belief in the formative influence of race, on the other hand, suggested that there was nothing new about the New World. The ethnic conflict between Latins and Anglo-Saxons, which travelers portrayed in America, could be witnessed as well on both sides of the Channel. It might have been possible to resolve the tension between these two schemes of analysis by qualifying both of them, but travelers were far more concerned about reporting their observations than they were about reconciling contradictions between them.

Moreover, the view that America was both an extension of Europe and in opposition to it was useful because in addition to providing a second scheme for ordering travelers' observations, it proclaimed the superiority of France. By contrasting American Anglo-Saxons unfavorably with their Latin counterparts, the observer, assuming the role of French nationalist, was able to reassure his audience of the essential virtue of France and the Latin race. This, in turn, reinforced the original, though somewhat different claim, of the antithesis between a feudal France and a modern America. Most observers—Jules Huret excepted—indicated only a dim awareness of this nationalistic function of the travel accounts. Ferri-Pisani had confessed, somewhat sheepishly, that French travelers, himself included, were "distracted from what they came to see and learn whenever they encountered a reminder of their motherland."[3] The references to the motherland were not, as Ferri-Pisani claimed, mere "distractions." The travelers' observations on life in foreign lands were the product of comparisons with aspects of life at home. The travel report was, in effect, a dialogue between two ways of life, which usually managed to confirm the superiority of the homeland.

While antithesis between Latin and Anglo-Saxon behavior was noted by every traveler, not all observers encouraged their readers to reject the values of the Anglo-Saxons or to endorse Latin attributes. The degree of hostility directed toward Anglo-Saxons varied with the state of Franco-American or Anglo-French diplomatic relations, and the values of the individual traveler. The gradual rapprochement between England and France, which began with the increasing threat from Germany in the 1890s, certainly affected the reactions of travelers. A turning point was reached in 1897 with the publication of Edmond Demolins's *A quoi tient la supériorité des Anglo-Saxons?* After its appearance, a number of Frenchmen began to regard the Anglo-Saxon character as a possible model for France, and this change naturally improved attitudes toward Anglo-Saxons. For the most part, however, travelers' opinions placed them clearly in the long tradition of French Anglophobia; whether Anglophobe or Anglophile, however, travelers regarded the United States as an extension of England.

The French perception of America as a province of Anglo-Saxon civilization had its origin in the colonial period. Already, in the eighteenth century, Anglomania stimulated an interest in America as Anglophobia was to do in the nineteenth century. Voltaire's creation of the Good Quaker was originally intended to describe the English, but it was also applied to Quakers in America.[4]

However, the philosophes' Americanism was based on an essentially nonracial view of man in the New World. The American was defined, not as an offshoot of the Anglo-Saxon race, but as a model of the enlightened man. A case in point was Benjamin Franklin, who was treated in France as a citizen of the world. However, French travelers and exiles in the New World as well as French observers in France soon helped to destroy this myth of the cosmopolitan American. The Jay treaty, the renewal of American trade with England after the Revolution, and the distaste for American habits provoked Frenchmen to reformulate their claim that France and America were partners in a common enterprise. Talleyrand, for example, remarked that "I have not found a single Englishman who did not feel at home among Americans and not a single Frenchman who did not feel a stranger." With proper allowance for the bitterness of a hostile émigré forced to find a home in the wilderness of America, there is evidence that this sentiment was widespread. According to Pierre Laussat, a diplomatic representative of Napoleon, "The Americans in general hate us. Even the least English of them is, in spite of his magnificent and hypocritical protests, much more English than French."[5]

The rise of nationalism after 1815 helped to accentuate the search for racial differences between citizens of France and the United States. In the nineteenth century, hardly a French traveler set foot on American shores without observing both the Anglo-Saxon character of American life and his own allegiance to the Latin way of life which was opposed to the former.[6] Tocqueville, whose own work dwelled primarily on the ideology of America, expressed most succinctly the conception of relations between races and continents which was prevalent after 1815. "The French of America are to the French of France as the Americans are to the English."[7] In the Civil War period, the cultural link between England and America was still unquestioned. Ferri-Pisani and Prince Napoleon were impressed by the "many traditions which outlived the War of Independence and which still attach through a thousand invisible bonds American mores to those of the former motherland."[8]

Such a position was easier to maintain during the Civil War than it was during the Progressive period when the United States had witnessed an influx of immigrants from the southern and eastern sections of Europe. Jules Huret, nonetheless, insisted that, despite the presence of "millions of Latins" in the United States, "the customs and the average mentality were not Latinized." When ex-ambassador Jules Cambon denied that America was Anglo-Saxon, Huret replied rhetorically, "Would he [Cambon] sustain the proposition as well that the ethics and the ideas of the Eastern American states on the seaboard from Canada to New York are not strongly impregnated with Puritanism?"[9] The "millions of Latins" who immigrated to the United States had not, in Huret's view, influenced the dominant culture of the United States. It remained a derivative of the Anglo-Saxon Puritan civilization. Ten years later, on the eve of World War I, André Siegfried confirmed this view. He called the United States "a new shoot from the old Anglo-Saxon trunk."[10]

The ethnic origins of Americans were apparent to travelers at different levels of the society and in various of its activities. Paul Bourget, who spent much of his time with the upper classes at Newport, saw their habits as evidence of "Puritan morality in a country of Anglo-Saxon traditions."[11] In at least three areas of American life—love, business, and cuisine—puritanical behavior was especially marked.

The analysis of romance in America inevitably began with a discussion of the American woman, her character and her habits. Most travelers noted the relative independence of women in America, compared to their European counterparts. Paul Bourget felt that this independence was combined with a desire to dominate which destroyed the romantic qualities of the woman.[12] Jules Huret was in essential agreement with Bourget. He lamented the absence of romantic appeal in "the American woman, who is so cold, so self-possessed, so narrowly realistic and calculating in all of her acts."[13]

This traditional assault on the frigidity of Anglo-Saxon women was extended to embrace the behavior of American men as well. There was an important difference, however. The American man's failure in romance was the result of timidity, not willfulness. Paul Adam opined that "the Yankee does not possess the gifts of seduction. Excessively timid, respectful, and sentimental, he is not obliged to resist the ardors of the Latin temperament." The mentality of the American male not only made it impossible for him to engage in amorous activity, but it destroyed his enjoyment in the contemplation of such activities. "Only a Latin could describe the finale of those dances where the male partner, while half undressed, demonstrates his obvious pleasure in pressing the female against him." This inability to enjoy erotic experiences was related to the mad pace of American life. Adam complained of the aggressive fashion in which American men boarded their buses. "No gallantry, no Latin sense of the erotic distracts the man from this warlike task."[14]

The inability of the Anglo-Saxon to enjoy his own and other bodies was judged a serious failure of the civilization, but it was not fatal. French travelers believed that other virtues compensated for this lack of sensuality. Frenchmen, particularly in the period after the 1890s, noted with some admiration the attributes of the successful American businessman. First of all, "the American of Anglo-Saxon origin," in contrast to his Latin counterparts, was self-sufficient. Paul de Rousiers suggested that the ability of Americans to withstand the loneliness of the West had enabled them to settle on the frontier where other races might have failed.[15] Such individualism, however, was combined with a kind of organizational ability which was also essential for exploiting the resources of the continent. Whereas the Latin might try to succeed alone, the American joined with others to attempt to bring his ideas to fruition. It was this energy and organizational sense of the businessman which, in Paul Adam's eyes, accounted for the strength of corporate enterprise in America.[16] While most travelers deplored the commercialism of American life, both de Rousiers and Adam believed that Frenchmen could learn a good deal from American businessmen without compromising the aesthetic qualities of French life.

Puritanism might produce positive attributes in the American businessman, but it was clearly not conducive to good habits in the realm of eating and drinking. There were numerous complaints from French travelers about American drinking practices. During the Civil War, Ferri-Pisani noted the provisioning of each railroad car with ice water. "Some of us cannot see one of these fountains, altars of temperance, without making a significant hydrophobic face."[17] The postwar period brought little change. When Paul de Rousiers

visited an American ranch which employed several Frenchmen, he
noted that his compatriots

drink together regardless of the hour, jeer at the prohibitionist Yankees, who
drink ice water and suffer from dyspepsia; if you want to see American life
from its least favorable side, go sit at these hospitable tables. You will hear it
criticized in all its details.[18]

In the last analysis, Puritan morality was most objectionable because of its crusading character. Anglo-Saxons sought to change the
beliefs and behavior of those who disagreed with them. Paul Bourget
noted "that fervor of proselytism which is so difficult for a Latin to
consider without some little suspicion. The history of the Anglo-
Saxon race would, however, be inexplicable without this hereditary
instinct of the missionary."[18]

The contrast between Latin and Anglo-Saxon mores, which appeared sporadically as the travelers reacted to the peculiarities of
American life, became most vivid and most systematic during the
encounters with Latin elements on the North American continent. In
the half century after the Civil War, travelers instinctively divided
the landscape of the New World into two geographic domains which
corresponded to ethnic groups. The largest areas were the province
of Anglo-Saxon culture, but there were significant enclaves in which
Latin customs flourished. Aside from Quebec, Cuba, and New Orleans, the preferred centers of Latin culture, the travelers met a
variety of groups and individuals of Latin origin scattered throughout
the United States. Visits to these areas provided not only an opportunity to describe them, but also an occasion for developing the
contrast between Anglo-Saxon and Latin behavior. This contrast,
almost invariably, clarified the superiority of the Latin way of life, by
permitting the French observer to identify with it, and thus with the
motherland.

Within the borders of the United States, travelers met a variety of
groups, but they were particularly impressed by the loyalty of immigrants from France to the French way of life. Despite the "uniform
mold" which shaped the personalities of immigrants and natives
alike, Frenchmen retained their old habits:

There is something touching in the singular persistence of our old national spirit. While the Germans, for example, acquire a new skin in several years, wherever they go, we remain ourselves.

This resistance to the pressure of Americanization was possible because "we prefer to permit ourselves to be smothered by the conquering race rather than accept its language and customs."[20]

Duvergier's encounter with loyal French immigrants was matched by the experience of the Bonapartist entourage. At one point, Prince Napoleon's party was stopped by "several Frenchmen, quite touched and speechless," who asked to speak with the prince:

They all long for the motherland. Of all the immigrants to America, the French are the only ones who cannot forget their flag, or the skies of the old country. They die with this memory engraved in their hearts and bequeath it intact to their children.[21]

Earlier, Ferri-Pisani had expressed some concern about a group of French volunteers "who came to the New World to make fortunes and who, instead of working, put on the uniform of a Zouave and enlist for sixty francs a month in the Civil War." The adherence of these immigrants from France to a foreign cause seemed entirely out of character, given the loyalty of other immigrants to the mother country. However, first impressions turned out to be deceiving. "Like real Parisians [the soldiers] began to mock the cause they were serving." This behavior suggested to Ferri-Pisani "the wide divergence in mores between these jesters making fun of everything and the Northerners imperturbably serious and incapable of discovering ridicule within themselves or others."[22]

Loyalty to France at the level of the group was duplicated by individuals. Duvergier praised Regis de Trobriand, a career officer in the American army, who, "in spite of his long American naturalization, remains a true Frenchman."[23] So did General Frémont, who pleased Prince Napoleon's entourage by explaining that he always placed "an acute accent on his name when some Anglo-Saxon hand forgets it."[24] French culture was still vital and attractive in the New World.

Travelers' encounters with official representatives of France were also occasions for celebrating the virtues of the mother country. The sight of the French Consul in New York brought a feeling of "patriotic emotion" to the hearts of Prince Bonaparte and his entourage.[25] During his visit to Washington, Jean-Jacques Ampère met the French minister "who represents French urbanity and Parisian intelligence in the midst of American frigidity."[26]

With the exception of the city of New Orleans, however, France's presence within the borders of the United States was insignificant. Frenchmen who wished to applaud the achievements of French culture in the New World were obliged to leave the United States for Canada. All travelers agreed that Quebec, in cultural matters, was a continuation of the homeland. This was evident in the reaction of Duvergier as he crossed the northern border of the United States; he remarked, "I am no longer a foreigner,"[27] and when Ampère crossed the border in the other direction, he commented, "I am abandoning France again." After suffering from the language and customs of the United States, Ampère was "consoled by hearing French in the streets" of Montreal.[28]

The French presence, however, was not always easily recognizable. It might be obscured by a veneer of Anglo-Saxon dress or language, but the knowledgeable observer from France would not be fooled. "Under the English uniform," Duvergier discovered, "there are hearts which beat for France."[29] Fifty years later, André Siegfried, while listening to a session of the Canadian Parliament in Ottawa, found "that underneath this foreign verbal envelope, I feel the passage of a hot current of our Latin eloquence. Only the words are English; all the rest is ours." The tone of the French speaker was in striking contrast to the voice of a second orator. "He is an English Canadian from Ontario who has the floor; the pure nasal Yankee accent is appalling; the tone is vulgar and commonplace."[30] Despite the veneer, it was impossible to conceal true French behavior; French travelers welcomed their compatriots from Quebec even when they spoke English and wore Anglo-Saxon clothes.

The applause for the achievements of French Canadians and the pleasure in discovering French customs in the New World were slightly tempered by the concern for increasing Anglo-Saxon domination. In the conflict between Anglo-Saxon and Latin in Quebec, the French travelers' support was offered without hesitation to "the people of French origin who defend their nationality with touching perseverance against the double invasion of England and the United States."[31] The French noted with concern and disapproval the manner in which the superior human achievement of their compatriots was threatened by the commercial dominance of the Anglo-Saxons. They feared the disappearance of the Quebec farmers who were impoverished, but happy. And what would become of the gaiety of Montreal Sundays which contrasted with the dismal silence of the Sabbath in New York? Would Laval University, which granted fewer diplomas than American colleges but preserved the true liberal arts approach, survive the Anglo-Saxon onslaught? The French Jesuits, credited with "the miracles of patience and humanity" which had converted the Indians to Christianity while the Anglo-Saxons acted with "disdainful brutality," were already in decline.[32] In short, the power of the Anglo-Saxons to overwhelm French civilization in the New World would be a defeat for the highest values.

The search for French provinces on the continent of North America took many travelers south as well as north. In New Orleans, as in Quebec, there was a large Latin population which lived in close proximity to the dominant Anglo-Saxons. The travelers were again interested in the relationship between the two groups. Xavier Marmier called attention to the "hereditary antagonism of the Gaul and the Anglo Saxon":

United on the same soil, by the same laws and the same interest, the two have been unable to mix with each other. Like the Europeans and the Asiatics, they retain their nationality on each side of their Bosphorus, and when one crosses Canal Street, it is like entering an entirely different country.[33]

Jules Huret, on the other hand, was persuaded that this racial confrontation had disappeared as a result of the New Orleans climate:

The sun has melted and dissolved the absolute elements of the races, and if it has not yet amalgamated them, it has accomplished the miracle of rendering the Puritans gracious and of making the souls of Quaker sons voluptuous.[34]

In this formulation, racial differences could be tempered by a proper environment. They were neither absolute nor enduring. Moreover, the climate had not only changed the character of the inhabitants, but their physical appearance as well. "In every street we meet many southern faces with bright black eyes, black mustaches, a supple, easy gait, and none of the Anglo-Saxon stiffness which we are accustomed to in the northern states."

The charm of New Orleans was further enhanced for Huret by the Gallic sounds in the air. "What a pleasure to hear [people] suddenly express themselves in our language as purely and clearly as if they had just left France." In effect, New Orleans was a mere extension of the homeland, as New York and New England were provinces of England. This point was clarified at the Mardi Gras parade where the gaiety and exuberance were

enough to make us realize that we are far from New England. . . . This is truly Marseilles with its cosmopolitan mixture of bronze complexioned easterners, its animated wharfs, its blue sky and radiant sun.[35]

The sun, however, did not always succeed in modifying racial traits. While the Anglo-Saxons were "Latinized" by the New Orleans climate, Paul Adam was persuaded that the American occupation of Cuba had "Anglicized" the Latin inhabitants of the island. Here race triumphed over environment. "The indolence and the daily siesta are finished. In four years, the Americans have changed the customs of the middle class and the elite." While most French travelers would have deplored this transition, Adam applauded it:

Even the French, who, with their Latin sentiments, criticized the violent activity of the Yankee, his passion for success, his quite brutal pride, his scorn for the individual in opposition to the collectivity, his hatred of laziness and scepticism, . . .

must admit the achievements of the occupation. It had accomplished the "joining of Latin individualism and Nordic solidarity."[36]

While most travelers implied that Anglo-Saxon and Latin traits could not be mixed, Adam regarded such a marriage as both possible and desirable. The combination was not intended to destroy the virtues of Latin civilization, but merely to energize an indolent population. Adam was quick to point up the positive aspects of the Latin character with its "vivid sense of honor." He acknowledged in the buildings of Havana a symbol of the achievements of "the Helleno-Latin forces in the southern lands of the two Americas." Moreover, the buildings "attest in a sublime way to the progressive role of the Latin mind which opened the way for geniuses of European races and was the master of all their active thoughts."[37] For Adam, the Anglo-Saxon model was useful, because it would help the Latin to regain his former energy. It was a means to an end, which was the preservation of Latin values.

The enclaves of Latin civilization in the New World, though smaller in area, population, and power than their Anglo-Saxon counterparts, played an important role for French visitors to America in the prewar period. They provided an analytical convenience by which travelers could set off Anglo-Saxon traits against their opposites. They also helped to reassure French readers that in spite of the growing power of Anglo-Saxon countries, French civilization retained its virtues.

Although the antithesis between Old World and New, between Latin and Anglo-Saxon was frequently apparent in the observations of travelers, it is important to realize that these devices were used in a casual and sporadic fashion. The two forms of antithesis appeared whenever an encounter with some group or individual suggested their relevance. The travel volumes, however, were not organized to explore these themes but to demonstrate the diversity of the human and natural landscape of the New World. Each chapter in the reports treated a region, a city, or some natural wonder. In the process, of course, the observer was led to consider the ethnic elements which he encountered, but the dominant impression which emerged was one of variety. Only in the 1920s would the antithesis become a systematic mode of analysis. Only then would the impression of diversity, human and natural, give way to the concept of a uniform, homogeneous system. On occasion, prewar America appeared threatening to Frenchmen, and briefly they reported its behavior as systematic, but for the most part the United States was still a young giant which had not yet come of age.

NOTES

1. *Outre Mer* (Paris, 1895), 420, 227. The word "race," as used in this quotation and in the chapter, refers loosely to ethnic differences rather than to scientifically measured physical distinctions between peoples.

2. *Ibid.*, 226. It is likely that the timing of Bourget's visit, coinciding with the nativist outburst of the 1890s, led him to exaggerate racial conflict.

3. *Prince Napoléon in America, 1861*, trans. Georges Joyaux (Bloomington, 1959), 151.

4. Echeverria, *Mirage in the West* (Princeton, 1951), 18.

5. Quoted in *ibid.*, 193, 150.

6. Tocqueville's *Democracy in America* is an exception to the rule. The author's preference for disregarding race as an explanation for historical developments is well known. He did, however, regard the way of life of the Quebec peasant as superior to the traditions of the American farmer. *Journey to America*, ed. J. P. Mayer, trans. George Lawrence (New Haven, 1959), 189.

7. *Ibid.*, 189.

8. *Prince Napoléon in America*, 105.

9. *En Amérique* (Paris, 1904), I, 89.

10. *Deux mois en Amérique du Nord* (Paris, 1916), 91.

11. *Outre Mer*, 57.

12. *Ibid.*, 226.

13. *En Amérique*, II, 378.

14. *Vues d'Amérique* (Paris, 1906), 103, 161, 393.

15. *La vie américaine*, 146. De Rousiers discovered one Frenchman who was able to survive the isolation of the frontier. Mandat-Grancey, a neighbor of Theodore Roosevelt in South Dakota, and author of several volumes on the American West, was an exception to the rule.

16. *Vues d'Amérique*, 120.

17. *Prince Napoléon in America*, 83.

18. *La vie américaine*, 148.

19. *Outre Mer*, 380.

20. *Huit mois en Amérique*, II, 29.

21. *Prince Napoléon in America*, 149.

22. *Ibid.*, 78.

23. *Huit mois en Amérique*, II, 309.

24. *Prince Napoléon in America*, 241.

25. *Ibid.*, 41.

26. *Promenade en Amérique*, II, 43.

27. *Huit mois en Amérique*, I, 382.

28. *Promenade en Amérique*, I, 106, 155.
29. *Huit mois en Amérique*, I, 382.
30. *Deux mois en Amérique du Nord*, II.
31. *Promenade en Amérique*, I, 137.
32. *Huit mois en Amérique*, I, 397, 173.
33. *Les Etats-Unis et le Canada* (Tours, 1874), 216.
34. *En Amérique*, I, 336.
35. *Ibid.*, I, 351, 334.
36. *Vues d'Amérique*, 301, 309, 327.
37. *Ibid.*, 311, 323.

# PART II:

## The Changing World, 1917–1932

# chapter 4

# The Anti-Americans _____

> All of our writers are going to America and—
> happily—returning. Each, in turn, wants to
> help us discover her.
> —*Europe Nouvelle*, 1930

> After my return to Paris, I became aware that
> to be in fashion, one must criticize America.
> —Paul Hazard, 1931

The French image of America in the twenties was altered in response to three categories of events: broad changes in the world order, the evolution of diplomatic and cultural relations between France and America, and revolutionary developments within American society. The impact of these changes on French intellectuals stemmed in part from the character of the events and in part from the predispositions of the individuals who experienced and articulated them. While there is no simple formula for gauging the beliefs of intellectuals, they are reflected, however imperfectly, in such personal factors as political affiliation; they are also the product of educational background, taken in the broadest sense. In assessing these influences, it is essential to distinguish between the leaders and the followers of the anti-American movement. The backgrounds of those individuals who played a major role in articulating the new image must be assessed with special care.

It would be tempting to assume that the rising hostility to the United States in France was the product of the ignorance, hasty reactions, and radical political beliefs of French commentators. Yet, even a cursory examination of the roster of anti-Americans indicates that they were recruited, to a large degree, from the most knowledgeable French authorities on American life. Many of the commentators had lived in America for extensive periods of time and had published substantial studies of the United States in the prewar period. These observers were usually staunch French nationalists who believed in republican institutions. Many were spokesmen for Anglo-Saxon culture in France, and some had worked for the Franco-American entente.

In all of these respects, the new anti-Americans resembled closely the engineers, businessmen, and professors who had promoted the entente and mass production in the early twenties. Indeed, many of the key anti-American spokesmen were recruited from the moderate and conservative ranks of the pro-Americans, rather than from more radical elements in France. Of course, not all of America's defenders were alienated by the developments of the decade. Cambon, Schreiber, and Hyacinthe Dubreuil persisted in their strong commitment to mass production. Others, like Charles Cestre and Firmin Roz, were more ambivalent. They continued to applaud American idealism, while paying tribute to the new anti-American literature.[1] Their loyalty to the United States stemmed in part from a generation gap. They were considerably older than the new authorities on America.[2] In addition, they were professionally committed to the entente: Cestre, as holder of the only chair in American civilization in the French university system; and Roz, as editor of the journal *France-Amérique*. Only very strong ties of this sort prevented an even larger defection of conservatives and moderates from the ranks of the pro-Americans.

The authorities on Anglo-Saxon and American civilization were joined by other prominent intellectuals in their campaign against American power and institutions. The new recruits were largely drawn to the debate on American civilization by their concern for the future of Europe. The rise of the United States was, for these men, an explanation of the decline of Europe. Hence, the study of America became essential. This is not to suggest that Anglo-Saxon specialists were insensitive to the shift in power. Indeed, this was one of the developments which motivated them to abandon their pro-American stance.

The image of America was only marginally affected by the degree of past interest in the United States on the part of a given observer. Professional backgrounds, however, exercised an influence on the approach if not the image of French commentators. Professors and politicians were inclined toward a systematic consideration of the American economy and politics. They focused on the development of public issues. Novelists and some journalists, on the other hand, investigated the effects of these developments on the behavior of the individual. Their accounts were impressionistic and anecdotal.[3] In reality, these two approaches complemented each other. They permitted the French reader to discover both public policies and their effect on the lives of individual Americans.

In view of America's reputation as the leading capitalist nation, the paucity of books on the United States by communist and socialist critics may, at first, appear surprising. To some extent, Marxist observers were diverted from exploring American civilization by their primary concern with the development of Soviet Communism. The Revolution of 1917 was a fresh subject in the twenties and its possibilities were still to be explored. In any event, American civilization presented a far greater affront to traditionalists than it did to Marxists. The latter generally viewed the assembly line and modern technology as a positive contribution to the revolution. They, of course, wished to end capitalist control of the means of production, but they did not intend to abolish or limit those means as some traditionalists did. Moreover, Marxists, with their internationalist views, were less sensitive to the decline of French power and the rise of the United States. These developments might even be welcomed as progress toward the demise of capitalism and the coming of the proletarian revolution.

The origins of the anti-American position may be traced to the publication in 1927 of three major studies of the United States by André Seigfried, André Tardieu, and Lucien Romier. These sober accounts presented ideas which were disseminated in a somewhat more colorful and emphatic manner by other French intellectuals. Georges Duhamel, Luc Durtain, and Paul Morand were most responsible for familiarizing the literate public with the views of their three predecessors. Because of the important role they played in creating the new image of America, these six men deserve disproportionate attention from the student of anti-Americanism.

The influence of these authorities is evident from the recognition which they received from other travelers in America and from reviewers in the leading journals. Until 1925, the works of Jules Huret and Victor Cambon had been accepted by most travelers as the standard accounts of American life. Louis Thomas called Huret's *En Amérique* "the best introduction to modern America for a Frenchman." Three years later, Firmin Roz cited Huret, along with Paul Bourget, to substantiate his own views of American life.[4] Victor Cambon's *Etats-Unis—France* was just as highly regarded. Louis Thomas considered Cambon second only to Huret as an authority on the United States. Herriot cited Cambon on the joys of American life, and Charles Cestre used Cambon's testimony on American industrialism.[5]

The citations in the travel literature reveal clearly that new authorities were discovered after 1927. André Lafond offered testimony on this point. He claimed that

once we have read the books of André Tardieu, the *Qui sera le maître, Europe ou Amérique?* of Lucien Romier, skimmed the illustrated volume published by Larousse, *Les Etats-Unis*, accepted as a basic book the remarkable work of André Seigfried, *Les Etats-Unis d'aujourd'hui*, we are sufficiently prepared for making contact with the products and the peoples of the New World.[6]

The fact that Lafond's study is largely a compilation of quotations from Siegfried, Tardieu, and Romier suggests that he made more contact with his predecessors than with the New World.[7]

Testimony to the emergence of a new image was offered in the same year by Firmin Roz, who was himself regarded as a leading expert on the United States. Roz found the work of Siegfried and Tardieu a kind of watershed in the French interpretation of modern American life. He argued that these "two quite different books published in 1927 help to throw a clear light on the United States today, on the short and striking past which has made her a nation, and on her future orientation." The two books, moreover, had enabled "several thousand elite Frenchmen" to "develop an accurate idea of the United States, based on reason and reflection."[8]

Enthusiasm for the work of the new authorities was also evident in French periodicals. The *Mercure de France* dubbed Siegfried's book "one of the most remarkable," while the *Revue des Deux Mondes* considered it "a masterpiece."[9] On no less than two separate occasions *Europe Nouvelle* referred to Siegfried's work as "a fine book."[10] The praise for Tardieu was only slightly more restrained. *Europe Nouvelle* admired his rigorous logic and his pessimism. The *Revue de Paris* found Tardieu's new book up to the standard set by the author in his first study of the United States written almost two decades earlier[11]

While for years the work of Siegfried, Tardieu, and Romier continued to receive the praise of critics and travelers alike, many intellectuals read with enthusiasm other accounts of American life. Indeed, by 1930, Georges Duhamel, Paul Morand, and Luc Durtain had, like their predecessors, achieved the status of authorities on America. In 1931, when *Le Figaro* polled French intellectuals to find out if American civilization threatened France, Duhamel's *Scènes de la vie future* was cited by seven different authors as evidence of the threat. Critics in the periodicals were also prepared to accept Duhamel's work, although they cautioned against certain exaggerations in his argument.[12]

Paul Morand's study of New York was just as well received. The *Revue Universelle* called it "an excellent book." The *Mercure de France*, after greeting *New York* as "one of the great successes of the present season," maintained two years later that "Paul Morand remains a very useful, agreeable, and intelligent Baedeker" for New York.[13] Luc Durtain's opinions on the United States were implicitly praised by the *Revue Universelle*, but he was rebuked for exhibiting too much enthusiasm for the Soviet Union.[14]

By 1931, it was virtually impossible for a French traveler or commentator to think about the United States without reference to one or more of the six authorities who had emerged in the period between 1927 and 1930. In his study of America, Marcel Braunschvig cited the work of Siegfried, Duhamel, and Morand. In the same year, Charles Pomaret, writing on American imperialism in Europe, acknowledged his debt to Siegfried, Duhamel, and Tardieu.[15] André Maurois even complained that the very abundance of the new literature made it impossible to achieve an independent view of America:

As in our childhood recollections, the memory is formed by the tales of our parents, photographs, and paintings, so our travel memories are ruined by reading. Am I the one who saw the country? Is it Keyserling? or Siegfried? or Romier? or Luc Durtain?[16]

Because of the shrill tone of Duhamel's polemic and the great controversy which followed its publication, scholars and some reviewers have focused on him as the key anti-American spokesman of his generation.[17] This emphasis and the interest in Morand and Durtain seems somewhat exaggerated in the light of their acknowledged reliance on other sources. Duhamel considered *Les Etats-Unis d'aujourd'hui* an "excellent and critical work." Durtain, who denounced the pervasive ignorance among French intellectuals about America, agreed that the work of Lucien Romier and "the memorable *Etats-Unis* of Siegfried" were exceptions to the rule.[18] He dedicated a later volume, *Dieux blancs, hommes jaunes*, to "the penetrating observer of America, André Siegfried."[19]

The exaggeration of Duhamel's role would be less important if it did not obscure the origins of anti-Americanism. By tracing Duhamel's ideas to their source in 1927, it is possible to establish clearly the manner in which they were shaped by such political issues as debts and security. Siegfried, Tardieu, and Romier provide an important link between the events of the mid-twenties and the vehement anti-Americanism of 1930.

Of the six new authorities on America, three were conservative republicans whose anti-Americanism was moderate in tone. André Siegfried's long-standing interest in the Anglo-Saxon peoples can be attributed in part to his Protestant background, and in part to his father's connection with the United States. Siegfried liked to recall his father's account of a visit with President Lincoln in the White House; the meeting took place while the elder Siegfried, an Alsatian cotton merchant, was on a business trip to the United States.[20] André Siegfried was trained at the Ecole Libre des Sciences Politiques, whose faculty was strongly oriented toward Anglo-Saxon institutions. His dissertation on *La Démocratie en Nouvelle-Zélande* explored the spread of English civilization outside of Europe, a subject which was to interest him for the rest of his career.[21]

Siegfried made the first of many voyages to the United States in

1898. On the eve of the Great War, in 1914, he returned to America, this time to prepare a series of articles for *Le Petit Havre*, his hometown newspaper. These articles were collected into his first book on the United States.[22] During the war, Siegfried used his knowledge of English as an interpreter with the British army. It was only after the war, however, that he emerged as the authority in France on the Anglo-Saxon nations. In 1924, Siegfried published *L'Angleterre d'aujourd'hui*. In 1925 he spent six months in America preparing *Les Etats-Unis d'aujourd'hui*, which appeared two years later.

The enthusiastic reception of Siegfried's volume can be attributed to the author's sober, objective tone, and the manner in which he highlighted all of the major issues between France and the United States.[23] The book gave equal attention to diplomatic questions, particularly the rise of America as a world financial power, and American domestic problems such as the race conflict and the development of mass society. The book's reception helped secure Siegfried's growing reputation. In addition to his regular teaching duties at the Ecole Libre des Sciences Politiques, he was soon called upon (in 1933) to give courses on American civilization at the Collège de France. Siegfried's place in French literary circles was fully recognized with his election to the French Academy. Throughout the twentieth century, the author's political views never deviated. His belief in an orderly republic was expressed in his support for Raymond Poincaré. (It is true that Siegfried refused to vote for Georges Clemenceau, but his motivation was personal rather than political.)[24]

The career of André Tardieu paralleled Siegfried's at many points. Tardieu was raised in a traditional French Catholic household, but he, like Siegfried, attended the Ecole Libre des Sciences Politiques and later taught there.[25] Tardieu made his mark in French politics. In contrast to Siegfried, who on four occasions ran unsuccessfully for the French Assembly, Tardieu was elected to that body and also became an important figure in the Ministry of Foreign Affairs. An opportunity to play the role of unofficial diplomat brought Tardieu to Harvard in 1908 as visiting professor. His year there culminated in the publication of *Notes sur les Etats-Unis*, a study of American political and economic institutions.

Tardieu's experience in the United States proved especially useful during World War I. When Prime Minister Clemenceau needed a man to head the French High Commission in America, an organization of 1,200 men which was created to coordinate the American and French war efforts, Tardieu was a logical selection for the post. After a year in the United States, he returned to France to continue liaison efforts with American officials both during and after the war. It was Tardieu's special relationship with Colonel House which helped to salvage the Versailles conference after the development of a stalemate between Wilson and Clemenceau. In the twenties, Tardieu continued to support the hard-line policies which Poincaré now advocated. His increasing disenchantment with the American position on debts and disarmaments was expressed in *Devant l'obstacle*, an explanation of the breakdown in Franco-American relations.

In contrast to Siegfried, Tardieu focused heavily on developments in foreign affairs, leaving aside the issues of mass production and nativism. In no sense did he blame the demise of the Franco-American entente on American policies alone. France's failure to adopt a forceful negotiating posture had contributed to her present difficulties, he believed. However, Tardieu's portrait of an American giant trying to impose her values on a weak France helped to justify anti-American feeling in France. It is ironic that this defender of Americanization should have helped, in spite of himself, to create anti-American feeling which in turn stirred hostility to the new technology.

Lucien Romier displayed considerable ambivalence in his reaction to mass society. As former editor of *La journée industrielle*, the leading business daily in France, he was naturally sympathetic to the business community in France. However, like certain businessmen, he was not an unrestrained admirer of modernization. His views accorded well with those of the readers of *Le Figaro*. Romier, as editor of that leading Catholic daily in the late twenties, responded to the developments of the period by upholding traditional values.

Romier's interest in America was prompted not only by the emergence of mass society, but also by the fear of American imperialism. In 1925 and 1926, just before his departure for the United States, he completed *Explication de notre temps* and *Nation et civilisation*, both of which explored the theme of Europe's future. In October of 1926, after his return from America, Romier, along with Paul Claudel and Paul Valéry, attended the Pan-Europe Congress held in Vienna as a delegate from France.[26] His trip to America must be seen in the context of this continuing search for the solution to Europe's problems in the postwar period.

Romier's study of the United States was a measured attack on the problems of mass society. Leaving aside the diplomatic problems between France and America, he concentrated on the implications of mass production, the new consumer society, and standardization for the nation, the individual, and the elite. In the process, he made it clear that the United States must bear the responsibility for the extension of the concept of mass society.[27]

The studies by Duhamel, Durtain, and Morand differed in tone and emphasis from those of their three predecessors. Duhamel and Durtain were drawn to the United States, not by any long-standing concern with American affairs, but by their preoccupation with Europe's future. Prior to the twenties, their interest in the United States had been confined to an enthusiasm for Walt Whitman; they admired his work while participating in a commune for young writers (the Abbaye de Creteil) which was founded in 1906.[28] Other than this brief enthusiasm, an occasional appearance by Georges Duhamel at Sylvia Beach's Left Bank Book Shop, a hangout for American writers during the twenties, was the only indication of interest in America.[29]

After World War I, the two writers became deeply involved in working for a durable peace. Both men had served as doctors in the war, and both had been horrified by the suffering they witnessed. Duhamel expressed his anguish in *Vie des martyrs* and *Civilisation*; just after the war, he and Durtain helped to found *Clarté*, a left-wing journal committed to the establishment of a peaceful, socialistic Europe.[30] Although they refused to join the Communist party, their sympathy for radical causes earned them an invitation to visit the Soviet Union. Each author published an enthusiastic volume of travel notes describing various features of the new regime.[31] It was after their travels to Russia that the two authors visited America. Duhamel accomplished his tour of the United States in three miserable weeks; Durtain, who also made a swing through America in 1928, was renewing an earlier acquaintance with the country.[32]

Duhamel's *Scènes de la vie future* is justly celebrated for its vehement attack on almost every aspect of mass society, ranging from the automobile and the motion picture to mass production and advertising. Indeed, the author's distaste for the new technology was so strong that he largely neglected problems of race and diplomatic issues.[33] Durtain's remarks on America were somewhat more restrained and more thorough. In addition to his nonfictional account, *Quelques notes d'U.S.A.*, he explored the reaction of the individual to puritanism and materialism in his two novels, *Quarantième étage* and *Hollywood dépassé*.[34]

Paul Morand had far more extensive contact with Anglo-Saxon culture than either Duhamel or Durtain, although he too visited America for the first time in the twenties. Morand's studies at the Ecole Libre des Sciences Politiques, where André Tardieu was his teacher, helped to orient him toward England. In 1908, while Tardieu was teaching at Harvard, Morand spent the year at Oxford University. During the war, he returned to England as attaché at the French embassy in London.

Meanwhile, he was developing an interest in the United States through his frequent contacts with Jean Giraudoux, the playwright and diplomat, and Tardieu, both of whom visited America during the war.[35] Only in 1925, as part of a trip around the world, did Morand himself actually set foot in the New World. He made up for lost time by returning to New York on three occasions in the next four years. These visits helped Morand prepare his famous study of the city, which was published in 1930.[36] In addition, he had occasion to read nearly every major French traveler who had written on America from Talleyrand, Lafayette, and Clemenceau to Paul Bourget and Paul Claudel.

The product of these efforts was an apparently enthusiastic portrait of New York which emphasized its diversity and history; the spectacular features of the city, such as its skyscrapers and speakeasies, were presented along with its museums and ghettos. In his conclusion, however, Morand stigmatized New York as violent and vulgar and therefore typically American. These sentiments did nothing to allay the suspicions of his fellow intellectuals about the dangers of American civilization.

Nonetheless, Morand was alone among the six leading authorities in presenting some redeeming features in the new technology. It was, in fact, his zeal for portraying the dynamic aspects of the twentieth-century world which earned for him the reputation as "the model traveler" of the era. Jacques Chastenet explained that "Morand doesn't pause over nature's spectacles; he is only interested in the most modern aspects of customs."[37] The preoccupation with modernism was also evident in Morand's fictional work. *Champions du monde* (Paris, 1930) studied the disintegration of four American characters who could not withstand the pressures of modern society.[38] In a number of shorter works, Morand portrayed the tension between the environment of urban America and the instincts of Afro-Americans.[39] Despite his interest in Negritude, his friendship with Jean Cocteau and the surrealists, and a general sympathy for contemporary fashions, Morand remained at heart an advocate of traditional values. Both Morand and Duhamel, like Siegfried, were elected to the French Academy.

In addition to these six leading authorities, a large number of other Frenchmen contributed to the commentary on American civilization. For the purposes of this study, they may be divided into two groups: Frenchmen who actually visited America and those who did not. Among the former were a side variety of commentators, some offering serious studies of American society and others who preferred to dwell on the spectacular—usually seamy—elements of American life. Three recipients of grants—Bernard Faÿ, Jean Gachon, and André Philip—were among the most systematic observers of the United States in this period. Faÿ, who was later to lecture on American civilization at the Collège de France, received a fellowship in 1919 to do research in the United States on Franco-American relations in the eighteenth century.[40] Both Philip and Gachon were recipients of Rockefeller grants: Gachon to study American foreign policy and Philip, a member of the Socialist party, to do research for a book on American labor with the aid of John Commons of the University of Wisconsin.

Other French observers of the American scene in the twenties had even a longer association with the United States. Before publishing his observations on American life in 1929, Régis Michaud had spent twenty years at Berkeley, Princeton, and Illinois as a professor of French literature. Michaud was also a student of American literature and a correspondent for the reactionary *Revue Universelle*. Lucien Lehmen, who also published his views of the United States in 1929, had been there for a decade. The experience of André Maurois was somewhat different. While he made his first visit to America in 1927, he was already well acquainted with Anglo-Saxon culture. Maurois served with the British army as liaison officer during World War I and wrote extensively about nineteenth-century Britain in the twenties.[41] He, too, was elected to the French Academy.

Other French travelers of the decade were drawn to the United States, like Romier, Duhamel, and Durtain, by an immediate concern for the problems of Europe. Robert Aron and Arnaud Dandieu, whose personalist doctrine acclaimed traditional values in hopes of restoring the primacy of the individual, naturally saw the country as the most extreme threat to their beliefs. Marcel Braunschvig, professor of French literature at Lycée Louis-le-Grand in Paris, was a more careful student of the United States. He spent a year there before concluding that Europe should cherish her old culture. A more popular advocate of traditional (or "Oriental") values in the twenties was the Count de Keyserling. Although he was a German philosopher, his views of America, which were translated into French, are relevant to the creation of the French image because of their impact in France. Speaking of his book, *Europe Nouvelle* proclaimed, "No study offers a better opportunity for Frenchmen to organize, test, and broaden the ideas that our own travelers and economists have transmitted to us on the United States." [42]

There were a number of other authors who preferred to present America as a spectacle rather than analyze it as a civilization. Paul Achard, for example, divided his time largely between New York and Hollywood, those pleasure domes of the United States. Achard was a reporter for the reactionary *Ami du Peuple*. Novelist J. Joseph Renaud and journalist André Lafond spent most of their time in New York City. Lafond, the editor of the *Journal du Rouen*, was somewhat more concerned about public issues than Renaud.

Along with French travelers in America, two groups of French commentators, most of whom had never visited the United States, evinced a strong interest in the development of American civilization. Certain critics explored the decline of Europe in terms of rising American power. The most influential of these commentators on the European crisis were geographers René Grousset and Albert Demangeon, poet Paul Valéry, philosophers René Guénon and Henri

Massis, both of whom advocated the restoration of the medieval church, and literary critics Maurice Muret and Gaston Riou.

Other commentators studied the rise of American empire directly. Passionate polemics were written on this subject by two Radical-Socialists: deputy J. L. Chastanet and publicist Kadmi-Cohen. Conservative banker Octave Homberg, who had visited America briefly during the war, wrote an equally biting attack. Somewhat more scholarly assaults on American imperialism came from the pens of another Radical-Socialist deputy, Charles Pomaret, and two academic specialists, Jean Bonnefon-Craponne and Pierre Laurent.

It should be evident that anti-Americanism developed among different intellectuals in different degrees and different forms. Some critics, such as André Tardieu, were primarily concerned about the exercise of American power in the diplomatic sphere. Others, like Lucien Romier, focused on the dangers of mass society. Among those observers who adopted a tone of outrage in discussing America were Georges Duhamel and Kadmi-Cohen. Most, however, presented their accusations with more sobriety. Yet the commentators shared a common origin and a common concern. They had a strong commitment to the maintenance of some aspects of the prewar world; they were consequently unhappy with France's decline and the development of mass society. By contrast, the more radical elements in the French intellectual community were far less concerned with these two developments, because they were better attuned to change. The conservative impulse of the anti-Americans was reflected, as André Rousseaux pointed out, in their common acceptance of Duhamel's views. Frenchmen, he said, "recognized themselves in him [Duhamel], because they too are conservative, bourgeois, and attached to their property, especially if it is land or a house."[43] Thus, Radical-Socialists and conservative republicans, who were bitterly divided on some issues, were joined by the fear of American power and American culture in a defense of traditional values.

## NOTES

1. Their enthusiasm for the new literature was evident in the following reviews: Firmin Roz, "L'évolution des Etats-Unis et l'avenir des relations

franco-américaines," *Revue Universelle* (January 15, 1928); and Charles Cestre, "Scènes de la vie future," *La Quinzaine Critique* (July 25, 1930).

2. Cestre and Roz were respectively four and nine years older than Siegfried, who was himself a year older than Tardieu and ten years older than Romier.

3. Novelists including Georges Duhamel, Luc Durtain, and Paul Morand frequently serialized their fictional and nonfictional accounts of America in the *Revue de Paris*. The more systematic work of such scholars and journalists as André Siegfried and Lucien Romier was published in the *Revue des Deux Mondes* or *Europe Nouvelle*.

4. *Les Etats-Unis inconnus*, (Paris, 1920), 278. *L'Amérique nouvelle* (Paris, 1923), 11, 15.

5. *Les Etats-Unis inconnus*, 279. *Impressions d'Amérique* (Lyon, 1923), 27. *Les Etats-Unis* (Paris, 1927), 196.

6. *New-York 28* (Rouen, 1929), 13.

7. The involvement of Lafond with the work of his predecessors was also exemplified by his invitation to Lucien Romier to preface his work. Furthermore, his book was selected to receive the Ralph Beaver Strassburger Prize awarded annually to an author who helps to promote Franco-American relations. The awards jury was headed by André Tardieu.

8. "L'évolution des Etats-Unis . . . ," *Revue Universelle* (January 15, 1928), 175, 202.

9. Henri Mazel, "Science Sociale" (November 15, 1928), 182. André Chaumeix, "Revue littéraire.—Images d'Amérique" (June 15, 1930), 928.

10. "Les Etats-Unis se détournent de l'Europe.—Conséquences pratiques de la Doctrine de Monroe" (April 30, 1927), 562. "L'election de M. Herbert Hoover" (November 10, 1928), 1528. André Gide also praised Siegfried's study of the United States. *The Journals of André Gide* (New York, 1941-1951), III, 46.

11. Jean Boulan, "Les dernières publications américaines et sur les Etats-Unis" (June 4, 1927), 734. Ignatus, "La politique: M. André Tardieu" (June 1, 1927), 706.

12. Gerard de Catalogne, *Dialogue entre deux mondes* (Paris, 1931); René Lalou, "*Scènes de la vie future* par Georges Duhamel," *Europe Nouvelle* (June 14, 1930), 892; Henri Massis, "*Scènes de la vie future*," *Revue Universelle* (June 15, 1930), 737; Gabriel Brunet, "Georges Duhamel et la civilisation américaine," *Mercure de France* (January 1, 1931), 10.

13. André Rousseaux, "*New-York*, par Paul Morand" (March 1, 1930), 622; Claude Merki, "Voyages" (May 15, 1930), 184; René de Weck, "Bibliothèque politique" (February 1, 1932), 736.

14. Robert Kemp, "Les livres nouveaux" (April 1, 1928), 110.

15. *La vie américaine* (Paris, 1931), 29, 43, 361. *L'Amérique á la conquête de l'Europe* (Paris, 1931), VI.

16. *En Amérique* (Paris, 1933), 69.

17. See, for example, Paul Gagnon, "French Views of Postwar America" (Ph.D. dissertation, Harvard University, 1960).

18. *Scènes de la vie future* (Paris, 1930), 222; *Quelques notes d'U.S.A.* (Paris, 1928), 30. Of the three novelists, only Paul Morand preferred the testimony of such old authorities on America as Paul Bourget and Duvergier de Hauranne to the work of Siegfried and company. *New-York*, 74, 56.

19. (Paris, 1930). The dedication, in the opinion of one reviewer, symbolized the common goal of the two authors which was to show the moral and geographic split between the European and American branches of the white race. René Lalou, "*Dieux blancs, hommes jaunes*, par Luc Durtain," *Europe Nouvelle* (July 5, 1930), 1153.

20. Robert le Traz, "André Siegfried," *Revue de Paris* (January 15, 1938), 317. André Siegfried, *Mes souvenirs de la III<sup>e</sup> République* (Paris, 1946), 14.

21. (Paris, 1914).

22. *Deux mois en Amérique du Nord à la vieille de la querre* (Paris, 1916).

23. Excerpts from *Les Etats-Unis d'aujourd'hui* were published in *Europe Nouvelle* (January 1, 1927). The *Revue des Deux Mondes* also used a long essay on mass production by Siegfried, quite similar in content to certain chapters of *Les Etats-Unis* (April 5, 1930).

24. Robert le Traz, "André Siegfried," *Revue de Paris* (January 15, 1938), 313.

25. For information on Tardieu's career, I have relied heavily on Rudolph Binion, *Defeated Leaders* (New York, 1960).

26. J. B. Duroselle, *L'Idée de l'Europe dans l'histoire* (Paris, 1965), 274.

27. Three sections of *Qui sera le maître* were serialized in the *Revue des Deux Mondes*: "La civilisation de masse" (September 1, 1927); "Les moeurs" (September 15, 1927); and "L'avenir économique" (October 1, 1927). The same journal published three other articles by Romier on the United States: "Sur la frontière des deux Amériques" (November 1, 1927); "Questions économiques: sur l'impérialisme financier" (July 15, 1928); and "Les imprévus de la Bourse" (August 15, 1930).

28. M. L. Bidal, *Les écrivains de l'abbaye* (Paris, 1936).

29. Sylvia Beach, *Shakespeare and Company* (New York, 1959), 146-148.

30. David Caute, *Communism and the French Intellectuals* (New York, 1964), 42; the two authors were friends of Léon Blum who persuaded them that France must have her own socialism. *Ibid.*, 84.

31. Georges Duhamel, *Le voyage de Moscou* (Paris, 1927). Luc Durtain, *L'autre Europe* (Paris, 1928).

32. It is interesting to note that Jules Romains, the good friend of Duhamel and Durtain, participated along with Claudel, Valéry, and Romier in the Pan-Europe Conference of 1926 in Vienna. Duroselle, *L'idée de l'Europe dans l'histoire*, 274.

33. *Scènes de la vie future* appeared in the *Revue de Paris* in serial form (April 1, April 15, May 1, and May 15, 1930). The same journal published Duhamel's "Sur la querelle du machinisme" (April 15, 1933).

34. (Paris, 1927); (Paris, 1928). In addition to *Hollywood dépassé*, which was published in the August 15, September 1, September 15, October 1, and October 15, 1927, issues of the *Revue de Paris*, the journal ran two other novels by Durtain portraying the American scene: *L'Attentat de Market Street* (August 15, 1926); and *Captain O. K.* (March 15, April 1, April 15, May 1, and May 15, 1931). Moreover Durtain's *Frank et Marjorie* was also situated in the United States.

35. Morand's activities during World War I are discussed at length in Paul Morand, *Journal d'un attaché d'ambassade, 1916-1917* (Paris, 1947).

36. *New-York* was serialized in the *Revue de Paris* (November 1, December 1, and December 15, 1929; and January 1, January 15, and February 1, 1930).

37. *Histoire de la Troisième République: Les années d'illusions, 1918-1931* (Paris, 1960), 270.

38. "Champions du monde, par Paul Morand," *Europe Nouvelle* (July 5, 1930), 1000.

39. Two of Morand's short stories dealing with blacks in the United States were first published in the *Revue de Paris: Baton-Rouge* (November 15, 1927); and *Charleston* (February 15, 1928). *Syracuse* (Paris, 1928), which also portrayed blacks in America, was published elsewhere. Two other short stories by Morand involving the American scene, but not blacks, also appeared in the *Revue de Paris: Excelsior* (January 1, 1928); and *Adieu New-York* (June 1, 1928).

40. *L'esprit révolutionnaire en France et aux Etats-Unis à la fin du XVIII<sup>e</sup> Siècle* (Paris, 1925) was the product of his labors.

41. Maurois published *Ariel ou la vie de Shelley* (Paris, 1923); *La vie de Disraeli* (Paris, 1927); and *Byron* (Paris, 1930). Maurois's initiation to Anglo-Saxon civilization is described at length in *Mémoires* (Paris, 1970).

42. René Lalou, "Informations littéraires," *Europe Nouvelle* (November 8, 1930), 1609.

43. "Quatre voyageurs," *Revue Universelle* (April 1, 1931), 118. The passage of time has not altered this judgment. In his recent book, Theodore Zeldin called Duhamel "the old conservative French bourgeois." *France, 1848-1945*: Vol. 2. *Intellect, Taste and Anxiety* (Oxford, 1977), 136.

# chapter 5

# The Decline of Europe

> The diversity of countries and cultures, against
> the will of diplomats and governments, has
> elevated to the rank of supreme value the force
> of a specifically human creative spirit. Today
> they are attacking your unity and diversity,
> your flesh and your soul. Europe, wake up!
> —Robert Aron and Arnaud Dandieu, 1931

French intellectuals entered the postwar period with grave doubts about the future of their civilization. As early as 1919, Paul Valéry spoke of the "fragility" of the European way of life. In a widely quoted passage, he pointed to the central dilemma which was to occupy the thoughts of European intellectuals between the wars. "Will Europe remain preeminent in every field? Will she remain what she appears to be, that is, the precious part of the earthly universe, the pearl of the sphere, the brain of a vast body; or will Europe become what she is in reality: that is, the tip of the Asiatic continent?"[1] The spiritual crisis had its counterpart in the realm of matter. European political hegemony in the world had been eroded. "Everyone agrees," remarked Albert Demangeon, "that at the end of the nineteenth century, Europe ruled the world; now she is losing her supremacy to other countries; we are witnessing a shift in the world's center of gravity away from Europe; we see her fortune passing into the hands of the peoples of America and Asia."[2]

Just as the preeminence of European culture was being challenged around the world, French intellectuals found their values threatened by the development of new institutions at home. In fact, the two challenges were closely related. The exploitation of new methods of production had helped the United States, Japan, and other countries increase their power at the expense of Europe. These same methods, introduced in Europe, were causing a social revolution which appeared to threaten European culture and with it the supremacy of elites. The rise of mass production and the consequent flood of consumer items from the automobile, electrical, and cinematic industries increased the wealth of ordinary people and seemed to jeopardize the primacy of spiritual values. At the same time, of course, it rendered obsolete the creativity of the craftsman. The standardization of material goods and processes also threatened to destroy the autonomy of the individual. It was assumed that uniform products would find their best market in a society of uniform men. A materialistic, egalitarian culture would also diminish the respect for elites, particularly intellectuals.[3]

The perception of these threats to European culture and European domination of the world produced a widespread agreement among intellectuals that Europe was in a state of crisis. Paul Valéry introduced this concept in France with his two essays of 1919 entitled "La crise de l'esprit." Just one year later, Albert Demangeon discovered the political equivalent of this cultural turning point. He called it "Europe's crisis of hegemony and expansion."[4] Once launched, the concept of a European crisis was widely accepted by French intellectuals as an accurate description of the European condition during the entire period between the wars. In 1927, René Guénon entitled his study of European values *La crise du monde moderne*. In 1935, André Siegfried wrote a similar analysis of contemporary problems which he called *La crise de l'Europe*.

The persistent use of the term "crisis" suggested that Europe had reached a watershed in her history. However, for many intellectuals the crisis was more than a turning point; it was an apocalypse, a sudden termination of the civilization which they knew and believed in. René Guénon, denying the validity of the apocalyptic position, nonetheless affirmed that "the end of the world" spirit was widespread among his fellow intellectuals.[5] Frenchmen were, of course, aware of Oswald Spengler's *The Decline of the West*, published in 1918, which offered the most systematic statement of this position.[6] Similar views were expressed in France in a less systematic fashion.

André Gide, for example, believed that "we are watching the end of a world, of a culture, of a civilization; everything must be questioned."[7] For Gide, the apocalypse opened up new possibilities. For Henri Massis, it was an unmitigated disaster. He claimed that "the destiny of western civilization, of man in short, is today threatened."[8]

While the belief in the decline of European culture moved intellectuals in all European nations, it was especially distressing to Frenchmen. In some countries, such as Germany, the concept of change was more clearly associated with progress. In France, however, the improvements of the nineteenth century had coincided with the decline of French power. Moreover, in comparison to other Europeans, Frenchmen placed a higher value on stability, moderation, and the critical intellect. R. E. Curtius, the German specialist on French culture, contrasted the German and French attitudes toward the European crisis. "The Frenchman is in need of a maximum of permanence, which explains the strong opposition to Bergsonism manifested in France today. The notion of a European crisis has for us a theoretical value which is real. For the Frenchman, it has an opposite meaning. It is worrysome, troublesome, and threatening."[9] Curtius's generalization was certainly true for conservative elements in France. Henri Massis, for one, accused Spengler of deliberately spreading the doctrine of relativism which helped to undermine Europe's power and her belief in universalism.[10]

As the most astute critics recognized, however, the European crisis could not be dismissed as a German conspiracy or even as a product of the war. In the largest sense, it resulted from the success of Europe in spreading certain aspects of her culture to the rest of the world. The acceptance of European ways, particularly in the Orient, gave the lie to Rudyard Kipling's famous line that West and East would never meet. The two worlds now shared, among other things, a belief in technology and the principle of national self-determination, two instruments with which to undermine European power. While the shock of the war had accelerated this shift in power, it had begun with the stream of European immigrants to America in the early nineteenth century and was furthered by the European conquest of the globe after 1870.

In retrospect, it was apparent that the decline of Europe was already under way. The American victory over the Spaniards in 1898 and the Japanese defeat of the Russians in 1905 proved that non-European areas could exploit technology and nationalism, both inventions of the Europeans, to overthrow their rule.[11] The war merely accelerated this process. It reduced European power by opening markets and investments to non-European countries, while the Europeans were exhausting their resources fighting each other. The war also accentuated the sense of confusion about European cultural values. Already, in the prewar period, the value of scientific inquiry had been challenged. Now the war seemed proof that the Europeans had no common values. The spectacle of fratricidal conflict certainly emboldened non-European people to challenge European control. The harvest of the war was the rising nationalism of India, Turkey, Morocco, and other countries, which culminated in the revolts against European domination in the postwar period.[12]

The resistance to European control over these other areas contradicted the belief that the spread of European culture had "succeeded in uniting the human species."[13] Better means of transportation and communication reduced the distances between Europe and the rest of the world. There was widespread acceptance of the principles of applied science and national self-determination. However, non-European societies had accepted these principles as a means of liberating themselves. The world was smaller, according to French observers, but it was more dangerous because conflicts between cultures were now more visible. Henri Massis believed that the postwar world was witness to "the most complete rupture of equilibrium that we have ever known."[14] His view differed in degree but not in kind from the position of his compatriots.

With the shift in power and the decreasing size of the world, the perspective of European intellectuals changed fundamentally. Critics were forced to pay more attention to non-European areas. For Albert Demangeon, the rise of Japan and the United States created a tripartite division of the world.[15] Europe, once a world power, was now only one of three great regions. Other observers preferred a bipolar conception of conflict in the world. They could point to either the struggle between Orient and Occident or the revolt of the colored peoples against white domination. While Europe as a whole was still a factor in world politics, the individual European nation no longer played a major role on the world scene.

The debate on the decline of Europe moved through various phases in response to the different aspects of the problem which were discovered during the twenties. Each phase presented a different conceptualization of the relevant divisions of the world. The focus of early critics was on the relation between Europe as a geographical and historical entity and the rest of the world. Within this framework, it was possible to stress either the political or the spiritual decline of Europe. Critics of European materialism, however, found the terms "Europe" and "non-Europe" inadequate for their purposes. Because the European spirit also pervaded non-European areas such as Japan and the United States, they often preferred to speak of a conflict between oriental- and occidental-type societies. Observers of the decline of European power came to realize that other areas of the world were also being challenged. Since the rebellion was largely directed against white domination, the concept of a worldwide racial struggle was adopted as valid. In this formulation, America stood with Europe against the developing societies. By the end of the decade, however, the racial perspective was giving way to a more immediate threat: the rise of the Soviet Union and the United States. The two giants appeared to be undermining European power and values.

In the first phase of the debate, the emphasis was placed on the deterioration of Europe's position in the world in the twentieth century as a result of internal and external factors. Europe's strength in previous years had been based on her cultural uniqueness, according to Paul Valéry. No other region of the world had successfully integrated the traditions of Greece, Rome, and Christianity. This blend had yielded the most important product of the European mind—science. In its pure form, science was a combination of imagination, curiosity, logic, and scepticism, which made possible the disinterested pursuit of knowledge.

As Valéry recognized, science was also useful for the solution of practical problems. It helped men to work more efficiently and live more comfortably. [16] Seduced by the practical application of science, Europeans had come to regard it as a means to an end, rather than an end in itself. They placed more value on material advancements than on the development of pure knowledge.

The corruption of science, according to Valéry, was in part responsible for the decline of Europe. By emphasizing the practical advances produced by science, Europeans encouraged the exportation of technology to the rest of the world. Americans and Asians were now exploiting applied science to increase their own power. As a result, "the classification of the regions of the world tends to become such that the grandeur in simple material terms, statistical elements, numbers—population, surface, raw materials—determines exclusively in the end the ranking of the areas of the world."[17] The collapse of the European spirit was therefore indirectly responsible for the decline of European power.

In the years between 1920 and 1927, new concepts were used to identify the European crisis. "Snobism or fashion," explained John Charpentier, "demands that we move from the Occident to the Orient."[18] Certain intellectuals, who were appalled by the rising materialism of Europe, embraced the Orient as an affirmation of their belief in the human spirit. Unlike Valéry, however, these critics did not regard science as the supreme achievement of the West. Placing a higher value on faith than intellect, they accorded this distinction to the medieval Catholic church. The conflict between Orient and Occident was essentially, in their minds, a confrontation between modern civilization and the traditional way of life.

René Guénon embraced oriental life because he found in it an emphasis on contemplation. The stability and passivity of oriental society encouraged the attainment of a pure intellectuality which was no longer possible in the West. However, the art of contemplation was not the exclusive possession of Orientals. Certain institutions of the West, such as the medieval church, had attained a similar perfection. In effect, "oriental" values were formerly accepted in the West; the activism and worldliness which characterized the modern period of European history had undermined them. For Guénon, the oriental example was merely a way of restoring the West to her pre-Renaissance course.[19]

While the European way of life had degenerated substantially in Guénon's view, it had not yet fallen to the level of civilization in America. The United States exhibited

a more "advanced" phase, so to speak of the same civilization [as Europe]: mentally, as well as geographically, contemporary America is truly the

"Extreme Occident"; and Europe will follow her example, without any doubt, if nothing is done to stop the unfolding of the consequences implicit in the present state of things.[20]

Guénon's analysis suggested that the United States would spread her materialism unless a countervailing force appeared. The introduction of the oriental example was, therefore, historically necessary.

Guénon's condemnation of occidental values stimulated a vigorous debate in France on the future of western civilization. The most important rejoinder to his argument was Henri Massis's *Défense de l'Occident*. On almost every major point, the two authors were in apparent conflict. Whereas Guénon insisted that the West was corrupting the East, Massis believed that the West was threatened by eastern values. Guénon hoped to infuse Europe with the spirit of the East, while Massis, as his title suggested, urged the rejection of oriental ways. Protestantism, so long as it encouraged contemplation, was a legitimate expression of the spirit and Protestant nations, such as Germany, were part of the West, according to Guénon. Not so for Massis. He believed that the Reformation, particularly in Germany, was the source of the romantic individualism which was now afflicting that country.

The differences between the two positions were more apparent than real. Massis's Occident and Guénon's Orient were not areas on a map; each referred to a traditional way of life in which spiritual values were supreme. The two authors agreed that the materialism of the Bolsheviks and the Japanese in the East and the Americans in the West threatened their ideals.[21] In the great tradition of the medieval church, they found an institution which could serve to secure their values.[22] Only its revival would enable men once again to turn from the concern for transforming the world to a quest for self-knowledge.

The conflict between oriental and occidental values had its analogue at a different level in the revolt of the colored races against white men. With certain important exceptions, racial divisions in the world mirrored spiritual divisions. The rise of the colored races was most evident in Japan, Russia, and Turkey, countries which Massis and Guénon believed were threatening spiritual values. However, those two critics denounced the materialism of the United States, whereas the observers who called attention to the revolt of colored races welcomed the strength of America as a bastion against the new threat. In confronting the exotic character of colored civilizations, there could be no doubt about the essential unity of the "white way of life. Whites. A unique axis. One stem only. It may seem to you that this stem is divided, that our race is split, but the roots have grown beneath the Ocean and are grappling on both sides of the Atlantic with the soil of the earth."[23]

Moreover, the geographic position of America in relation to powerful colored nations, especially Japan, gave the United States a special strategic importance. The rivalry between Japan and the United States in the Pacific Ocean was now the focus of the struggle for world domination. According to Maurice Muret and René Grousset, the United States would have the primary responsibility for controlling the Japanese effort to find new sources of raw materials and an outlet for their excess population. (The exclusion of all Orientals by the American Immigration Act of 1924 not only exacerbated the problem of finding an outlet for the Japanese population, but it also created ill feeling between the two countries.) To achieve their goals, the critics expected the Japanese to assemble a coalition of colored nations, including the Chinese and the Russians. In the light of this threat, the United States was an indispensable instrument for defending the white race; Muret acknowledged the American role while at the same time condemning the United States as a "mediocre" civilization. [24]

A recent off-spring of western civilization, North America has rapidly and elegantly developed into an exemplary and unique civilization, more occidental in some ways than Europe. It would seem that as the advanced sentinel of the white world on the Pacific coast, North America wanted to demonstrate to the nearby colored races the capabilities of the white nations. What is North American civilization if not European civilization with all its possibilities realized, European civilization at its height?[25]

In the battle between races, Europe could only survive with America's help; in the spiritual realm, America was corrupting European civilization. In either case, the critics agreed that European hegemony was in danger.

The United States was at once the strongest of the "white" nations and the most vulnerable. While the revolt of the colored races against European powers was occurring either in Asia or Africa, far from the mother countries, America was experiencing racial conflict as an internal problem. In Mexico and South America, the revolts were a response of the discontented Indian population to European rule. In the United States, it was the militancy of the blacks which jeopardized white control. The Chicago race riots of 1919, as well as Marcus Garvey's Back to Africa movement, were taken as evidence of a serious threat to white domination in the United States. In the long run, the power of the white race in America was less secure than it was in Europe; this uncertainty, in turn, undermined the claim that the United States would, in fact, become the bulwark of white civilization against the colored nations of the world.[26]

After 1927, when the situation in Asia and Africa had become somewhat more stable, the colored domination of the world was discussed less frequently and less intensely. Critics continued to identify themselves as part of the white race, but they turned to the more immediate problem of the ideals which would direct the development of the race. In so doing, they merged the question of power with that of values. Whereas the oriental-occidental debate had focused only on values, and the race issue was concerned exclusively with power, the conflict between European countries and their extra-European offspring raised both issues. The United States and the Soviet Union threatened the hegemony of Europe and, at the same time, defended values which seemed foreign to many Europeans:

The United States and Russia appear today like two new centers of power around which the white race can cluster; they are totally different in their concepts of society; both are turned exclusively toward the future and thus are destined to resemble each other in their goals. The whole world regards them with a curiosity which mingles repulsion and attraction. [27]

Most French critics agreed with Romier that the apparent opposition between Russia and the United States on matters of social organization was an illusion. Despite appearances, the two societies were absorbed in material concerns and indifferent to the protection of the individual personality. Alfred Fabre-Luce illustrated metaphorically the similarity of social goals in the two countries. With reference to French travelers to the Soviet Union and the United States, he remarked: "The French embarkation hesitates between two contrary directions, but as the earth is round, they suggest the same goal."[28] Despite the fear of Bolshevism among conservative critics, neither they nor their liberal counterparts were prepared to defend the American way. Count de Fels offered a striking expression of this resistance to both systems. "Ford or Lenin?" he queried. "Neither Ford nor Lenin."[29]

French intellectuals reacted in a strong fashion to the postwar situation because it appeared to jeopardize their own position in two closely related ways. The shift in power to extra-European nations relegated European nations to the status of second-rate powers. The intellectuals naturally were sensitive to this change, but it could not be separated from an equally profound shift of power within the European nations. The new technology, which non-European societies had exploited to overthrow European control, was also subverting the domination of the older elites in Europe. With the rise of an egalitarian consumer society, intellectuals feared that their position would be eroded. The apocalyptic sentiments, so characteristic of intellectuals of this period, reflect the dual challenge to the primacy of the intellectuals which came simultaneously from within and outside of Europe.

However, the apparent despair with which French intellectuals faced the decline of Europe belied the point of writing about it. In reality, the recognition of the problem was the first step toward its solution. The particular character of the solution, moreover, would be elaborated, in large part, to respond to the nature of the problem as it was articulated by the intellectuals. The detection of Europe's decline launched the campaign for her defense. (See Part V, chapter 14.)

NOTES

1. "La crise de l'esprit" first appeared in English translation in *Athenoeum* (April-May 1919). It then appeared in the *Nouvelle Revue Francaise* (August 1919). A lecture on the same subject was given at the University of Zurich,

November 15, 1922. The three essays were then published in *Variété* (Paris, 1924). "La crise de l'esprit" was considered by Henri Massis as "the point of departure for all reflections on such a subject" (i.e., the decline of Europe). In 1961, Denis de Rougemont, in analyzing the ideological origins of the movement to unify Europe, spoke of the "determining influence" which Valéry exercised on subsequent studies of Europe. *Vingt-huit siècles d'Europe* (Paris, 1961), 334.

2. *Le déclin de l'Europe* (Paris, 1920), 12.

3. The coincidence of the perception of Europe's decline as a center of the world with the growing confusion over social values is discussed at some length in Guy Michaud, "La crise de la civilisation européene," Max Beloff, et al., ed., *L'Europe du XIX⁰ et du XX⁰ siècle* (Milan, 1964), 368-369.

4. *Le déclin de l'Europe*, 15.

5. *La crise du monde moderne* (Paris, 1927), 13.

6. Spengler published his book in 1918, but he chose its title in 1912, before the war. This suggests that the sense of Europe's decline preceded the war, at least among certain Europeans. Denis de Rougemont, *Vingt-huit siècles d'Europe*, 312.

7. Quoted in Maurice Muret, *Le crépuscule des nations blancs* (Paris, 1925), 7.

8. *Défense de l'Occident* (Paris, 1927), 1.

9. Quoted in *ibid.*, 67-68.

10. *Ibid.*, 31.

11. René Grousset, *Le reveil de l'Asie* (Paris, 1924), II.

12. Muret, *Le crépuscule des nations blancs*, 22, 37.

13. *Défense de l'Occident*, 5.

14. *Ibid.*, 5.

15. *Le déclin de l'Europe*, 313.

16. *Variété*, 27, 40, 46, 52.

17. *Ibid.*, 30.

18. "Les romans," *Mercure de France* (January 15, 1927), 412; also in 1927, André Duboscq spoke of "certain intellectual circles" which were obsessed with the question of eastern influence on western philosophy, art, and literature. *Le problème du Pacifique* ( Paris, 1927), 66.

19. *Orient et Occident* (Paris, 1924), 22, 92, 169.

20. *Ibid.*, 22.

21. In responding to Massis's volume, Guénon insisted that Massis did not know any true Orientals; otherwise, he would not have believed them to be a threat to the West. *La crise du monde moderne*, 214.

22. *Défense de l'Occident*, 255-257.

23. Luc Durtain, *Dieux blancs, hommes jaunes* (Paris, 1930), 8.

24. René Grousset, *Le reveil de l'Asie*, 208. Maurice Muret, *Le crépuscule des nations blancs*, 196. André Duboscq, *Le Problème du Pacifique*, 101.

25. Muret, *Le crépuscule des nations blancs*, 209, 138.

26. *Ibid.*, 153, 139. Demangeon, *Le déclin de l'Europe*, VII.

27. Lucien Romier, *L'homme nouveau* (Paris, 1929), 109.

28. "Trois écrivains francais en Russie," *Europe Nouvelle* (November 19, 1927), 151.

29. "Tour d'horizon 1932," *Revue de Paris* (January 1, 1932), 211. Of course, socialists as well as communists would have found this formula unacceptable. However, even extreme conservatives opposed the new system of mass production as an alternative to communism. (See Part IV, chapter 11.) In this regard, the conservative banker Octave Homberg was as adamant as Count de Fels: "Between these two gigantic transmitters of constraint [Russia and the U.S.] France is still an oasis where a man can breathe a certain air of liberty. But make no secret of it: we are threatened." Quoted in Gerard de Catalogne, ed., *Dialogue entre deux mondes*, 105.

# chapter 6

# The Rise of American Empire _____

> The conquest of Europe has advanced and the little
> outposts of the American invasion have already been
> installed at the gates of France, Italy, Germany,
> and all the nations of the Old World. Another few
> years of European anarchy and we will become an
> enslaved continent. Perhaps we will have the
> consolation of repeating along with the poet that
> captive Greece conquered its conqueror, and our
> last artists will depart to teach the Beaux-Arts
> to the children of Babbitt as the Greeks'
> off-spring taught grammar to the children of the
> heroes of Pydna and Cynoscephalae.
> —Charles Pomaret, 1931

The perception of a European crisis was inseparable from the recognition of the rise of extra-European powers. The United States, in particular, had demonstrated her strength by intervening in the war and the postwar settlement. However, in the early postwar period, the attention of Frenchmen was diverted from America by the development of Japanese, Russian, and Turkish power which was, in certain ways, a more immediate threat. By 1927, in the wake of the debt agreements of the previous year, the rise of American empire in the world seemed beyond dispute. J. L. Chastanet maintained that "Uncle Shylock and American imperialism look so strangely alike as to appear to be one and the same person."[1] For the next five years, or until the depression had clearly undermined American economic power, French observers reacted vigorously against American domination.

French interest in American empire was in no sense a product of the 1920s. In the first volume of *Democracy in America*, Alexis de Tocqueville remarked that the United States, along with Russia, "seems marked out by the will of Heaven to sway the destinies of half the globe."[2] Tocqueville's belief in the future power of America was shared by other travelers of the mid-nineteenth century. During the Civil War, Ferri-Pisani inquired rhetorically: "Will America some day be Europe's protector and master, just as a hundred years ago Europe was America's?"[3] By 1900, Europeans thought they knew the answer to Ferri-Pisani's question. The European economy was beginning to feel the impact of American industrial competition just as the United States emerged from the Spanish-American War an imperial power in her own right. Many observers on both sides of the Atlantic believed that the era of American domination of the world had arrived.[4] According to John Hay, "The financial center of the world which required thousands of years to journey from the Euphrates to the Thames and the Seine seems passing to the Hudson between daybreak and dark."[5]

The fear of American control over Europe soon disappeared in France as it became clear that the United States was far more interested in dominating the Caribbean than the Continent. Moreover, Frenchmen were increasingly preoccupied with their enemies in Europe. The long war and the early postwar period brought a hiatus in the discussion of American power. As long as the United States was an ally or a potential ally, American imperialism was not a popular concept. By 1926, however, the French situation had changed substantially. The Locarno Pact diverted attention from the German threat. The problems in Asia with Japan, Turkey, and the Soviet Union had subsided momentarily. It was the power of the United States which increasingly disturbed French statesmen and intellectuals.

Of course, these negative factors do not account for the belief that the United States had become an empire. Such a conception had to be verified by producing evidence of a systematic expansionist policy in Washington. The American position on debts, disarmament, loans, and tariffs provided some evidence to this effect. (See Part III, chapters 7-9.) It was equally clear, however, that the United States did not use such common instruments of imperial control as troops.

Indeed, the accusations against American imperialism coincided with complaints about American isolationism. In effect, French critics were groping toward a new concept of empire which was based on financial, rather than military or political control. The United States, through this system, could dominate Europe without directly intervening in European politics. Charles Pomaret maintained that "since the Roman legion, no force has arisen in the world which is so powerful as American finance: for two thousand years, no world empire has demonstrated the capacity to rule the world like the empire of the Kings of Bank and Industry from across the Atlantic."[6] United States control of European finances led inevitably to influence over other aspects of European life. Lucien Romier argued:

The entire civilization, however independent its deeper sources, is subject to the influence and attraction of its creditors. The surprising diffusion of Americanism in the world for the last ten years has no other cause. Financial imperialism dictates customs and tastes, and after annexing material values by means of constant, competitive bidding, it will perhaps conquer human values.[7]

For many Frenchmen, American investment and the debt policy were merely the outward signs of a power which undermined the basic values of European life.

It was understandable that French critics should react most vigorously to the rise of American empire in Europe. They were not, however, indifferent to the development of American power in other parts of the world, especially Latin America. Indeed, expanding American interests in various parts of Latin America inevitably competed with European interests there. Even before the recognition of America's imperial status in Europe, French critics were commenting on the growth of "Yankee imperialism" in the "American Lake,"[8] as they called the Caribbean. However, sensitivity to American influence in Latin America increased rapidly after 1926. In part, Frenchmen were simply reporting the rising anti-Americanism in Latin America which culminated in 1928 in the presentation of a resolution at the Havana Conference condemning unilateral intervention in the affairs of member states.[9] In part, they saw in Latin America a model of their own relations with the United States. Such a conception was reflected in *Europe Nouvelle's* rhetorical question: "Have they at last heard in Washington the cry of alarm which all free-spirited Europeans and South Americans utter to anyone who asks them for their reactions to the situation of the United States in the world?"[10] By 1927, many French critics felt obliged to denounce American control over Latin America as part of a general plan for an American global empire.

A minority of critics, after examining the accusations against American empire in Europe, concluded that they were untrue. These critics agreed that the United States was an imperial power in the New World, especially in the Caribbean, but they found only piecemeal American control in Europe. The minority critics maintained that the world was divided into two empires. The United States ruled the New World, while Europe and Britain dominated Asia and Africa. This conception notwithstanding, the minority critics admitted American influence over Europe. Most French readers would, therefore, infer that American empire was rising everywhere, if somewhat more rapidly and more systematically in Latin America than in Europe and Asia.

The titles and contents of articles and books on America indicate that not until 1927 did the concept of America as an empire become popular in France. An occasional observer, such as Jean-Marie Carré, recognized American imperialism before 1927. It is significant, however, that Carré's assessment of American empire was deliberately republished in 1927. Three years earlier, he discovered in the United States an

intoxication with unity and expansion. Everywhere we find the same feelings. A great empire rises through the prosperity of an avid and enterprising people; a collectivist democracy is inspired by a spirit of imperialism. Idealism loses ground and the United States enters into a dangerous crisis of growth.[11]

The first use of the term "empire" in the title of a book or article on the United States came just two weeks after the signing of the debt agreement in April 1926 when Bernard Faÿ published three articles called "L'empire américain et sa démocratie."[12] In 1927, the concept of an American empire became firmly fixed in the French mind. The publication of J. L. Chastanet's polemic against the United States entitled *L'Oncle Shylock ou l'impérialisme américain* was less influential in converting Frenchmen to a new view of the United States than the more careful work of André Tardieu and André Siegfried. Tardieu spoke of the "foundation of a new empire" in America, while Siegfried warned of the development of a "form of imperialism which is subtle and unprecedented."[13] Two other studies in the same year focused French attention on American expansion. Jacques Crokaert's *La Méditérranée américaine* denounced American domination in the Caribbean while André Duboscq recognized the rise of American power in the Pacific in *Le problème du Pacifique*.

The accusations against American empire continued in France for an additional four years. In 1929, Octave Homberg published *L'impérialisme américain*; in the same year, Jean Gachon's study of *La politique étrangère des Etats-Unis* pointed to the American demand for raw materials as a reason for American expansion. In 1930, two more studies focused on the extension of American control in the world. Jean Bonnefon-Craponne's *Le pénétration économique et financière des capitaux américaines en Europe* portrayed American expansion in its economic dimension, while Kadmi-Cohen's *L'abomination américaine* denounced American cultural and political domination of Europe. In 1931, two more titles diagnosed the effects of American economic development on Europe. Pierre Laurent's *L'impérialisme économique américain* and Charles Pomaret's *L'Amérique à la conquête de l'Europe* both exposed the threat to European hegemony posed by American capital.[14]

The accusations against American empire raised serious questions about American motives in entering the war. If, indeed, the United States was imperialistic in 1927, was it not also in search of an empire in 1917? If so, then Frenchmen had been duped in supposing that the United States entered the war for idealistic reasons. The reassessment of American motives for intervening in 1917 began with the work of André Siegfried and André Tardieu. Both critics maintained that self-interest rather than idealism motivated American decision makers.[15]

Only two authorities went so far as to claim that American entry into the war was a product of imperialistic motives. Octave Homberg and Kadmi-Cohen both used American interest in dominating

Europe as an explanation for the decision to intervene. Homberg saw American motives as "resolutely imperialistic." The United States had become "even more imperialistic because she felt richer every day." American entry into the war had given the nation exceptional bargaining power which was soon exploited at the Versailles Conference:

The United States under President Wilson acted in an imperial fashion, which is condemned in the Monroe Doctrine, by imposing herself as an arbiter in the negotiations for a peace treaty, by dealing categorically with problems completely foreign to the United States . . . by remaking the map of Europe, and by intervening in favor of the conquered nation; moreover, this intervention threatened the security of the conquerors because the guarantee treaty was not implemented.[16]

A similar conception of American behavior during the war was presented by Kadmi-Cohen. His chapter on American intervention, entitled "Préméditation," supported the view that the United States was exploiting European vulnerability in order to build an empire on the Continent. A seat at the Paris Peace Conference was the means to this end. Intervention was, therefore, essential, although not necessarily on the side of the Allies. The preference for Britain and France over Germany was not based on ideological considerations. It was the result of a calculation on the part of the Americans that the Allies were weaker than the Germans and could more easily be dominated. Even the timing of American entry was planned to produce the maximum American control over European affairs. The United States could have ended the war in 1917 by sending a small expeditionary force; instead, she waited until 1918 and gathered an enormous army which would give her additional strength at the peace conference. Substantial American control of Europe began at Versailles. "Since 1919, all of Europe had been watching America and the government of the United States. Since this date, the wishes and decisions of this government have been expressed in all of the various international agreements."[17]

This conception of America's behavior was rejected by most French critics who were convinced that American empire had developed logically but unintentionally out of the relative wealth and productivity of postwar America. The policy of the new empire was paradoxically to maintain control over Europe while abstaining from involvement in European politics. Such a policy contrasted with the cooperative intervention of the wartime period. In this regard, Henri Bérenger complained that the Americans "insisted on directing Europe" but were content to play the role of "observers."[18] The curious combination of American imperialism and isolationism was noted earlier in *Europe Nouvelle*. The journal remarked that "America increasingly turns her back on old Europe." Meanwhile, "the greatest empire in the world was being built piece by piece."[19] This conception was reinforced by an examination of the basic reactions of Herbert Hoover toward the Old World after his election in 1928. He believed in "America for the Americans . . . and the world for America."[20]

The isolationism of the American government, most critics argued, applied only to the question of European security. On financial matters, the American government was prepared to support the interests of her investors and the American public. This aggressive policy was essentially a product of the postwar era, as Charles Pomaret maintained in 1930. "The Americans aspire to world empire, and for ten years they have set themselves the task of conquering one."[21] The date for the inception of American empire, then, is 1920.

The absence of American troops in Europe, and the refusal of the United States to participate in most postwar European conferences forced critics to redefine the concept of empire for their readers. They, accordingly, stressed the unique features of American domination. It was not, said Chastanet, "a military imperialism, booted and helmeted, but rather an economic and financial imperialism."[22] A year later, *Europe Nouvelle* used almost the same language: "Imperialism takes many forms. It is not always armed and helmeted; it can appear under the apparently pacific guise of the banker and teller."[23] The American empire was perfectly adapted to the circumstances of the modern world where new forms of power were replacing old ones. "In the century in which we live, it is no longer with soldiers that one enslaves the world, but with bars of gold and bank credits."[24]

The evidence of American control over European life was located in the realm of finance and industry in Europe. French observers frequently noted that New York had replaced London as the financial center of the world.[25] The growth of the American merchant fleet was regarded as another source of American power. It was rapidly approaching parity with the British fleet.[26] However, maritime and financial strength were less important than the abundance of American resources and the efficiency of American factories in shifting the balance of economic power in the world. André Siegfried recognized that "by the pure weight of its greater wealth, make no mistake about it, America is likely to become the economic center of gravity of the planet."[27]

Europeans were already feeling the effects of American economic domination of the world by the mid-twenties. André Siegfried pointed to one instance of such control involving the purchases of American cotton. Because the European purchaser needed an American loan to buy the cotton, "the New York lender finds himself in the naked and brutal relation to the old continent of a wealthy man who has helped a poor man and expects to recover his advance." In such circumstances, "America can do anything. . . ." She has the power to

strange men and governments, help them in situations she chooses, watch over them, and finally—the thing which she likes above all—judge them from the height of her moral superiority and impose her lessons on them.[28]

The French were even more sensitive about private American loans to municipal, state, and national governments in Europe. They believed that American ownership of such public securities permitted the United States to influence policy decisions of these debtor governments. As a result, Americans could "exercise with the minimum of risks and the maximum of revenue, political control."[29] Under these circumstances, Europe had lost her sovereignty. Charles Pomaret explained that "a people in debt is no longer an independent people, because her creditors rise up against certain of her acts and attitudes for fear of their repercussions on the regularity of the service on their stocks."[30]

André Tardieu also complained about the "authoritarian diplomacy" of the American government. He and Achille Viallate were annoyed by the requirement of the United States government that foreign merchants' account books be submitted to customs. He also criticized the pressure of the American government on Belgium and France to reduce the size of their armed forces and thus pay their war debts.[31]

The fact that economic control was less blatant than political or military domination was no consolation to the French critics of American imperialism. Pomaret insisted, all the same, that Europe was being "enslaved," while *Europe Nouvelle* claimed that American domination was only "apparently pacific."[32] Indeed, there was reason to argue that the Roman and Napoleonic Empires were far more benign than the American system:

American imperialism is more subject to condemnation than all the old imperialisms because the latter at least compensated for their control by efficient protection and substantial aid, while American imperialism is synonymous with an all-encompassing national egotism and is implemented without any cooperation from the other nations which it seeks to dominate.[33]

In short, America's political isolationism and economic imperialism were better suited to increasing American wealth than they were to satisfying the needs of the European people.

Financial domination by the United States was especially onerous for Frenchmen because it was considered inseparable from cultural control. As Albert Demangeon noted in 1920, World War I marked the end of an era. The direction of cultural influence had ceased to run from east to west. The arrival of the American army in Europe and the end of European immigration to America were important turning points in modern history:

America advances toward Europe; the march of civilization changes direction. The men who return to Europe have sometimes lived long years in the United States; they carry with them the habits, the tastes, and the ideas of America; they are going to spread them widely; they become, in a manner of speaking, the representatives of America, its missionaries, its commissioners; by creating close relations between their country of adoption and their country of birth, they will contribute to enlarging the circle of American influence.[34]

Other critics were less concerned with the flow of men than they were with the flow of money. It was American financial control, they felt, which would destroy cultural self-determination for Europeans. André Tardieu pointed out that "because America is now a lender rather than a borrower as she was before the War, she is entitled to meddle with this European life whose motives she knows nothing about, disdains, and condemns."[35] Such meddling would ultimately lead to the development of an American empire, according to André Siegfried. "The concerns of the sheriff, the missionary, and the influence-seeker arise surreptitiously, and from this situation an empire with an unusual and subtle form may take shape."[36] The *Mercure de France*, on the other hand, felt that American expansion was anything but subtle. "The United States has another ambition: that of 'civilizing' the old world which she has economically enslaved. . . ." The prospect of such a development led the editors to plead: "God preserve us from such a calamity."[37]

Not all critics, however, were persuaded that the United States had built or was likely to build an empire in Europe. They could agree that Americans had increased their investments in Europe and had taken a hard line on the debt question without regarding this as evidence of an imperial design. It was in the New World, according to these critics, that, consistent with the Monroe Doctrine, the United States was becoming an empire. Asia and Africa, meanwhile, remained under the domination of Europeans. The world was now a duarchy, with an American empire organized around the Panama Canal and the British and European empires relying on the Suez Canal. André Siegfried maintained:

Since the War, the United States forms a system independent of Europe. For more than a century she has tended to do this, but now, consciously or not, for good or for bad, a whole group of countries, which up to now gravitated more or less around the old Continent, are undergoing an economic attraction which orients them toward this new center; this has been evident for Canada for a long time, and for Central and South America.[38]

The proponents of duarchy argued that nowhere in Europe (with the possible exception of Germany and Russia) did the United States exercise the kind of systematic control which she maintained over certain Caribbean nations. As a consequence, she would never dare to intervene militarily in Europe to protect her interests as she did in Latin America.[39]

The French recognition of an American empire in the Caribbean had preceded by several years the threat of United States domination in Europe. As early as 1920, Albert Demangeon had denounced the Monroe Doctrine as a form of "Yankee imperialism."[40] In 1923, Louis Gilaine called it "the Doctrine which strangles while affirming that it protects them [the Latin Americans]."[41] Five years later, *Europe Nouvelle* complained that "Neo-Monroeism is a means of domination through gold."[42]

As the decade progressed, more frequent and more specific criticism of United States' actions in Latin America appeared in French journals. Within a space of two months, *Europe Nouvelle* condemned American control over Panama and Cuba. The journal was particularly adamant in denouncing a clause in the Panamanian constitution which allowed the United States to intervene and assure "justice" in Panama's elections. By virtue of this clause, Panama was considered "a state practically annexed to the United States." The Cuban problem was similar. It was described as "American domination of Cuban domestic politics."[43]

In 1929 and again in 1930, the *Revue des Deux Mondes* warned its readers that French interests in Mexico were being replaced by American investments. Moreover, United States control of the Mexican economy was leading to cultural domination through the film.[44] In Mexico, the French opposition to American control was based in large part on the harm which it was doing to French interests, as well as a distaste for American culture.

The two conflicting views of American empire, which were presented to the French reader in the late twenties, were never reconciled by French writers. The conflict was especially glaring in the work of André Siegfried; *Les Etats-Unis d'aujourd'hui* presented two views of American empire. On the one hand, Siegfried argued that the United States, with its isolationist mentality, was only interested in domination over the New World; on the other, he claimed that America was beginning to exercise imperial control over Europe. These two claims were not necessarily in contradiction, but Siegfried failed to recognize the tension between them.

In any event, even those critics who denied that the United States had established an empire in Europe agreed that American control had increased substantially. The French reader could not avoid the impression that American domination was rising around the world. The United States was by common consent an empire in the New World, and most critics agreed that America was gaining imperial stature in Europe as well.

## NOTES

1. *L'Oncle Shylock ou l'impérialisme américain à la conquête du monde* (Paris, 1927), 11.
2. Vintage edition (New York, 1957), I, 452.
3. *Prince Napoleon in America, 1861*. Trans. by Georges Joyaux (Bloomington, 1959), 40. An interesting discussion of nineteenth-century French views of American empire is contained in Henry Blumenthal, *France and the United States: Their Diplomatic Relations, 1789-1914* (Chapel Hill, 1970), 71-74. By the mid-nineteenth century, the idea of American cultural imperialism was already taken seriously by Europeans. In 1851, Philarète Chasles spoke of the "Americanisation" of Europe. Four years later, Baudelaire lamented "this century americanised by its zoocratic and industrial philosophers." Theodore Zeldin, *France, 1848-1945*. Vol. 2. *Intellect, Taste and Anxiety* (Oxford, 1977), 127.
4. See p. 42.
5. Quoted in Achille Viallate, *Economic Imperialism and International Relations during the Last Fifty Years* (New York, 1923), 37.
6. *L'Amérique à la conquête de l'Europe* (Paris, 1931), 189.
7. *L'homme nouveau* (Paris, 1929), 139.
8. These expressions were used by Albert Demangeon, *Le déclin de l'Europe* (Paris, 1920), 249, 94.
9. The resolution was, in the end, defeated, but only after strenuous efforts by the American delegation.
10. "Les Etats-Unis se détournent de l'Europe" (April 30, 1927), 562.
11. "Trois mois dans une université californienne," *Revue Universelle* (February 15, 1927), 227.
12. *Correspondant* (April 25, May 10, and June 10, 1926).
13. *Devant l'obstacle* (Paris, 1927), 279; *Les Etats-Unis d'aujourd'hui* (Paris, 1927), 227.
14. This list does not include the large number of volumes such as Georges

Duhamel's *Scènes de la vie future* which were primarily concerned with the danger of American cultural imperialism. Those studies are discussed at length in later chapters.

15. *Les Etats-Unis d'aujourd'hui*, 319. *Devant l'obstacle*, 157.

16. *L'impérialisme américain*, vi, ix.

17. *L'abomination américaine*, 35, 37, 42-43, 46, 53.

18. "Dettes et réparations," *Revue de Paris* (June 1, 1932), 489.

19. "Les Etats-Unis se détournent de l'Europe"(April 30, 1927), 562, 536.

20. L'élection de M. Herbert Hoover," *Europe Nouvelle* (November 10, 1928), 1528.

21. *L'Amérique à la conquête de l'Europe*, v. J. L. Chastanet argued in similar fashion that it was American finance which was the basis of the empire, and that its manipulations had begun in 1919. *L'Oncle Shylock*, 22.

22. *L'Oncle Shylock*, 11.

23. "L'action des Etats-Unis en Amérique du Sud"(December 15, 1928), 1714.

24. Charles Pomaret, *L'Amérique à la conquête de l'Europe*, 284.

25. Maurice Lewandowski, "La puissance financière des Etats-Unis et son expansion mondiale," *Revue des Deux Mondes* (February 1, 1918), 664. The same article was cited in Albert Demangeon, *Le déclin de l'Europe*, 58.

26. William Oualid, "La richesse des Etats-Unis," *Europe Nouvelle* (February 22, 1919), 377. Albert Demangeon, *Le déclin de l'Europe*, 84.

27. *Les Etats-Unis d'aujourd'hui*, 204.

28. *Ibid.*, 226.

29. Octave Homberg, *L'impérialisme américain*, 15. Pierre Laurent, *L'impérialisme économique américain*, 214.

30. *L'Amérique à la conquête de l'Europe*, 186. As early as February 21, 1925, *Europe Nouvelle*, in an article entitled "Indépendance financière, liberté politique," had cited Prime Minister Herriot on the danger of French dependence on other nations. "A debtor state is no longer completely an independent nation in an era where economic affairs weigh so heavily in the conduct of policy . . . ," 236-237.

31. Tardieu, *Devant l'obstacle*, 298-300. Viallate, *Le monde économique* (Paris, 1928), 178. Jean Gachon mentioned no particular instances of American intervention in European affairs, but he feared that "the American government might use its enormous economic power to exercise diplomatic pressure on us." *La politique étrangère des Etats-Unis*, 147.

32. *L'Amérique á la conquête de l'Europe*, 189. "L'action des Etats-Unis en Amérique dù Sud" (December 15, 1928), 1714.

33. Homberg, *L'impérialisme américain*, envoi.

34. *Le déclin de l'Europe*, 47.

35. *Devant l'obstacle*, 283.

36. *Les Etats-Unis d'aujourd'hui*, 227.

37. Auriant, "Bibliothèque politique" (July 1, 1930), 239.

38. *Les Etats-Unis d'aujourd'hui*, 207-208. The concept of duarchy was also accepted by the following authors: Pierre Laurent, *L'impérialisme économique américain*, 187; and Achille Viallate, *Le monde économique*, 87, 41-42. Jacques Crokaert offered a different version of duarchy. He saw Britain and the United States competing around the world for domination of trade routes, rather than dividing the world into two parts. *La Méditerranée américaine*, 27.

39. Gachon, *La politique étrangère des Etats-Unis*, 145. Bonnefon-Craponne, *La pénétration économique et financière des capitaux américaines en Europe*, 204.

40. *Le déclin de l'Europe*, 249.

41. "Le centenaire de la doctrine de Monroe," *Europe Nouvelle* (March 31, 1923), 393.

42. "L'action des Etats-Unis" (December 15, 1928), 1712.

43. Léon Rollin, "La république de Panama entre les Etats-Unis et la Société des Nations" (February 2, 1929), 148. Léon Rollin, "Cuba en 1929; 30 ans d'indépendance à l'ombre des Etats-Unis" (April 27, 1929), 553.

44. Jacques Kulp, "Le problème mexicaine: Les Etats-Unis et nous" (October 15, 1929), 921. Jacques Kulp, "La pénétration des Etats-Unis en Amérique Latine" (October 15, 1930), 842, 856.

# PART III:

# Franco-American Relations, 1917–1932

# chapter 7

# Security and Disarmament _____

> French Governments of the Right, the Left, the
> Center, French Cabinets dominated by Nationalistic
> and Radical sentiments, had succeeded one another;
> the Left had but recently returned to power after
> a shining triumph, but for fourteen years France
> itself had met each foreign proposal with the
> unvarying response that security preceded all
> else. . . . If America continued to preach, France
> still remained unconverted.
>
> —Frank Simonds, 1932

The discovery of American empire by French critics in 1927 coincided with the deterioration of relations between the two countries. Three issues were particularly provocative to French observers: the American position on securities and disarmament, the agreements on debts ,and reparations, and the rise of American investment in Europe. The acrimonious discussion of these issues, as André Siegfried pointed out, rendered obsolete the wartime symbol of the Franco-American entente, Lafayette.[1] Relations between the two countries were no longer characterized by a collaboration of equals. The entente was giving way to American empire.

While the issues of debts and security are analytically separable and have been treated in separate chapters of this section, they were, in fact, linked by their impact on each other and by their effect on Franco-American relations. The solution to the debt problem was closely intertwined with the achievement of security. Both Americans and Frenchmen realized that savings on arms could be spent on payment of the war debt. There was, however, substantial discord on the way in which security could be achieved, short of French expenditure on arms.

The two issues were also related because they were regarded by Frenchmen as evidence of the rise of American empire. Grievances over debts were inseparable from irritation over disarmament demands. In the midst of discussions on the war debt in 1925, *Europe Nouvelle* catalogued for its readers the mistreatment of France by the United States since the war:

In six years, France has witnessed successively the rejection of the Treaty of Versailles by the United States and the abandonment of the Anglo-Franco-American guarantee pact. After six years of default, France's credit in Germany has been consolidated by the Dawes Plan into annuities of less than 1,200 million marks which does not even cover the interest on the sums needed for the reconstruction of the devastated regions.[2]

Grievances over the failure of America to secure France's borders were mingled with annoyance over American financial policy. Eight years later, the two issues were just as inseparable and equally as irritating. In the *Revue Universelle*, Saint-Brice asked rhetorically: "Who then has led the world for fifteen years, if not the nation which determined the shape of the peace, imposed the Dawes Plan, the Young Plan, the Hoover Moratorium, provoked the naval conferences and directed disarmament? . . ."[3] The issue of American power served to connect debts and security in the French mind after 1924.

Because the two issues were so intertwined, it is difficult to assess the relative importance of each in generating anti-Americanism in France. The task is also complicated by the quantity and intensity of the discussion over debts. It would be misleading, however, to overemphasize the importance of the debt question and underestimate the influence of the issue of security and disarmament. Speaking of the American position at Versailles and the Washington Naval Conference, André Tardieu remarked:

The debate on the debts has brought them back to life. Through it, France relives a shortened version of the long series of her deceptions: the uselessness of the sacrifices agreed to by her and her allies in accordance with the American ideas in 1919, the rejection by the Senate of the treaty of solidarity; a separate peace with Germany without an effort of prior adjustment with her wartime friends; the Washington Conference so hard on the French navy and colonies . . . .[4]

The impact of the war debt issue, in Tardieu's view, cannot be measured without reference to the context in which it was considered. That context was shaped, in turn, by prior disagreements and deceptions at Versailles and Washington. The debt question might best be regarded as a kind of catalyst which "operates within a bad context like a coefficient of aggravation."[5] To fully understand the reaction against the debts, it is essential, then, to return to the question of security and disarmament which first alienated French observers from the wartime entente.

The Washington Naval Conference was an important turning point in Franco-American relations because it brought Frenchmen for the first time to an acute realization of their loss of power to the United States. Léon Archimbaud, an observer and chronicler of the conference, who was also a member of the French Assembly, confessed that at Washington

we were certainly not treated with high regard. On different occasions, France, the victor of the Marne and Verdun, was humiliated . . . by her exclusion from the "big three." France is the "new poor man" among the nations; the United States and Japan are "the new rich."[6]

This first impression was not finally confirmed until later in the decade when the cumulative impact of the debt question and the renewed efforts of the United States to pursue the question of disarmament compelled Frenchmen to recognize their inferiority. Henri de Jouvenel accordingly justified France's refusal to attend the Geneva Conference of 1927. "There is no reason to be embarrassed about taking the side of the poor nations in response to a memorandum which seems to us a bit like the manifesto of the *nouveaux riches*."[7] The conflict between the American and French positions on security and disarmament was thus exacerbated by the conviction among French observers that the United States was a superior power, capable of imposing her own position on France.

On the security issue, the seeds of discord were sown between the two nations only a few months after American entry into the war, at the peak of the entente relationship. Wilson's enunciation of the fourteen points in 1918 brought the American position on peace into conflict with French views on at least two important issues. The proposal to replace the prewar alliance system with an international organization charged with enforcing the peace was acceptable to France only if the new system protected her against future German aggression.[8] The League of Nations was inadequate in this respect.

The disagreement over the nature of the new security system was compounded by Wilson's ideas on disarmament. In the fourteen points, he had argued for a reduction of arms consistent with the internal security of each nation. The disarmament of Germany at Versailles was to be the first step toward world disarmament. When the Americans proceeded in the postwar period to pursue this goal, they encountered the opposition of France. Disarmament was untenable to Frenchmen without adequate security arrangements. The French were particularly alarmed by the failure of England and the United States to ratify the treaties which guaranteed France protection against German aggression. To compound matters, the Bolshevik Revolution had ended the possibility of an alliance with Russia. Disarmament would simply expose France to the superiority of the German population and industrial capacity. Therefore, French leaders found Anglo-Saxon talk of disarmament hypocritical—in view of the rejection of the guarantee treaties—and against the interests of France.[9]

In spite of their vigorous opposition to disarmament, however, French leaders and the French press greeted the calling of the Washington Naval Conference with enthusiasm. After Versailles, there had been considerable apprehension that the United States would withdraw entirely from participation in world affairs. The conference, therefore, was welcomed by Frenchmen as evidence that isolationism had not yet triumphed in America.[10] French leaders also hoped that the conference would provide a forum for presenting their own views on the security question. Since land as well as naval disarmament appeared on the agenda, and since land forces were so obviously related to national security, it seemed certain that this issue would be raised at the conference. Moreover, the naval arms race between England and the United States, which had strained their relationship, seemed to offer an ideal opportunity for French mediation. By siding with the Americans, France might even be able to revive the entente of 1917.[11]

All of these hopes, however, were based on a fundamental illusion: that France could influence the debate on naval disarmament even though the French navy had deteriorated during World War I and had not been rebuilt after the war.[12] French hopes were soon dashed. The Big Three naval powers—England, the United States, and Japan—moved into secret meetings to discuss the critical issue of tonnage limitations on ships in various categories. The exclusion of the French delegation from these discussions not only prevented France from mediating between England and the United States, but also dealt a cruel blow to the prestige of the nation. In a conference of world powers, France had been relegated to a second rank position.

The report of the Big Three on December 15, 1921, further dismayed the French delegation. In the category of capital ships, France was to be allowed to build little more than one-third the tonnage of the Anglo-Saxon powers and slightly better than one-half the tonnage allotted to Japan. The cruelest blow to French pride, however, was the provision for parity between France and Italy.

The French delegation immediately protested to Secretary Hughes that France, as a two-ocean power, needed a larger navy than Italy. In a moment of irritation, Hughes angrily replied: "Why, you can't even pay your debts."[13] The remark, touching as it did on a second sensitive area of Franco-American relations, served to inflame the French delegation even further.

In reality, the ratios for capital ships were of far less concern to French leaders than the attempt to place limitations on auxiliary ships. As long as Anglo-French relations remained in a state of uncertainty, France needed an inexpensive and reliable means of assuring her coastal defense and that of her empire, namely, the submarine. The British proposal to abolish submarines altogether, therefore, angered the French delegation. Happily for France, other powers were also opposed to it. The alternate proposal of applying ratios for capital ships to auxiliary categories was also unacceptable to France. The French delegation raised eyebrows at the conference by demanding parity with the United States and Britain in submarines.

Only an appeal from Secretary Hughes to Prime Minister Briand brought about French acceptance of limitation on capital ships, at the expense, however, of agreements to limit any auxiliary ships.[14]

As if the official deliberations were not painful enough, the French delegation was subjected to irritating attacks in the American press. Shortly after the conference opened, Edwin James of the *New York Times* reported that France was seeking parity with Japan in capital ships and with the Anglo-Saxon powers in submarines. The report, implying French militarism, stirred strong negative reactions in the United States and abroad.[15] The source of another article on the French position was a British diplomat who deliberately leaked information to the American press. The article summarized French objections to the tonnage limitations recommended by the Big Three in an obvious effort to establish France's responsibility for blocking disarmament.[16] On another occasion, Lord Lee of the British navy read an article written by a Captain Castex of France, which appeared to justify the use of submarines as commerce destroyers.[17] The alleged French position was especially damaging because it appeared to be identical to the German policy on submarine warfare during World War I. Despite French denials, the American public now believed that France had succeeded Germany as the chief advocate of militarism.

French critics of the Washington Conference were most deeply concerned about France's loss of prestige. Her navy, in fact, had not suffered at all. The tonnage of existing capital ships was still below the tonnage allotted to the French navy at the conference.[18] Moreover, the submarine, a cheaper and a more dangerous weapon than the capital ship, had escaped limitation altogether. If the French navy came through the conference unscathed, however, French pride did not. Frenchmen were humiliated by the reactions of the American public and Anglo-Saxon leaders. The French press, naturally, reflected the bitterness of the government by denouncing the failure of the Anglo-Saxon powers to consider French needs.[19] Several critics were more explicit. They insisted that, until the Anglo-Saxon powers signed the guarantee treaties, France would accept no form of disarmament.[20]

The French were particularly sensitive to the repeated accusations of militarism in the American press. Admiral de Gouy remembered the cartoons in American newspapers which pictured French soldiers in Prussian helmets. The shift in American opinion was both bewildering and irritating to Frenchmen.[21] Firmin Roz blamed the change in attitudes on the "frightening versatility of American opinion." He was particularly outraged by Mark Sullivan's claim that French policy at the Washington Conference was militarist in character. "How can an American dare to express himself in this manner about a people who have been so recently and enthusiastically praised by his whole country as martyrs and heroes?" The only explanation which Roz could offer was the resurgence of the isolationist tradition.[22]

Other critics accounted for Franco-American differences in terms of long-standing conflict between Latin and Anglo-Saxon mentalities. André Siegfried, for one, believed that language and cultural differences were at the root of the problem. In Washington, British delegate Balfour "maneuvered just as he would have in his own country, while our delegates, isolated in their hotel, were complete foreigners, out of touch and misunderstood."[23] Léon Archimbaud agreed with Siegfried. He pointed out that

French thought, the classic Latin genius, which has done so much for the collective culture of nations, was absent at Washington. The meddler prevailed: American empiricism, building and destroying without intellectual direction, without a juridical, much less a philosophical guide.[24]

While Frenchmen reacted bitterly to their treatment in Washington, they did so without entirely abandoning hope for the entente. Franco-American differences were serious but not yet fatal. Nonetheless, as Robert Ferrell has observed, the Washington Conference left its mark on Frenchmen. "The ruffled pride of France took years to soothe and it [the conference] had frequent unfortunate manifestations in later French diplomacy."[25] One such manifestation was the refusal of France to accept President Coolidge's invitation to a second naval conference in 1927, this one designed to extend the Washington ratios to auxiliary craft. French opposition to the Geneva Conference also reflected the continued resistance to limitations on auxiliary craft, especially submarines. Moreover, France was already engaged in the opening discussions of the League Preparatory Commission on Disarmament. This body, consistent with a principle enunciated by the French government, was considering disarmament as a whole rather than separating its land and naval components.

The stalemate between England and the United States over limitations on cruisers not only prevented an agreement at Geneva, but provoked gleeful accusations of Anglo-Saxon hypocrisy in France.[26] The bitterness of Frenchmen over the Geneva Conference stemmed in large measure from the connection of disarmament with the debt issue. Almost a year before the conference, and just two weeks after the signing of the debt agreement, the *Revue des Deux Mondes* published an anonymous article denouncing the Anglo-Saxon nations for their campaign to disarm France in order to dominate the world.[27] Three months later, in the same journal, Firmin Roz attacked the United States for trying to disarm France while Germany was still a military menace. For Roz, disarmament was consistent with the American effort to collect war debts; both policies were leading toward American domination of France.[28]

The Geneva Conference of 1927 served to remind French leaders of this growing American imperialism. Henri de Jouvenel considered the "Anglo-Saxon navalism," advocated in disarmament conferences, as a form of "inexpensive imperialism."[29] An editorial in *Europe Nouvelle* expanded on Jouvenel's argument:

The American boy has begun to realize his strength; vaguely, he senses that he has become master; what he will do with his power, he does not know; the main thing is that if the spirit moves him, he can exercise it: the young giant is awake. That is the revelation of Geneva; but is it really a revelation after the interallied debt affair which is, after all, the same thing?[30]

In the face of rising American power, French critics could feel some measure of satisfaction in the united reaction of their compatriots. Saint-Brice, writing in the conservative *Revue Universelle*, noted that, regardless of party, Frenchmen were unanimous in their opposition to both the debt agreement and American efforts to disarm France.[31]

The deterioration of Franco-American relations was temporarily arrested in 1927 and 1928. As a result of negotiations over the Kellogg-Briand Pact, the diplomatic atmosphere improved sufficiently to justify the remark of one spokesman that "after the élan of 1917-1918, and the dispute over the debts, here is a new swing of the pendulum."[32] In fact, the swing was short both in duration and distance; the Kellogg-Briand Pact failed to resolve either of the two outstanding differences between France and America: debts and the security issue.

Foreign Minister Briand's original proposal was intended to counteract anti-French feeling in America which had increased after France refused to attend the Geneva Conference. It provided for the renunciation of war as an instrument for solving Franco-American problems. While the proposal was calculated to please the members of the peace movement in America, it was worded exactly like the defensive alliances which France had signed with Yugoslavia and Romania;[33] for this reason, American officials ignored Briand's initiative. Nonetheless, pressure from the peace movement forced Secretary Kellogg to respond to Briand. He found a way out of his dilemma by proposing that a multilateral renunciation of war be substituted for Briand's bilateral treaty. The new treaty would satisfy the peace movement without committing the United States to a defensive alliance with France. In fact, as the French government and French opinion recognized, the Kellogg-Briand Pact did little more than postpone the resolution of the issues dividing the two countries.[34]

By the summer of 1928, even before the signing of the Kellogg-Briand Pact, an Anglo-French agreement, permitting France to construct an unlimited number of small submarines and Britain to build as many small cruisers as she chose, had already disturbed the American government.[35] In retaliation, President Coolidge signed a bill authorizing the construction of fifteen large American cruisers. This action provoked Vladimir d'Ormesson to protest "the attitude of the American Congress which quickly passed a meaningless Kellogg Pact in order to devote its careful attention to studying an explicitly imperialistic naval program."[36]

The prospect of a renewed naval race in 1928 frightened England and the United States into calling still another naval conference, this one to be convened in London in early 1930. Once again, France was reluctant to participate. A 1929 summer meeting between President Hoover and Prime Minister MacDonald to discuss differences between the two countries on the disarmament issue again raised the specter of an Anglo-Saxon front against France.[37] The French also protested that the conference was redundant, indeed retrogressive, because the issue of disarmament was already being handled in its entirety by the League Preparatory Commission. However, the chief obstacle to French participation in the conference was again the conflict between disarmament and security.[38] France would agree to limit the construction of submarines only if Britain would guarantee her against a Mediterranean attack by the Italians.

The absence of a British guarantee was the key obstacle to limitations on auxiliary vessels at the London meeting. The British would produce such a guarantee only if the United States, in turn, agreed to consult with the European states over any violation of the Kellogg Pact. After some wavering on this critical issue, the American government refused to commit itself to such a violation of the isolationist tradition.[39] When this became clear, France, followed by Italy, withdrew from the conference. The Big Three agreement to limit the construction of auxiliary ships was not applicable to France. Nonetheless, French critics were irritated by the belief that the Anglo-Saxon disarmament policy was designed to achieve naval superiority at the expense of French security.[40]

The climax of the interwar effort to find a satisfactory means of reducing armaments was the World Disarmament Conference, sponsored by the League of Nations.[41] The conference differed in two important respects from previous meetings. It was the product of initiatives taken by league members rather than the United States and reflected their belief that naval and land disarmament were inseparable issues. These two factors made participation more palatable to Frenchmen, but they did not remove any of the substantive differences between France and America on this issue.

These differences were revealed at the opening of the conference when France unveiled the Tardieu Plan calling for a league with a strong international army. Nations were expected to turn over their arms to the league, but could recover them in the event of an invasion. The nine-point plan, presented by the Americans, differed radically from the Tardieu proposal. It called for a reduction of arms, both land and naval, in all categories, but its most controversial feature was the proposal to ban all submarines.[42] The clash between the two positions at the outset of the conference was reinforced when President Hoover presented a new proposal in June of 1932 in an effort to save the conference. He invited all nations to accept an across-the-board, one-third reduction of armaments in all categories. The difficulty with Hoover's scheme was that it hardly affected the Germans, who were lightly armed, while a substantial portion of the French military would have been disarmed. Such a proposal seemed to mock the French concern for security.[43]

When the Tardieu ministry was replaced by the more liberal Herriot government, the new prime minister offered his own plan for disarmament in November of 1932; it, too, stressed the role of a strong league in enforcing the peace. The agreement of right and left on this issue supports Henri de Jouvenel's claim that "there is only one idea . . . on which all parties in France agree: that the League of Nations will only exist when it will have the strength to apply sanctions."[44]

As in 1927, so again in 1932, the clash between France and America on disarmament coincided with strong differences over the debt issue. In each case there was evidence of systematic interference in European affairs, a situation which was denounced in an editorial in *Europe Nouvelle*.[45] The *Revue Universelle* also saw a connection between the two issues. The journal maintained that the Hoover disarmament scheme was designed to fail and thus give the United States an excuse to insist on the resumption of debt payments in the fall of 1932.[46]

From World War I to the Geneva Disarmament Conference, the differences in principle between France and America on disarmament and security remained constant. The French insisted that the United States provide a substitute for the guarantee treaty before undertaking disarmament. The United States argued that after disarmament had taken place, the guarantee treaty would be less significant. If the principles did not change, however, the context in which they were argued was altered. After the debt agreement of 1926, the American interest in disarmament was viewed in France as one element in the American imperial scheme. The policy of the United States on security and disarmament had irritated Frenchmen before 1926. In the late twenties, it appeared to be a genuine threat to French independence.

## NOTES

1. *Les Etats-Unis d'aujourd'hui* (Paris, 1927), 313.

2. "Les négotiations de Washington" (October 3, 1925), 1310.

3. "Les mirages de Washington" (May 1, 1933), 484.

4. *Devant l'obstacle* (Paris, 1927), 286.

5. *Ibid.*, 285.

6. *La conférence de Washington* (Paris, 1923), 349.

7. "Conférence du désarmement ou conférence des armements?" *Europe Nouvelle* (February 19, 1927), 227.

8. On this point, see W. M. Jordan, *Great Britain, France, and the German Problem, 1918-1939* (London, 1943), 206.

9. Etienne Fournal, "Points de vue . . . ," *Europe Nouvelle* (September 17, 1921), 1207.

10. "Les Etats-Unis et la paix," *Revue de Paris* (August 1, 1921), 667. Although only the discussions on disarmament are considered in this chapter, the conference also dealt with Far Eastern issues, especially the question of the Open Door in China and the Anglo-Japanese alliance.

11. Harold and Margaret Sprout, *Toward a New Order of Sea Power* (Princeton, 1940), 178.

12. The French government had been so preoccupied with the reconstruction of the northern part of France, which had been devastated during the war, that it had delayed making a decision about the appropriate naval policy for postwar France. See *ibid.*, 169-170.

13. Merlo Pusey, *Charles Evans Hughes* (New York, 1951), II, 483.

14. French demands for parity with the Anglo-Saxon powers in submarines were primarily calculated to raise the question of guarantees for security which had not been discussed at the conference. Sprout, *Toward a New Order of Sea Power*, 291.

15. *Ibid.*, 180.

16. *Ibid.*, 183.

17. *Ibid.*, 201. Archimbaud, *La conférence de Washington*, 145.

18. Archimbaud, *La conférence de Washington*, 332. Contre-Amiral Degouy, "Après Washington et après Gênes," *Revue des Deux Mondes* (June 1, 1922), 658.

19. A survey of opinion in the French press at the end of the conference indicates that all Frenchmen were angered by the failure of the conference to consider the problem of French security. Sprout, *Toward a New Order of Sea Power*, 257.

20. Etienne Fournal, "Points de vue . . . ," *Europe Nouvelle* (September

17, 1921), 1207. Amiral Wister Wemiss, "La marine et la conférence de Washington," *Revue de Paris* (March 1, 1922), 149.

21. Contre-Amiral Degouy, "Après Washington et après Gênes," *Revue des Deux Mondes* (June 1, 1922), 651.

22. Roz, *L'Amérique nouvelle* (Paris, 1923), 232, 235-236.

23. *Les Etats Unis d'aujourd'hui*, 310.

24. *La conférence de Washington*, 110.

25. *Peace in Their Time* (New Haven, 1952), 43-44. Frank Simonds reached a similar conclusion about the effect of the conference on France, although he stated it in rather extreme terms: "For France, the Washington Conference was a moral disaster without limit . . . ." *Can America Stay at Home?* (New York, 1932), 154-155.

26. Frank Simonds, *Can America Stay at Home?*, 193. The British delegation insisted that large cruisers (10,000 tons with 8-inch guns) were offensive weapons and should be limited, while the American delegation maintained that small cruisers (8,000 tons with 6-inch guns) should be limited for the same reason. The arguments were based purely on self-interest since the Americans needed larger ships to reach their more widely dispersed possessions, while the British could service their empire with smaller ships. *Ibid.*, 193.

27. "A propos du désarmement" (May 1, 1926), 129.

28. "L'attitude des Etats-Unis" (August 1, 1926), 531, 537.

29. "Conférence du désarmement ou conférence des armements?" (February 19, 1927), 227.

30. L'échec de la conférence navale" (August 6, 1927), 1014.

31. "Le coup de Washington" (March 1, 1927), 617.

32. "Le traité d'arbitrage franco-américaine," *Europe Nouvelle* (February 11, 1928), 162.

33. Indeed, Briand invited two leaders of the American peace movement, James Shotwell and Solomon Levinson, to discuss the proposed treaty while they were in France. The language in which the Briand initiative was couched attempted to appeal to both the Levinson and the Shotwell wings of the peace movement. Robert Ferrell, *Peace in Their Time*, 71, 89-90.

34. Saint-Brice, "En marge du pacte Kellogg," *Revue Universelle* (August 1, 1928), 358. "Du traité de Versailles au Pacte Kellogg," *Europe Nouvelle* (August 25, 1928), 1142.

35. Saint-Brice, "L'heure américaine," *Revue Universelle* (November 15, 1928), 484. Edmond Delage, "Les difficultés du désarmement naval," *Europe Nouvelle* (November 17, 1928), 1577.

36. "Politique des pactes ou politique des croiseurs?" *Europe Nouvelle* (January 19, 1929), 66-67.

37. *Le Matin* expressed virulent hostility to the Hoover-MacDonald meeting, while *Le Temps* and *Journal des Debats* were suspicious. Raymond G. O'Connor, *Perilous Equilibrium* (Lawrence, 1962), 47. The two statesmen agreed to reduce destroyer tonnage to 150,000 if France would accept a corresponding reduction in her submarine tonnage. *Ibid.*, 48.

38. French willingness to participate in the London Conference was in some measure the result of a conciliatory move on the part of the United States at the League Preparatory Commission for Disarmament. The American delegate, Hugh Gibson, had agreed that there could be some shift in tonnage from one category to another. Previously, the Americans had insisted on a fixed limitation in each category. The new agreement would allow France to exceed somewhat her submarine tonnage limitations. *Ibid.*, 25.

39. Secretary Stimson at first indicated that the United States would be willing to consult, but was forced to back off from his initial offer when President Hoover was reluctant to commit the country to such a course. *Ibid.*, 91. Robert Ferrell, *American Diplomacy in the Great Depression* (New Haven, 1957), 95.

40. Saint-Brice, "De Washington à Londres," *Revue Universelle* (November 1, 1929), 358-363. René La Bruyère, "Les étapes du désarmement naval de Washington à Londres," *Revue des Deux Mondes* (January 15, 1930), 419. "Conclusions à Londres," *Europe Nouvelle* (April 19, 1930), 615.

41. The United States, while not a member of the league, had been participating informally in the discussions of the Preparatory Commission and was invited to take part in the Disarmament Conference as well.

42. W. M. Jordan, *Great Britain, France, and the German Problem*, 167.

43. Simonds, *Can America Stay at Home?*, 231.

44. Arnold Wolfers, *Britain and France between Two Wars* (New York, 1966), 170.

45. "Tournant dangereux pour l'Amérique et l'Europe," *Europe Nouvelle* (December 3, 1932), 1395.

46. E. N. Dzelepy, "Dettes de guerre: l'Amérique et la crise," *Revue Universelle* (December 1, 1932), 557.

# chapter 8

# Debts, Reparations, Tariffs, and Loans

> The "no entanglement policy" has become a dogma
> for the masses overseas. However, it is only
> serviceable for unthinking crowds. Preaching
> abstention at the very time when observers,
> experts, and traveling statesmen from the
> United States are in all the European capitals,
> even Moscow, is dishonest. Dishonesty turns to
> cynicism when the American press advises our
> creditors to abandon us to our fate while their
> bankers and businessmen are colonizing and besieging us.
> —Régis Michaud, 1931

The hostility of the French public to the American position on war debts is usually regarded as the key element in the disintegration of the wartime entente. The importance of the issue stems, on the one hand, from its duration. As Jean Prévost noted, "The continual hope of Frenchmen to see the United States abrogate or at least reduce the debt has distorted relations between the United States and France from 1919 to 1931." On the other hand, the issue generated an intense emotional reaction among Frenchmen. Prévost pointed out that "the public considered our debt obligation toward America, not just with concern, but with a kind of fury."[1] After the euphoria of the entente period, when France believed in American idealism, the insistence on collecting the debts helped to establish the French image of a selfish, materialistic America.

In retrospect, it is clear that the French response to the debt issue cannot be isolated from the prior disillusionment with the American position on security; even more obviously, the debt issue was ensnarled with other aspects of the financial difficulties which gripped the world after 1919. The most important of these were the reparations problem, the tariff issue, the monetary situation in France, and the availability of credit. As often as not, French hostility to America was provoked by these issues in themselves or in combination with the debt problem. Sometimes, moreover, reaction against the debts was triggered by an issue only indirectly related. In such instances, the debt question was a convenient means of expressing resentment against the financial situation as a whole. This would account for the frequent identification of Franco-American problems in terms of the effort to collect the debts.

While the debt issue was often debated in purely moral terms, in point of fact the moral argument was grounded in the realities of postwar financial conditions in France and America. Because France's total debt had grown rapidly before and after the war, particularly in relation to the resources available for payment, its settlement became all the more agonizing. That France owed four billion dollars to the United States was a serious matter. Her obligation to Britain was of a similar magnitude. Moreover, the French prewar investment of four billion dollars in Russia had been seized by the Soviet government. At the same time, the obligations of the government to creditors within France had risen dramatically. In the event that there were insufficient funds to pay both domestic and foreign creditors, a choice would have to be made.[2] The financial burden of the government was also increased by the need for credit to reconstruct the northern region of France, which had been completely devastated during the war. In principle, this money was to come in the form of German reparations payments. However, if the money should not be forthcoming, the French government would have to divert the funds for payment of the foreign debt to accomplish the task of reconstruction.

While the American government pretended there was no link between debts and reparations, it acted in a different fashion. Secretary Hughes attempted to forestall the French invasion of the Ruhr in the fall of 1922 by proposing in his New Haven address that a commission of experts be established to determine Germany's capacity to pay. The commission was to have the advice of American financial experts, serving as private citizens. The Hughes initiative was taken in large part because the American government realized that debt settlements would occur only when the reparations issue had been resolved.[3]

Hughes's recommendation was accepted only after the French occupation of the Ruhr. The Dawes Commission, headed by American financier Charles Dawes, completed its work in the summer of 1924. The commission recommended the resumption of reparations payments on a regular basis, but provided no definitive schedule for the payments. The German economy, which had ground to a halt, was to be revived by a massive infusion of American investments. In short, the money to pay for reparations would come from the United States. This solution, which demonstrated the financial preponderance of the United States in Europe, signaled an important turning point in Franco-American relations. Charles Pomaret called attention to the fact that "for the first time, in 1924, Europe sensed its dependence. For the first time, American finance was a power in the back rooms of the London Conference."[4] *Europe Nouvelle* spelled out more specifically the implications of the Dawes Plan for Europe:

European governments today are faced with a problem of a very specific character; they can continue to waste their energy fighting among themselves and lose both power and prestige; in the end, exhausted, they will have to accept without protest Wall Street's conditions, which will in fact mean the end of the modern state, the product of the Revolution; or by agreeing to abandon hope and pretentions, in order to save what they can still save, they will understand that the mediocre agreement which they can still reach is infinitely better than the one they will have to accept in several months if they separate without concluding anything. However, it is essential that they understand this.[5]

While the increase of American power was perhaps the most critical revelation of the Dawes negotiations, the French were also disturbed by the willingness of Americans and the English, despite commitments at Versailles and London, to scale down the reparations. André Tardieu lamented "the Anglo-Saxon dogma that before repairing the devastation, it is necessary to reestablish the devastator."[6] However, the bitterness over the reduction in reparations was most strongly expressed only after the conclusion of the debt agreement. Only then were the French in a position to argue that the Germans had been treated more leniently on reparations than they were on debts. In any event, the French response to the debt settlement was made with one eye on the Dawes Plan.

The debt controversy was also linked with the monetary situation in France after World War I. As a result of the pressure of wartime expenses, which were financed by enormous borrowing, the franc had begun to fall rapidly during the war. With the exception of the recession years of 1921-22, obligations mounted in the postwar period and the fall of the franc continued; from 1924 to 1926, the franc's value declined so rapidly that the question of monetary stability became a major public issue. Unable to solve the problem, one government after another fell.[7]

The coincidence of this rapid decline of the franc with the negotiations over the debt did not escape observers in France. The lack of confidence in the franc was obviously increased by the likelihood that huge new obligations would be imposed without the prospect of additional income. Moreover, it was widely believed that there were calculated efforts to weaken the franc. Prime Minister Poincaré spoke of the "criminal machinations of international finance."[8] Others insisted that these machinations were part of a scheme to force France to ratify the debt agreement. Roger Picard pointed out that "many people in France accused the speculators in foreign markets of responsibility for this sharp decline of the franc and insisted on interpreting these maneuvers as the expression of a means of pressure destined to force us to ratify."[9]

The relation between the debts and the monetary crisis was also evident in the State Department ban on private loans. It not only put pressure on Frenchmen to ratify the debt accords, but also eliminated a much needed source of revenue. Indeed, the Committee of Experts, which had been created in the spring of 1926, recommended, among other solutions, that the French government ratify the debt accords immediately to make available American private loans. It was the one part of the report, however, which the Poincaré administration rejected.[10]

In the light of the connection between debts and the monetary issue, it is exceedingly difficult to interpret the reaction to the debt issue by French critics. Nonetheless, the evidence indicates that the strongest expression of anti-Americanism came in July of 1926 during the crisis of the franc rather than in April when the debt accords were signed. Maurice Muret, just a year later, recalled that anti-Americanism peaked in July. "The Parisian mob abused American tourists a bit with scornful remarks and provocative gestures."[11] Americans countered by pasting French money on their cars. Not until July 11, 1926, did the silent parade of wounded war veterans in Paris protest the debt accords.[12] Apparently, the injustice of the debt agreement was felt more acutely after the fall of the franc, even though anti-Americanism was blamed entirely on the former event.

The ban on loans, a third element in the financial situation, was also linked with the French monetary problems and the debt issue. It too produced strong public reaction which was frequently directed at the effort to collect debts. The loan policy of the American government developed in the wake of substantial investment by American citizens in European countries. To prevent a conflict between the government effort to collect debts and the concern of private sources to maintain the strength of their loans, bankers were expected to consult with the State Department before lending abroad.[13]

The new loan policy had no effect on Franco-American relations until the United States began to insist on the funding of the debt in 1924. Indeed, from 1918 to 1924, the French government had received loans amounting to more than $500 million from private sources in the United States. When, in late 1924, the French government sought an additional loan, the State Department urged Morgan and Company to withold the funds until (1) the American government received its share of reparations collected under the Dawes agreement and (2) the French government began paying for American army supplies which had been purchased at the end of the war.[14] The use of these pressure tactics by the American government was successful, but it caused considerable irritation in France. The insistence of the United States that an agreement must be reached on the debt led to accusations of miserly behavior. "Shylock," said Octave Homberg, "takes his small commission from the payments of the debts to his old associates for the damages which they have suffered."[15] Similar resentment was evident in the columns of *Europe*

*Nouvelle.* "There is something tragic in the situation of the great trans-Atlantic nation. It is overflowing with gold which it uses badly but always asks for more."[16]

The loan issue came to a head in January of 1925 after Finance Minister Clémentel failed to include the French obligations to America in his list of public debts. The American government's protest provoked Louis Marin, a conservative republican deputy, to denounce the American debt policy in a speech before the Assembly. The speech was as provocative to the American government as it was to Marin's compatriots. Only one day later, the State Department banned all American loans to France.[17] While the issue received little attention from travelers or commentators in the elite journals, there is no question that it helped to compound the monetary situation, to make the collection of the debts even less palatable, and thereby to stimulate the rise of anti-Americanism in France.

The other important factor which affected repayment of debts was the tariff policy of the United States. Through the Fordney-McCumber Tariff of 1922 and the Smoot-Hawley Tariff of 1930, the United States established the highest trade barriers in American history.[18] The new tariffs blocked the sale of French products to the United States, thus eliminating the most feasible method of paying off the war debts.[19] This policy of exclusion naturally provoked French opinion. Charles Pomaret pointed out that the tariff permitted America to control her own market, while, at the same time, exercising leverage on the markets of other countries. He deplored "America's unilateral conception of the problem and the resulting infringement on the sovereignty of foreign states."[20] Other spokesmen were more alarmed about the effects of the American tariff. *Europe Nouvelle* protested that "the role of a creditor is not to ruin her debtors,"[21] while Kadmi-Cohen saw the tariff as evidence that the United States intended to enslave Europe.[22]

Because there was often no way of dissociating the tariff issue, the loan policy, or the monetary situation from the debt question, it is difficult to determine to what extent French opposition to the American position on debts stems from hostility to American financial policy in general. Anti-American sentiments were certainly stimulated by all of these developments. It therefore seems unlikely that the debt policy, unburdened by the American position on tariffs, reparations, and loans, would have caused such a vehement reaction in French opinion.

Nonetheless, the debt question was, in its own right, a thorny issue. As a substantial financial burden for the French to carry during the postwar period, it was an important national concern. In addition, and equally serious, the debts had become a symbolic issue during the war. Although their legal status was never in doubt, they had come to represent both for Americans and Frenchmen the entente spirit. In 1917 and 1918, when American troops were only present on the front lines in small numbers, the American contribution to the war effort was largely financial. At the time, Senator Cummins of Iowa, as well as other public officials and private citizens who were carried away by wartime zeal, had argued that the loans should be a gift to France.[23]

It is no wonder that many French officials, along with the French public, had the strong impression that the money would never be repaid. The impression was reinforced by the deliberate pace at which the United States proceeded to collect the debts. Not until February of 1922 did Congress pass legislation setting up the World War Debt Commission, which was charged with the responsiblity of collecting all debts.[24] Even then, the American government did not press the debtors to negotiate; and, after the German default on reparations in the spring of 1922, the solution to that issue became the first order of business. Indeed, Assistant Minister of Finance Parmentier, during a visit to the United States in July of 1922, pointed out that while France recognized her debt obligation, payments could only begin after reparations were forthcoming. Former Prime Minister Clemenceau, on an unofficial tour of the United States four months later, went further than Parmentier. Arguing the immorality of charging an ally for a contribution to the joint effort in the war, Clemenceau urged the complete cancellation of the debt.[25]

In 1923, England became the first nation to negotiate a settlement of the war debts. With the establishment of this precedent, French hopes of cancellation, based on the possibility of a united European front against the United States, were ended. In their place, another Anglo-Saxon agreement had emerged.[26] As at the Washington Conference, Frenchmen again felt that cultural differences were creating, or at least reinforcing, policy differences.

Franco-American conflict over the debt issue reached serious proportions only after the Dawes settlement had been accepted by the major powers. Then, the United States adopted the ban on loans as a weapon to coerce France into negotiations. After an abortive effort to reach a settlement in the summer of 1925, the Mellon-Bérenger agreement was signed in April of 1926, funding the debt at full value, but reducing the interest rate to 1.67 percent.[27] The controversy over the debt, which had erupted periodically before 1926, was set off more intensively by the settlement.

There were three major grounds for protesting the Mellon-Bérenger agreement. Those who felt that the repayment of a loan to a wartime ally was immoral generally urged the complete cancellation of the debt. This position was advanced most dramatically in Louis Marin's speech before the French Assembly in January of 1925. Marin maintained that the American loan was a contribution to the Allied cause in lieu of American soldiers. The sacrifice of French soldiers at the front, therefore, represented the repayment of the loan in blood. The popularity of Marin's position was evident in the reaction of the French Assembly to his speech. It was greeted by thunderous applause from all sides.[28] The deputies proceeded to vote almost unanimously to placard the speech throughout France at public expense.[29] The debt issue, like disarmament, was a matter which united spokesmen from all parties.

The insistence of the United States on repayment of debts went far toward establishing the image of America as a materialistic power, immune to moral arguments. André Siegfried contended that "when the time for settling the Allied debts arrived, the evocation of the great work accomplished in common was coldly put aside as one discards from a counter documents useless for settling interest."[30] Siegfried agreed with Marin that France had paid her debt in blood. The same sentiments were reflected in a café song which invited Americans to come drink in France: "Fill up your lamp over here, Sam, and then you'll forget such a little thing as money."[31] "Uncle Sam" soon became "Uncle Shylock" to many Frenchmen. J. L. Chastanet went so far as to entitle his study of American financial policy *L'Oncle Shylock*.[32]

The moral argument derived additional strength from the fact that the European powers used their loans to purchase arms and materials in America. As Germaine Martin and Charles Pomaret pointed out, these purchases helped the Allied cause, but they also contributed to the growth of the American economy. By asking for repayment of the debts, the United States would reap further profits, while France would bear an increased burden.[33]

The second argument against the American debt policy was technical rather than moral. Spokesmen for this position expected France to reimburse the United States, but argued for a special standard to calculate the debt totals. Ironically, the use of economic criteria had originally been proposed by the Anglo-Saxons to determine the reparations payments of the Germans and was severely criticized in France. Now, certain Frenchmen insisted that debts and reparations were linked in practice, if not in theory. Caillaux and Parmentier had adopted this position in their negotiations with the American government. Moreover, it had been implicitly recognized by Secretary Hughes's intervention in the reparations affair.[34] The refusal of American leaders to officially accept the link between the two issues raised the specter of a German default on reparations during which France would be expected to meet her debt obligations.[35]

After the Dawes agreement, Frenchmen felt that the reduction in reparations had established a precedent for an equal reduction in France's debt burden.[36] While the American government would agree to cut the interest rate, France was expected to pay the entire principal of the debt. The United States seemed to accept the principle of "capacity to pay" in dealing with German reparations, but not in considering the French debt.[37]

When Frenchmen attempted to explain why the United States was acting in such a selfish and unjust fashion, they discovered substantial evidence of imperialism in the American posture. Many felt that the debt settlement was a convenient way to gain informal control over the European economy or additional territory. Georges Clemenceau, in a bitter letter to President Coolidge on August 8, 1926, accused the United States of territorial ambitions. "It is an open secret that in this affair there are only imaginary dates of payment, which will lead to a loan with solid security in the shape of our territorial possessions as was the case of Turkey. Such a thing, Mr. President, I am bound to tell you, we shall never accept."[38]

Most critics were more fearful of American economic domination in France. J. L. Chastanet saw the debts as "a double-edged sword for Uncle Shylock. The revenue . . . is all in all of little importance for him. What is more attractive is the possibility of exercising permanent extortion on us."[39] Two years later, Octave Homberg painted a more precise picture of the developing American control over France. He asked rhetorically:

Isn't it painful to see so many art objects, old houses, and beautiful land in our country pass into the hands of foreigners? We have the impression that we are being colonized. At stake in this progressive dispossession is everything which was part of the living personality, the charm, even the appearance, and the spirit of France, the salt of this earth. Thanks to the payment of the debts for sixty-two years, we are the ones who will furnish this people, already gorged with gold, the new means of enslaving us.[40]

Even if Franco-American conflict had abated after 1926, it is clear that irreparable damage had already been done to the entente by that date. The Dawes Plan, the ban on loans, the Mellon-Bérenger agreement, and the monetary crisis taken together had convinced Frenchmen that the United States was conspiring to secure domination of France. This belief, however, was reinforced over the next six years. A series of confrontations between France and America further exacerbated the diplomatic situation.

Both the debt issue and reparations were revived again in 1929. The debt issue, in fact, had never been fully resolved, because Poincaré had decided in 1926 not to present the Mellon-Bérenger accord for ratification to the French Assembly. The decision had been made in hopes of renegotiating the original pact on a basis more favorable to France. By 1929, these hopes were no longer realistic and, with the principal of a loan for $500 million falling due in that year, France would either have to ratify the original agreement or pay the entire sum at that point. The debt accord, therefore, was presented to the Assembly as an issue of confidence in the Poincaré government; on these terms, it was accepted by a margin of eight votes.[41] At the same time, the Assembly ratified a similar agreement with England; in both cases, however, France's agreement to pay her debts was predicated on the receipt of reparations from the German government. The debate over ratification produced still another outburst of anti-American feeling in France.[42]

The year 1929 also witnessed a new chapter in the saga of reparations. To replace the Dawes Plan, which was only an interim solution, a definitive settlement was needed. As in 1924, a committee of experts, headed by American financier Owen Young, was the vehicle for the task. The Young Plan used the debt agreements as a model, providing that regular installments would be paid over a period of fifty-nine years. The agreement attempted to commercialize Germany's debt by selling bonds to private investors, thus insuring regular payments on part of the loan. The most controversial aspect of the Young Plan was the proposal to create a Bank of International Settlements. It was not only to assume the role of transferring reparations payments from Germany to the Allies, but more generally to coordinate monetary operations between governments. These functions were to be overseen by a board of directors composed of both European and American representatives.[43]

To some Frenchmen, the proposal for the Bank of International Settlements seemed still another aspect of the American campaign to dominate Europe. Kadmi-Cohen felt that the bank "permits the businessmen of New York and Washington to control all of Europe."[44] Octave Homberg agreed. He contended that the bank "conceals the plan to Americanize Europe," and that, in regulating international exchanges, it "would become above all the docile instrument of American greed." The process would be a subtle one, according to Homberg. The bank would "oversee—to use the expression which the Anglo-Saxons mouth so willingly—the day-to-day existence of every European state. . . . soon the state banks of these different nations will be only its vassals."[45]

The financial arrangements of 1929, which seemed to settle once and for all the payments problems plaguing Europe since the war, were barely in place when the depression rendered them unworkable. By early 1931, it had become clear that the Germans would be unable to meet their obligations that summer. The collapse of the German economy, moreover, was certain to undermine American investments, as well as the Young Plan. To prevent further harm, President Hoover intervened suddenly in June of 1931 to recommend a moratorium on all intergovernmental payments. Although the moratorium applied to debts as well as reparations, it was strongly opposed in France as a precedent for the Germans to withhold the unconditional portion of the reparations payment. Hoover's failure to consult France before announcing the plan was another factor in French opposition.[46] In addition, many Frenchmen believed that the moratorium was designed primarily to help the Americans save their investments in Germany and only secondarily to enhance the resumption of reparations payments.[47]

The moratorium not only failed to solve the financial crisis, but it created expectations which could not be fulfilled. During a meeting with Prime Minister Laval in the United States in October of 1931, President Hoover apparently conveyed the impression that the moratorium established the long-awaited official link between debts and reparations.[48] In any event, the European powers, assuming that the financial situation of Europe would not permit the resumption of intergovernmental payments, agreed at Lausanne to a 90 percent reduction in reparations on the condition that the United States accede to a similar cancellation of debts.

It was in this context that the Hoover administration, with a mandate from Congress, announced that debt payments would be resumed in full on December 15, 1932. The Herriot government accordingly recommended that France meet her obligation, but the Assembly balked, causing the fall of the government, and France defaulted. The strong opposition of the Assembly to the payment of debts without the receipt of reparations was echoed in French opinion. Raoul de Roussy de Sales, looking back to 1932, spoke of the "violence of the French reaction."[49] There was indeed rioting by right-wing groups in Paris, including the Action Francaise and Croix de Feu in protest against the American demands.[50] Violence, in the metaphorical sense, was also evident. One article in the *Revue Universelle* was entitled "Shylock Wakes Up."[51] Georges Lechartier indicated his opposition to the American position by acclaiming the end of the Hoover administration. "Whatever the policy adopted by the Democratic President, a friend of France and the Allies, it cannot be worse than the one followed for four years by the Republican President."[52] *Europe Nouvelle*, looking to the past rather than the future, found the American position in 1932 a perfect reflection of

American policy during the entire postwar period. "Surely the Americans can claim a rare consistency in the narrowest and most egotistical attitude. Right from the peace conference on, their manner of insisting on their rights has had tragic repercussions on the position of the reparations problem."[53]

It is clear, once again, that French opinion reacted to each development as part of a series of related events. The resumption crisis of 1932 was exacerbated by the memory of the Dawes Plan, the Young Plan, and the debt crisis. The major turning point in the twenties was reached with the Mellon-Bérenger agreement of 1926, although it alone would not have produced such a dramatic effect. Each subsequent crisis over debts and reparations tended to further alienate French opinion. By 1932, after the failure of the moratorium policy, Franco-American relations reached their low point. It was with considerable eagerness that Frenchmen awaited the inauguration of Franklin Roosevelt.

## NOTES

1. *Histoire de France depuis la guerre* (Paris, 1932), 272, 246.

2. Robert Murray Haig, *The Public Finances of Post-War France* (New York, 1929), 63.

3. Jean-Baptiste Duroselle, *From Wilson to Roosevelt* (New York, 1968), 148-149.

4. *L'Amérique à la conquête de l'Europe* (Paris, 1931), 187. The claim that the acceptance of the Dawes Plan marked a major turning point in European history has been abundantly documented in two recent studies: Stephen A. Schuker, *The End of French Predominance in Europe: The Financial Crisis of 1924 and the Adoption of the Dawes Plan* (Chapel Hill, 1976); and Charles S. Maier, *Recasting Bourgeois Europe: Stabilization in France, Germany, and Italy in the Decade after World War I* (Princeton, 1975).

5. "Les conditions de la finance privée" (July 26, 1924), 951.

6. *Devant l'obstacle* (Paris, 1927), 194.

7. Haig, *The Public Finances of Post-War France*, 142.

8. *Ibid.*, 91.

9. *Le problème des dettes interalliées* (Paris, 1934), 97.

10. Haig, *The Public Finances of Post-War France*, 145-154.

11. "L'opinion américaine et la France," *Revue de Paris* (March 1, 1927), 25.

12. *Literary Digest* (July 24, 1926), 7.

13. Herbert Feis, *The Diplomacy of the Dollar* (Baltimore, 1950), 8.

14. Benjamin H. Williams, *Economic Foreign Policy of the United States* (New York, 1929), 89-90.

15. *L'impérialisme américain* (Paris, 1929), 38.

16. "La conférence financière" (January 1, 1925), 34.

17. Feis, *The Diplomacy of the Dollar*, 21-22. The ban on loans was rescinded in 1928 after the French government had signed an agreement extending most-favored-nation treatment to Germany. To avoid trade discrimination, the United States withdrew the ban on loans and in return was also granted most-favored-nation status by the French government. Williams, *Economic Foreign Policy of the United States*, 278-279.

18. The twenties was a period of high tariffs all over the world and France was no exception. The French tariff level on manufactured goods rose to 21 percent during the decade. William Ogburn and William Jaffe, *The Economic Development of Post-War France* (New York, 1929), 543.

19. The only other means of paying an intergovernmental debt are to transfer gold, of which the Europeans had only a small supply during the twenties; to receive money from foreign tourists and military personnel; or to accept investments from the creditor. It was the last of these options which enabled the Europeans to pay off some of their debt to the United States.

20. *L'Amérique à la conquête de l'Europe*, 38.

21. "Les négotiations commerciales franco-américaines" (October 22, 1927), 1408.

22. *L'abomination américaine* (Paris, 1930), 92.

23. Williams, *Economic Foreign Policy of the United States*, 220.

24. Congress insisted that the entire principal must be repaid by debtors along with 4.25 percent interest. No other terms were to be accepted. In reality, the commission had to scale down the interest in order to obtain agreements with the debtor nations. Harold Moulton and Leo Pasvolsky, *War Debts and World Prosperity* (Washington, 1932), 77.

25. *Ibid.*, 83.

26. "L'entente Anglo-Saxon," *Europe Nouvelle* (November 29, 1924), 1578. England agreed to pay the full principal of her debt and 3.33 percent interest.

27. Finance Minister Joseph Caillaux had attempted to negotiate a settlement in the summer of 1925, but the United States would not agree to a link between the payment of debts and reparations. Caillaux did succeed in negotiating a temporary settlement by which the French would begin regular payments on the debts. "La semaine de Washington," *Europe Nouvelle* (October 17, 1925), 1376.

28. Williams, *Economic Foreign Policy of the United States*, 90.

29. Louis Levine, "The French Point of View," in Harold Moulton and Cleona Lewis, *The French Debt Problem* (New York, 1925), 258.

30. *Les Etats-Unis d'aujourd'hui*, 204.

31. *New York Times* (November 22, 1925), XII, 13.

32. (Paris, 1927).

33. "Le problème des dettes en France et aux Etats-Unis," *Revue de Paris* (November 1, 1926), 148; *L'Amérique à la conquête de l'Europe*, 59.

34. The claim that the American government had implicitly recognized the link between debts and reparations was advanced by Char es Pomaret, *L'Amérique à la conquête de l'Europe*, 59; and Kadmi-Cohen, *L'abomination américaine*, 64.

35. C. J. Gignoux, "Du Plan Dawes aux dettes interalliés," *Mercure de France* (January 15, 1925), 397.

36. *Ibid.*, 397; *Devant l'obstacle*, 259.

37. Pomaret, *L'Amérique à la conquête de L'Europe*, 60-61.

38. Quoted in Benjamin Williams, *Economic Foreign Policy of the United States*, 229. Clemenceau's allegations are reminiscent of Herriot's anger in 1924 when he was informed of the House of Morgan's conditions for European loans. The French would first be required to adopt a plan for withdrawal from the Ruhr. To this condition, Herriot responded with vehemence "that perhaps he should offer two French provinces as security." Schuker, *The End of French Predominance*, 351-352.

39. *L'Oncle Shylock*, 78.

40. *L'impérialisme américain*, 22.

41. The margin of eight votes is somewhat deceptive. A number of Radicals who voted against the debt accords would have changed their votes, if the proposal had been in danger of defeat. "De Poincaré avec Briand à Briand sans Poincaré," *Europe Nouvelle* (August 3, 1929), 1056.

42. These issues were raised by Saint-Brice in "Où reparait 'Pan Europe,'" *Revue Universelle* (August 1, 1929), 363.

43. The role of the bank is discussed at length in Frank Costigliola, "The Other Side of Isolationism: The Establishment of the First World Bank, 1929-1930," *Journal of American History* (December 1972). Under the Dawes Plan, an American, Parker Gilbert, had taken charge of transfer payments.

44. *L'abomination américaine*, 74.

45. *L'impérialisme américain*, 47-48. Saint-Brice also inveighed against the bank on the grounds that it would bring an end to the hegemony of national states. "A l'américaine," *Revue Universelle* (April 1, 1929), 106. A somewhat different view was presented in *Europe Nouvelle*. Its editors

agreed that Europe must resist American power; however, they expected the bank to advance European unity and thereby provide a counterweight to the American presence. Y. de Boisanger, "Après le plan Young: du règlement des réparations au règlement des dettes" (June 15, 1929), 790.

46. Robert Ferrell, *American Diplomacy in the Great Depression* (New Haven, 1957), 113-114.

47. David Landes, *The Unbound Prometheus* (Cambridge, 1969), 376, cites Jacques Chastenet's opinion that the United States was primarily interested in protecting her investors in Germany. The same claim was raised by Jean Allary, "Les Américains ont parlé," *Europe Nouvelle* (June 27, 1931), 875.

48. Duroselle, *From Wilson to Roosevelt*, 202.

49. "Le problème des dettes franco-américaines," *Europe Nouvelle* (December 26, 1936), 1259.

50. *New York Times* (December 14, 1932), 18.

51. Saint-Brice (December 15, 1932), 731.

52. "Le Président Roosevelt," *Revue des Deux Mondes* (December 1, 1932), 519.

53. "Le refus de M. Hoover" (November 26, 1932), 1370.

# chapter 9

# American Investments in Europe ____

> The incredible profits of the American economy
> since the War have enabled the United States to
> invest capital in the countries which Europe used
> to finance and in the same Europe which fifteen
> years ago still financed American enterprises.
>
> —Charles Pomaret, 1931

The European debt to the United States after World War I was comprised of a number of elements. The most visible portion was the money loaned by the American government to the Allies during and after the war. As an intergovernmental matter, the loan was funded through diplomatic channels and became a public issue. The less obvious portions of the debt were the direct and indirect investments of private American sources. Indirect investments, usually in the form of loans to European governments, were not regarded by French critics as essentially different from intergovernmental credits such as war loans. Direct investments, which financed subsidiaries of American firms in Europe, were another matter. The growth of American-controlled multinational corporations was considered a serious threat to the independence of France and Europe.

Not all Frenchmen were opposed to American investment. In the period after World War I, when credit was not readily available in France, American loans and investments were welcomed. In 1920, Louis Thomas, a French businessman, regarded the United States as the best source of credit for France.[1] As late as 1924, Senator Louis Dausset, addressing the American Club in Paris, argued that

America's excess profits should be invested in France.[2] Even after the debt agreement, some Frenchmen continued to ask for American credit, although they were increasingly wary of the dangers of American control.[3]

As early as 1920, a few critics had recognized that danger. Albert Demangeon, for one, welcomed American loans for reconstructing the devastated areas and supporting public works, but not American investment in French industry. He maintained that "American expansion in France must be a collaboration and not a colonization."[4] By 1926, Frenchmen no longer believed in the possibility of collaboration, although they recognized the inevitability of American investment. *Europe Nouvelle* explained this predicament:

After the wartime destruction, Europe is in dire need of credits to revitalize herself, to put her machine in order; she is like an automobile which must have a full tank before starting a trip; everyone goes to the only source from which credit flows, namely, Wall Street.

In this respect, the American government is the master of Europe; it controls us as much by the certificates which it grants us as by the credits which will be granted to us.[5]

The American corporations which established European subsidiaries were active in the new and technologically advanced industries. American companies played an important role in the marketing of oil and electricity; these forms of energy helped to sustain the automobile, telephone, and movie industries in which American control was also substantial. In other areas of the European economy, American investment was sporadic. The concern of French critics, despite the relatively small total investment, must be understood, in part, in terms of the strategic character of these industries.[6] In a national emergency, France would be at the mercy of American-controlled companies for its oil supply and parts for the telephone system.

The opposition to American control was also intensified by the cultural implications of the new industries. American companies often used new methods to make products which were unfamiliar to the French public. Mass production, the telephone, and even the automobile were still relatively rare in France in 1919. As Marcel

Braunschvig explained, the spread of American industry could not be separated from the rise of a new technology. "When Ford creates branches in Europe, it is not so much (if we believe him) to increase his profits as to display, before an enraptured Europe, model factories which are rationally organized."[7] The success of the American film industry was also deplored because it "is organized according to the principles of Ford."[8]

The new products of the assembly line, such as the automobile, the telephone, and the cinema, were as disturbing to French critics as the new methods. They threatened to disrupt the traditional organization of French society. This was particularly true of the film, which exposed Frenchmen to the American language, American dress, and the American scene. In this sense, movies were becoming a vehicle for cultural imperialism. As Marcel Braunschvig explained, "The film is in the process of Americanizing the world."[9]

Of course, opposition to the film industry was not unanimous in France, nor did it necessarily entail the uniform rejection of all American movies. Charlie Chaplin and his films were widely hailed by Frenchmen during this period. Moreover, avant-garde French artists accepted the cinema as an art form to be taken seriously. They were particularly impressed with what they believed to be the imaginative use of the motion-picture medium by American directors. Such convictions, however, were exceptions to the rule. For most intellectuals, the rise of the film was a disturbing development which threatened their own primacy and the survival of French culture.

The French reaction to American investment was also intensified by the coincidence of the clash over repayment of the debt with the recognition of increased American investment. The conflict over debts and disarmament convinced Frenchmen that Americans were trying to control the French economy. The rise of investments merely reinforced this impression. It is equally true that the existence of American-controlled companies in France helped to exaggerate the response to the debt issue and others.

The pattern of American control differed in each of the five major industries, although American investment increased substantially in all of them during the twenties. American control of the electrical industry was largely confined to the manufacture of electrical products. In the distribution of electrical power, European companies retained control. The most dynamic force in the field of electrical equipment production, not only in France but throughout Europe, was the International General Electric Company. In 1928, the merger of the French Thomson-Houston Company and the Société Alsacienne de Constructions Mécaniques brought over 50 percent of electrical equipment manufacturing in France under the control of a new company, Alsthom. While it is true that General Electric owned only 14 percent of the Alsthom stock, the control of the company was nonetheless assured by an agreement giving Alsthom the exclusive right in France to exploit General Electric patents and processes. The company remained under French management, but in the words of French Minister of Postal, Telegraph, and Telephone Services Mallarmé, it was "American controlled."[10]

The second largest French firm in the field of electrical equipment was the Schneider Company; like Alsthom, Schneider had an arrangement with an American company, Westinghouse, giving it exclusive rights to their patents. Moreover, Westinghouse owned 45 percent of the Schneider stock.[11]

With the notable exception of England, European nations maintained control over the distribution of electrical power.[12] In France, the American company, International Power and Securities Corporation, had small holdings in the Union d'Electricité and had loaned $4 million to help it construct a high-voltage ring around Paris, providing additional power to that city.[13] The loan led to unfounded accusations of American control, notably by J. L. Chastanet; he quoted the *Wall Street Journal* on the interest of American financiers in offering loans to "six or eight giant electrical energy companies in France."[14]

In their patterns of development, the electrical and telephone industries were quite similar. American control was exercised primarily over the manufacture of telephone equipment rather than the distribution of services.[15] The consolidation of the telephone industry was accomplished by a single giant, International Telephone and Telegraph Company. Its subsidiary, Le Matériel Téléphonique, a company with two factories and 4,000 employees, was the major producer of telephone equipment in France. The other active firm in the industry was French Thomson-Houston. In 1926, ITT purchased the telephone division of that company, which consisted of two factories with 2,500 workers. In addition, ITT had an arrangement for "close technical collaboration" with the Grammont Company, a producer of automatic telephone equipment. Grammont, however, denied any financial control by ITT.[16]

Largely because the government had awarded several contracts to French subsidiaries of ITT, American control of the telephone industry became more of an issue in France than similar control in the electrical equipment business. In 1928 and 1929, Le Matériel Téléphonique was chosen by the French government to modernize the telephone system of Paris. French Thomson-Houston, also under ITT control, was already involved in automatizing the phone systems of Morocco and Tunis. More controversial was the selection of ITT by the French government to install 180,000 automatic lines throughout France. By these decisions, modernization of the entire French telephone system was entrusted to American-controlled companies using equipment made in their factories.[17]

Already in 1926, at the time of the merger of ITT and French Thomson-Houston, rumors of an American takeover of the French telephone system had spread. Le Temps, one of the most reliable dailies in France, was one source.[18] French financial dailies were quoted by J. L. Chastanet to the same effect. They, in turn, got their information from the New York Herald, which claimed that ITT would float an international loan after the stabilization of the franc in order to cover its purchase of the French system.[19]

Controversy surfaced again in 1930 after ITT received the contract to modernize the French system. Senator Jean Philip accused the government of sacrificing the interests of France by awarding the job to an American company.[20] The Minister of the Postal, Telegraph, and Telephone Services attempted to minimize the dangers by arguing that ITT was an American company under French management.[21] Many Frenchmen were not satisfied with this response. Jean Bonnefon-Craponne and Charles Pomaret believed that the country was "in the presence of an American enterprise of enormous energy; the stakes would be nothing less than the independence of the telephone service of Paris and France." In time of war, the foreign control of the system would be particularly dangerous.[22] The fears of an American takeover, however, proved to be groundless.

In the telephone and electrical industries, American companies were able to dominate their European rivals through technological superiority. In the competition for control of oil resources, American firms benefited from State Department support. When it appeared that the exploitation of the Mesopotamian oil fields would be restricted to European companies, Secretaries Colby and Hughes argued for the application of the Open Door. The pressure from the department resulted in an agreement in 1925 which forced the French and British companies to concede a 23.75 percent share of the oil produced in the area to American companies.[23] Irritated by the American demand for the Open Door, Roger Lévy pointed out that Americans refused to make similar concessions in their own colonies. He called the new oil policy an example of "Yankee egotism."[24]

France was even more directly affected by the pressure tactics of American oil companies in France. When the French attempted to regulate oil imports through the Klotz Plan of 1919, Standard Oil lowered its prices, thus forcing French importers to sell out. The Anglo-American companies then obtained an agreement from the French government by which their firms would supply two-thirds of the oil used in France, although half of this oil was to be marketed by French companies.[25] Standard of New Jersey and Vacuum together accounted for 26 percent of the total oil marketed in the country. In 1929, when the French government decided to reward oil companies which refined their product in France by lowering the duty on the crude oil they imported, Standard, Gulf, and Atlantic pooled their resources to establish a refinery in France, the Société Franco-Américaine de Raffinage.[26]

French critics took special notice of two aspects of the oil situation. One was the involvement of the American government in promoting the interests of American companies, a situation which Jean Gachon characterized as "economic imperialism."[27] The American control over the supply of oil throughout the world was also threatening to Frenchmen. Such control could render an oil-rich country like Colombia dependent on the American companies.[28] J. L. Chastanet complained that "America is almost the absolute master of all the oil in the universe," while Charles Pomaret spoke of "the quasi monopoly of the world production of oil" enjoyed by the United States. Both critics acknowledged the strength of such non-American firms as Royal Dutch Shell and Anglo-Persian, but maintained that both companies were dependent on Standard of New Jersey for their supply of oil.[29]

The automobile industry presented different problems for Frenchmen. While America dominated world production, France was the leading producer of cars in Europe during the twenties. In contrast to the situation in the oil industry, American interests in France in the automobile industry were relatively minor. Ford had one assembly plant at Asnières, 370 dealers, and 3,000 garages, while General Motors maintained a warehouse in Marseilles and controlled a sparkplug factory (the Société des Bougies A. C. Titan). The two companies together employed only 11,375 men. A Morgan and Company loan to Citröen did not jeopardize the autonomy of that company or of other large French automobile manufacturers in the twenties.[30]

American companies threatened the French industry only indirectly by their activities in other countries. In 1929, General Motors announced its purchase of the Opel plant in Germany, which was expected to produce 200,000 cars a year. Ford adopted a different strategy for establishing his company in Europe. Rather than purchase a European firm, Ford built the Dagenham plant near London, also with a capacity of 200,000 cars. The operation of these two plants would enable American manufacturers to supplant the French as the leading producers of small cars.[31] Moreover, in November of 1929 it was rumored that Citröen and Peugeot would be purchased by General Motors. Although this rumor was untrue, critics noted that Fiat had borrowed $10 million from New York bankers who were given the option to acquire 400,000 shares of Fiat stock.[32]

The French reacted to these initiatives from America with expressions of concern. Marcel Braunschvig regretted "the very grave menace for European producers of automobiles, among which French producers were in first place up to now."[33] Pomaret, while concerned about the construction of new factories and the purchase of old ones by American producers, was even more alarmed by such "insidious forms" of domination as the custom of shipping parts to Europe and assembling them there to avoid tariff payments.[34]

American domination of the French film market was more than a fear; it was a reality. Before World War I, the French film industry had led the world in the production of motion pictures. During the war, the industry had collapsed, and, in the immediate postwar period, the production of films suffered from the diversion of capital to the reconstruction of the devastated areas in northern France. In the absence of French-made films, a market for foreign films arose, which American producers were quick to exploit. By 1924, fully 85 percent of feature-length films shown in France were American-made. American control was still substantial by 1927, although it had declined to 63 percent.[35] According to J. L. Chastanet, Americans were "inundating the entire world with their films."[36]

As the French film industry began to recover from the war, its representatives turned to the government for protection against the flood of American films into France. In 1927, Edouard Herriot, then Minister of Public Instruction and the Fine Arts, worked with French producers to set up a Cinema Commission. This body had the power to ban foreign films regarded as unsuitable for the French public and to enforce a quota system by which only four foreign films could be shown in France for each film produced in the country.[37]

The quota, established in March of 1928, provoked the Motion Picture Producers and Distributors of America, representing the American film industry, to vote a boycott of the French market. American films would not be shown in France, and French films would not be viewed in America. Under the pressure of the boycott, the French government agreed in September of 1928 to accept seven foreign films in France for each French film produced.[38]

American domination of the French market was not always achieved in fair competition with French films. Indeed, many observers were concerned about "the bold and tyrannical commercial techniques" which the subsidiaries of American companies were using in Europe.[39] American producers would offer European movie houses one or two popular features, essential for the commercial success of these theaters, in return for an agreement to show a large number of less popular American movies.[40] Independent movie theaters, which attempted to resist American control by refusing second-rate American films, were boycotted by distributors of American films and found it impossible to operate at a profit.

To make matters worse, American distributors showed little interest in French-made films. Even after a group of French producers toured America to promote their films in 1927, the situation did not improve. In 1929, only nineteen French films were shown in America. While French producers complained of discrimination against their product, American distributors maintained that audiences in the United States were simply not receptive to French films.[41]

The market for American films in France was swelled by other factors. American companies owned about three-fourths of the best movie theaters in France including establishments in Paris, Le Havre, Bordeaux, Toulon, Toulouse, Lyon, Strasbourg, and Rouen. These theaters provided a natural outlet for American films and further reduced the market for French movies.[42]

While outright control of European companies was common in other industries, American film producers preferred the device of the marketing agreement. The most famous of these arrangements involved the German Universum Film A. G. and Metro-Goldwyn-Mayer and Paramount. Signed in 1926, the pact obligated the German company to market fifty American films per year in return for an American loan and an agreement to market twenty German films per year in America.[43] French critics were naturally alarmed that these arrangements would establish a precedent in France.[44]

American control was a reality in the movie equipment industry. Kodak alone manufactured 75 percent of the world's film. Western Electric Company, a subsidiary of ITT exercised a similar monopoly over the production of equipment for sound films. In France, Western Electric products were distributed through a subsidiary of another American company, the Société de Materiel Acoustique.[45]

The American domination of the film industry was more disturbing to Frenchmen than similar control over the oil, electric, and telephone industries because of the cultural impact of the film. While the automobile and the telephone threatened to disrupt certain aspects of French life, the film raised the specter of Americanization in the most fundamental sense; it threatened language, dress, and the very life style of Frenchmen. The American control of this industry was, therefore, a more controversial matter than American domination of other French industries.

Frenchmen were especially annoyed by the tendency of Americans to exploit and corrupt personnel, inventions, and material of French origin. As Marcel Braunschvig pointed out, the film itself was an invention of the Lumière brothers. Braunschvig believed that Americans had exploited a basically artistic medium for commercial purposes.[46] A more recent discovery such as the method for synchronizing sound, also a product of French ingenuity, was the foundation of Hollywood's commercial success in the era of sound films.[47]

Americans were also exploiting French and European personnel for Hollywood productions. Critics complained that directors such as Jacques Feyder, Mauritz Stiller, and Ernst Lubitsch were lured to the United States by her riches and then required to work in the commercial atmosphere of Hollywood, a fate shared as well by such actors as Maurice Chevalier and Greta Garbo. Their consequent misuse by American directors was compounded by the pain of seeing Chevalier sing in English.[48]

Hollywood's use and corruption of European inventions and talent was a relatively mild threat to French culture compared to the possible indoctrination of the entire French public in American mores by the American film. René Jeanne, for one, was convinced that American producers nourished grandiose cultural designs. He accused Will Hays of believing that "the only way to assure peace is to Americanize the thoughts, the language, and the souls of the inhabitants of 'little, old Europe.' "[49] Jean Allary traced the effort to disseminate the American way of life from the film back to its antecedents in the nineteenth century:

Formerly the preachers of Cincinnati or Baltimore deluged the world with pious brochures; their more cheerful offspring, who pursue the same ends, inundate it with blond movie stars; whether as missionaries loaded with Bibles or producers well supplied with films, the Americans are equally devoted to spreading the American way of life.[50]

Certain aspects of French life were particularly vulnerable to the imperialism of the film. Lucien Romier attributed the increasing uniformity of styles in France to the power of the American cinema. Hollywood was replacing Paris as the fashion center of the world. René Jeanne argued more generally that the American film was a vehicle for familiarizing French audiences with American products. A taste for these items would, of course, stimulate the demand for them, perhaps at the expense of French products.[51]

The advent of the talkie in 1927 raised an issue which was of special concern to French intellectuals: the survival of the French language. Jean Allary represented the thoughts of many critics when he asked: "Must we already look forward to the day when American sound films will spread over the old world, submerge it, and drown national productions?" In his own opinion, that day was not likely to arrive. France would be protected by the language barrier, while England would be more likely to suffer from an invasion of American films. Marcel Braunschvig agreed. He pointed out that the silent film was actually a more universal medium of communication.[52]

Other critics, however, were deeply alarmed about the future of the French language. René Jeanne accepted the opinion of an unnamed American film maker who claimed that "the sound film will not reduce our market in France, because, in six months, all those people who are interested in movies will speak American."[53] Other critics were more concerned about the use of dubbing in American films, because it might threaten the purity of the French language and allow the films in which it was used to be considered "French," thus bypassing the quota system. Charles Pomaret called his readers' attention to an American producers' organization, "Ciné-Studio Continental," whose task is to produce on European soil the French, German, Spanish, and Italian versions of sound films recorded in English in Hollywood."[54] This development might prolong American domination of the film industry, which had seemingly been undermined by the talkie.

Although the film was intended to be a medium of entertainment, French intellectuals discovered that American movies, on occasion, spread distorted views of French life. They were particularly sensitive to films depicting some aspect of World War I. *Beau Geste* was denounced in France because it portrayed the cruelty of an officer in the French Foreign Legion, who, in one scene, stripped his dead soldiers of all their worldly belongings. The film was considered so objectionable that after protests in the French press it was banned by French censors; the German government, in turn, at the request of the French ambassador, agreed not to allow the film to be shown in Germany.[55] There was milder criticism of *Enemies of Women*, which showed only American troops marching under the Arch of Triumph after World War I. No less than three French dailies denounced the film for implying that the American army was singlehandedly responsible for winning the war. Metro-Goldwyn-Mayer reacted quickly to the critics. The scene at the Arch of Triumph was filmed again to show French and British, as well as American, troops.[56]

On other occasions, Frenchmen protested that American films were instruments of government policy. The territorial ambitions of the United States in the Pacific Ocean were believed to be responsible for *White Shadows*, which showed the natives of the Marquésas Islands in the process of being corrupted by their French colonial masters. Such a portrait was assumed to undermine French control of the area.[51] Homberg found a similar political motive in other American productions, particularly films which showed America at war. In his view, *Wings, What Price Glory*, and *The Fleet's In* deliberately stressed the power of America's navy and air force in order to impress viewers with the military strength of the United States.[58]

The depiction of French life in American films was also a subject of concern to French critics. *The Girl from Montmartre*, for example, was considered objectionable because it portrayed Paris as dirty, dingy, and impoverished. In *They Had to See Paris*, René Jeanne criticized the stereotyped view of Parisian women as promiscuous and therefore dangerous to foreigners. Commenting on these distortions of French life, Jeanne contended that they were part of a general plan for American domination of the world. "This is how Mr. W. H. Hays, 'Czar of the American cinema,' uses the film which is supposed to be the 'instrument of pacification among peoples'; this is how he expects to teach people to know, understand, and love each other."[59]

By virtue of their domination of the film industry, Americans also had the power to interpret European history. Edouard Herriot pointed out that in the American films "our European folk tradition, as well as the history of our continent, is translated by some honorable citizens of Los Angeles. Joan of Arc might be played by a young Californian, and a native of Illinois with the features of his region might appear as Napoleon."[60] Here was a more subtle problem than the deliberate denigration of Europe. If Europeans no longer had the power to interpret their tradition, they would cease to have an identity of their own.

The opposition to American control, both in films and in oil, electricity, automobiles, and telephones, was generated by a similar desire to assure French independence. Basically, the campaign proceeded at two levels. The French, along with other Europeans, feared an American economic takeover. As Benjamin Williams remarked:

Since the War there has been a general crystallizing of European feeling against the United States as the great commercial rival and financial dictator of Europe, and as the general exponent of an allegedly severe capitalism.[61]

The threat of economic control helped to stimulate fear of American cultural imperialism. Since the film epitomized both forms of power, it became the special focus of French concern. In the atmosphere of the late twenties, with the conflict over debts, disarmament, and investment at its peak, some Frenchmen found it compelling to believe that the film was the instrument of the American people trying to enslave France and Europe.

## NOTES

1. "La commerce extérieur des Etats-Unis et l'entreaide financière américaine," *Europe Nouvelle* (January 10, 1920), 24.

2. "Les rapports financiers entre la France et les Etats-Unis," *Europe Nouvelle* (December 6, 1924), 1650.

3. Lucien Romier, "Questions économiques sur l'impérialisme financier," *Revue des Deux Mondes* (July 15, 1928), 448.

4. *Le déclin de l'Europe* (Paris, 1920), 221.

5. "Les Etats-Unis, créanciers de l'Europe" (February 20, 1926), 237.

6. American direct investments in Europe at the end of 1929 totaled $1,352,753,000, while direct investments in France were only $145,009,000. American investment in Germany and Britain exceeded substantially the investment in France. Frank Southard, *American Industry in Europe* (Boston, 1931), 193.

7. *La vie américaine* (Paris, 1931), 31. Mira Wilkins maintains that the technology and efficiency of American corporations constituted a kind of "American challenge" to Europe during the twenties. *The Maturing of Multinational Enterprises: American Business Abroad from 1914 to 1970* (Cambridge, 1974), 74.

8. "Cinématographie," *Mercure de France* (August 1, 1924), 793. Films

were considered the second industry of the United States in one case, *ibid.*, 793, and the third industry after meat and automobiles, in another. Braunschvig, *La vie américaine*, 355.

9. *La vie américaine*, 359.

10. Frank Southard, *American Industry in Europe*, 28-29. The Compagnie des Lampes, the largest corporation producing electric lights in France, was a subsidiary of French Thomson-Houston and had working agreements with International General Electric. *Ibid.*, 29.

11. *Ibid.*, 29.

12. The Greater London Counties Trust Company, the largest English distributor of electric power, was known to be a subsidiary of Utilities Power and Light Company of Chicago. *Ibid.*, 37.

13. *Ibid.*, 38.

14. *L'Oncle Shylock*, 136.

15. In smaller European countries, however, such as Spain, Romania, and Turkey, American companies did operate the telephone system. Southard, *American Industry in Europe*, 42.

16. *Ibid.*, 44-45.

17. *Ibid.*, 45-46.

18. Pomaret, *L'Amérique à la conquête de L'Europe*, 99-100; and Jean Bonnefon-Craponne, *La pénétration économique et financière des capitaux américains en Europe* (Paris, 1930), 152.

19. *L'Oncle Shylock*, 132-133.

20. Bonnefon-Craponne, *La pénétration économique et financiére des capitaux américains en Europe*, 150.

21. Southard, *American Industry in Europe*, 46.

22. *La pénétration économique et financière des capitaux américains en Europe*, 152; *L'Amérique à la conquête de l'Europe*, 99.

23. Herbert Feis, *The Diplomacy of the Dollar* (Baltimore, 1950), 59.

24. 'Le pétrole et la rivalité anglo-américaine," *Europe Nouvelle* (March 5, 1921), 321-322.

25. Jean Gachon, *La politique étrangère des Etats-Unis* (Paris, 1929), 168-169.

26. Southard, *American Industry in Europe*, 64.

27. *La politique étrangère des Etats-Unis*, 170.

28. "L'action des Etats-Unis en Amérique du Sud," *Europe Nouvelle* (December 15, 1928), 1712.

29. *L'Oncle Shylock*, 100; *L'Amérique à la conquète de l'Europe*, 112-113.

30. Southard, *American Industry in Europe*, 73, 74, 78; Bonnefon-Craponne, *La pénétration économique et financière des capitaux américains en Europe*, 154.

31. Southard, *American Industry in Europe*, 72, 77. American automobile manufacturers already maintained a lead in the production of large vehicles for the European market with 150,000 per year. *Ibid.*, 79.

32. *Ibid.*, 74.

33. *La vie américaine*, 245-246.

34. *L'Amérique à la conquête de l'Europe*, 108.

35. Carlton J. H. Hayes, *France: A Nation of Patriots* (New York, 1930), 186.

36. *L'Oncle Shylock*, 98.

37. Hayes, *France*, 188-194; Southard, *American Industry in Europe*, 99. Both the Germans and the British had introduced quotas restricting the importation of foreign films.

38. Hayes, *France*, 195.

39. Braunschvig, *La vie américaine*, 356. MGM operated sixty-eight subsidiaries in Europe, while Paramount had forty-seven offices, including eight in France. Southard, *American Industry in Europe*, 95.

40. Braunschvig, *La vie américaine*, 356.

41. Hayes, *France*, 190. Charles Pomaret claimed that some French films were purchased by American companies and then deliberately withheld from the public to prevent Americans from developing an interest in French films. *L'Amérique à la conquête de l'Europe*, 104.

42. Hayes, *France*, 183; Southard, *American Industry in Europe*, 95. It is evident that the operation of American theaters in France was not a culturally neutral affair. Frenchmen objected to the technique of rapid ticket selling and the abolition of the custom of tipping ushers. Hayes, *France*, 183.

43. Southard, *American Industry in Europe*, 97.

44. Charles Pomaret suggested the possibility of a link between Franco-Film and Metro-Goldwyn-Mayer, and suspected a similar connection between Aubert and Warner Brothers, but offered no evidence of either. *L'Amérique à la conquête de l'Europe*, 105. Americans were also supposed to have gained considerable influence in the Chambre Syndicale Francaise de Cinématographie, the organization which represented French film makers. René Jeanne, "L'invasion cinématographique américaine," *Revue des Deux Mondes* (February 15, 1930), 868.

45. Pomaret, *L'Amérique à la conquête de l'Europe*, 101-102; Southard, *American Industry in Europe*, 99-102. French critics applauded the lawsuit filed by Klangfilm A.G. against Western Electric in Germany to prevent the company from eliminating competition for sound film equipment. Pomaret, *L'Amérique à la conquête de l'Europe*, 102.

46. Braunschvig, *La vie américaine*, 355. Nothing was said about the role of Thomas Edison in the development of the movie.

47. René Jeanne, "La France et le film parlant," *Revue des Deux Mondes*, (June 1, 1931), 536. Later in the decade, Jeanne also lamented the fate of two Frenchmen, Georges Melies and Emile Cohl, who discovered the animated cartoon but died impoverished, while Walt Disney grew rich on their invention. "De Melies à Walt Disney," *Revue des Deux Mondes* (March 15, 1938), 424-428.

48. Pomaret, *L'Amérique à la conquête de l'Europe*, 103; Octave Homberg, *L'impérialisme américain* (Paris, 1929), 19.

49. "L'invasion cinématographique . . . ," 872.

50. "Hollywood menaçant . . . ," 603.

51. *L'homme nouveau* (Paris, 1929), 193; Jeanne, "La France . . . ," 535. Some Americans did indeed advocate the doctrine of "trade follows the film." See Robert Sklar, *Movie-Made America* (New York, 1975), 216.

52. "Le film sonore et ses problèmes," *Europe Nouvelle* (February 9, 1929), 167; Braunschvig, *La vie américaine*, 358.

53. Jeanne, "L'invasion cinématographique . . . ," 878.

54. Pomaret, *L'Amérique à la conquête de l'Europe*, 106.

55. Hayes, *France*, 186.

56. Jeanne, "L'invasion cinématographique . . . ," 879-880. A similar protest was made against *The Big Parade*, a film about the life of an American soldier at the front; in this case, too, French critics denounced the producer for implying that the Americans won the war alone. *Ibid.*, 879-880.

57. *Ibid.*, 857; Homberg, *L'impérialisme américain*, 19.

58. Homberg, *L'impérialisme américain*, 19.

59. "L'invasion cinématographique . . . ," 879-882.

60. *L'Europe*, 213.

61. *Economic Foreign Policy of the United States* (New York, 1929), 242. This feeling is not entirely without foundation, as Mira Wilkins makes clear. She considers World War I a "watershed" in the development of the American multinational corporation. The 1920s mark the beginning of the "dramatic U.S. corporate challenge to European enterprise worldwide." *The Maturing of Multinational Enterprises*, viii.

_____ PART IV:

# The American Scene:
# The Assault on Liberty,
# 1917–1932

# chapter 10

# The Racial Conflict:
# Anglo-Saxons Versus Foreigners _____

> Some little Yankee shoe-shine boy, a kid with a rat's face, half
> Saxon, half Jew, with a trace of Negro ancestry in his maddened
> marrow, the future King of Oil, Rubber, Steel, creator of the Trust
> of trusts, future master of a standardized planet, this god that the
> universe awaits, god of a godless universe.
>
> —Georges Bernanos, 1931

The deterioration of Franco-American relations in the early twenties
created an atmosphere in which French observers were prepared to
discover and emphasize some of the less attractive aspects of American life. This change in the diplomatic climate was accompanied by a
social revolution within the United States. The most important aspects of this revolution were the conflict in values between native
Americans and immigrants and the spread of new industrial processes such as the moving assembly line and the Taylor System. Even
without the disintegration of the entente, these new developments
would have justified French observers in creating a new image of
America. However, the emphasis which was placed on the two
revolutionary aspects of American life can only be explained by the
context in which they appeared. The rising power of the United
States in Europe made mass society and the racial conflict particularly relevant to Frenchmen. In addition, the negative reactions of
American writers helped to reinforce the predispositions of
Frenchmen on these matters.

The simultaneous recognition of the racial conflict and the rise of mass society by French observers is understandable not only in terms of the realities of contemporary America, but also in relation to the history of the image. The two developments were regarded as consistent by Frenchmen because both suggested the oppressive character of American society. In this sense, they reinforced the impression Frenchmen had obtained from their experience with American policy on debts and security. Moreover, the conception of America as a mass society immersed in racial conflict seemed perfectly consistent with the two major prewar approaches to American life. The rise of a race problem indicated that America remained an Anglo-Saxon culture, beseiged by minority groups from within. The spread of mass production confirmed the view that America was essentially a New World, that is, a society formed according to new principles including the primacy of the collectivity and the production of material goods.

While these two approaches were consistent in some respects, they produced important contradictions in the French image of America. As in the prewar period, Frenchmen continued to regard the United States as a cultural extension of Great Britain while at the same time they perceived American civilization as totally independent of Europe. Moreover, one approach stressed the differences between ethnic groups within the United States, while the other focused on homogeneity as the central feature of American culture. Some more serious critics attempted to resolve these contradictions. Bernard Faÿ spoke of the "peaceful rivalry" between the races which permitted the Anglo-Saxons to rule "with taciturn prudence and resourceful dignity," while Lucien Romier referred to "the common and voluntary forgetting of history" which "results in all these races associating together in a new task."[1] Unity could also be explained as the result of coercion. André Siegfried bemoaned the fact that "assimilation, like a steamroller, ruthlessly crushes the finest flowers of the older civilizations and as a rule allows to survive an individual who is sadly childish and implacably standardized."[2] These explanations, however, contradicted earlier assertions of these same authors regarding the insoluble character of racial hostility in the United States. They do indicate that the image of a homogeneous America took precedence over the picture of the United States engaged in racial strife. For the most part, however, the two conceptions of American life were sustained simultaneously by French critics.

The central importance which French observers attached to the racial conflict in America was evident in André Siegfried's contention that "the essential charactertistic of the postwar period in the United States is the nervous reaction of the original American stock against an insidious subjugation by foreign blood."[3] As early as the 1890s, critics such as Paul Bourget had predicted the emergence of race as the most difficult problem for Americans to solve.[4] However, the nativism of the nineties had given way to the more harmonious racial atmosphere of the Progressive era, and French travelers turned their attention primarily to the expansion of the American economy. They failed to note that the influx of immigrants during these years was augmenting the "foreign" population in America.

The renewal of racial conflict in the United States came about during the war and the early postwar years. National Prohibition and immigration restriction were originally legislated on a temporary basis as war measures. The Ku Klux Klan emerged in this period and achieved its greatest popularity in 1924, the year in which permanent restriction of immigration was voted. The Scopes trial of 1925 and the execution of Sacco and Vanzetti in 1927 were also interpreted as evidence of racial conflict. Only in 1927 did the cumulative impact of these events lead French observers to see racial struggle as an integral part of American life. By partial coincidence, it was in this same year that Franco-American diplomatic relations reached their nadir and the campaign against mass society began to gather momentum, thus eliminating two barriers to the discussion of racial conflict.

From these developments with a racial dimension, Frenchmen singled out for special treatment Prohibition and immigration restriction. Some attention was given to the Scopes trial and the Sacco-Vanzetti affair in the French press. The latter was the occasion for strong left-wing protest activity, but went almost unmentioned in the travel literature.[5] On the whole, travelers stressed developments which had a long-run impact on the daily lives of Americans. Both immigration restriction and Prohibition, for example, were debated throughout the twenties. Moreover, the personal experience of the traveler who passed through customs or visited a speakeasy directed his attention to the wider implications of both measures.

The emergence of racial conflict had two somewhat different effects on French observers. On the one hand, they recognized and deplored the accentuation of puritanism in American society. This response was consistent with traditional French Anglophobia which had been strengthened by the postwar falling-out between France and the Anglo-Saxon countries. Frenchmen also sympathized with the persecuted minorities in America, an extension of their prewar practice of supporting the beleaguered Latin elements in America. On the other hand, they feared the rising foreign population which further jeopardized the possibility of ethnic unity in the United States. The large proportion of "exotic" races in America also made Frenchmen uneasy. While they criticized Anglo-Saxon persecution of blacks, Orientals, and Jews, they regarded the emergence of these races as evidence of "the rising tide of color."[6] This added a new dimension to the French distaste for the American racial situation in the postwar period.

In view of their harsh condemnation of prohibitionist tendencies in nineteenth-century America, the negative reactions of French observers to the Prohibition experiment of the twenties were predictable. Individual habits, which they found distasteful earlier, had now received the official blessing of the state. As a constitutional amendment, Prohibition was a blatant affront to French sensibilities. In this regard, J. Joseph Renaud remarked, "A Frenchmen, even if he chooses to drink only water for reasons of economy or diet, considers any criticism of wine a personal offense. He finds it impossible to accept the idea that a great nation could suppress this essence of the sun." A ban on whiskey made good sense, but "wine, beer, and cider are light beverages which are healthy; why are they not excluded from Prohibition?"[7] Marcel Braunschvig agreed. He pointed out that "with our habit of regarding wine, beer, and cider as 'hygienic' beverages, we do not understand their prohibition along with whisky."[8]

The sympathy among Frenchmen for selective restriction of alcoholic consumption was based not only on a desire to align American and French practices in this area, but also on the belief that the American climate and the Anglo-Saxon temperament appeared to require such a policy. Most Frenchmen agreed with American advocates of Prohibition that alcoholism was a problem in America. André

Siegfried blamed it on "the dry enervating climate" of the New World.[9] Régis Michaud preferred a racial explanation of the matter. "The Anglo-Saxon has always held himself aloof from the semi-epicurean and poetic tradition tracing its ancestry to Horace, which encourages the Latin race to seek moderate euphoria *inter pocula*." In contrast to this tradition, Michaud deplored "the taste of Americans for violent sensations."[10] In either event, a legal barrier to alcoholic consumption was a necessary substitute for the absence of self-restraint in Americans.

The evidence of immoderate behavior was, of course, multiplied during the period of Prohibition by the appearance of speakeasies, moonshine, and bootlegging. Under these circumstances, the opportunities for observing Americans under the influence of alcohol increased markedly. As Georges Duhamel explained, such occasions were extremely unpleasant:

For ten years, since the War, I haven't seen a single drunken scene in my own country which has filled me with such sadness and such anger as this one. I know that we Frenchmen are guilty of showing excessive indulgence for the man who drinks too much wine, for Silenus, for the drunkard who retains his sense of humor. However, we rarely witness in our own country this dramatic, stultifying, and mortal intoxication which seems to be quite sought after in your country.[11]

The manner in which alcohol was consumed during Prohibition called attention to the fundamental contrast between two national characters: the French, imbued with moderation, and the American, which sought extreme sensation. It also dramatized the conflict between two ways of life. After an evening in a speakeasy, Luc Durtain lamented the existence of

2,000 of these morose cellars! I can't keep myself from envisioning the proud grape harvests of the South, the faces of pretty girls bending over rows of vines, the great wine presses with their screws lined like pages of poems, the vats where the new wine ferments. I seem to hear vibrant cries and songs which float like the edge of a cloud suspended in the air. What a melancholy thing virtue and the law have made of alcohol here.[12]

Alcoholic consumption in America reminded Durtain of the dominant urbanism of American life, which he contrasted with the rural character of France. The drinking atmosphere in France was linked with the gay and poetic experience of the grape harvest, while in America it was dampened by dingy cellars, as well as the belief that alcohol was immoral.

While French travelers rarely passed up an opportunity to visit a speakeasy, they were uniformly critical of what they saw there. The stories of poisonous alcohol which blinded or killed consumers convinced Durtain, to the surprise of his American companions, that a glass of lemonade would be preferable to whiskey.[13] Paul Morand ordered water rather than an alcoholic beverage for the same reason, while J. Joseph Renaud accepted a drink only to avoid disappointing his American friends.[14] The principal role of the speakeasy, according to Luc Durtain, was to provide a cheap thrill for Americans who enjoyed breaking the law without having to face the consequences of their actions.[15]

At the speakeasy, Frenchmen were also able to assess the behavior of American public officials and the criminal element. Paul Achard watched a local policeman enter a speakeasy and accept a free glass of beer. Instead of enforcing the law, the officer had broken it himself.[16] Somewhat more serious was the activity of "a very important figure in the world of American politics." This gentleman, according to André Lafond, apologized for having to carry his bottle of champagne to a restaurant, because, in the process, the champagne had been shaken before it could be drunk.[17] Perhaps the fullest account of illegal activities in connection with Prohibition was offered by J. Joseph Renaud. One night he stood by a New York dock watching bootleggers unload their cargo of whiskey from a boat. This experience was followed by a visit to a speakeasy where Renaud saw several well-dressed gangsters divide the proceeds from a recent delivery of their product.[18]

Prohibition was also offensive to French observers because it appeared to violate the constitutional rights of minorities. These minorities, moreover, shared either a religious, racial, or cultural kinship with Frenchmen. Prohibition, according to André Siegfried, was really a cultural outgrowth of the Puritan faith. Its imposition on non-Anglo-Saxon ethnic groups was both a form of cultural imperialism and a violation of religious liberty as guaranteed under the Constitution. "Inflicting customs in the name of a belief which is fundamentally religious is an intolerable interference in the autonomy of one's private life."[19] The right of an individual to worship according to his own beliefs without interference from the state, which was a principle of Anglo-Saxon origin, was now placed in jeopardy ironically by the Anglo-Saxon zeal to spread Puritan culture.

Other critics were equally distressed about the violation of constitutional rights. Lucien Romier insisted that Prohibition "has no precedent of equal magnitude in all history." The law was "evidence of a collective disposition toward moral and social fanaticism" in the United States.[20] Georges Duhamel believed that Prohibition was only an extreme example of a worldwide trend. "America makes me sensitive to the tendency of states to exceed their rights: that is, to permit legislators to consider a series of issues, which, up to now, man debated with God or himself in the sanctity of his own soul."[21] In this sense, the contest between Anglo-Saxons and foreigners was also a struggle between the individual and the state.

Only one critic, Paul Achard, believed that Prohibition constituted a direct threat to the European continent. "The fact that there are on this earth ninety million people who don't drink creates an immense question mark for the world, especially since these people comprise the most modern and powerful civilization." It was therefore possible that "in fifty years, we will follow America's example."[22] Achard's line of reasoning was in most instances reversed. Instead of believing that American power would be used to spread Prohibition, critics asserted that Prohibition was a way of maximizing the nation's power by increasing the efficiency of the American worker and making the economy more productive.[23]

French critics of Prohibition were irritated, although infrequently, by more tangible problems than the clash of values. Only an occasional writer mentioned the decline in the American purchase of French alcoholic beverages. The elimination of the legal market for French wine in the United States was compensated to some degree by the purchases of the growing number of American tourists in France during the twenties.[24] Prohibition did create one minor diplomatic issue between the two countries. The conflict arose after a 1923 Supreme Court ruling that ships carrying alcoholic beverages would not be permitted in American territorial waters. This decision, as the French government pointed out, conflicted with the right of French sailors to receive daily rations of wine. It is hardly surprising that the French were angered by reports that the American government intended to seize all ships violating the ruling. Not until 1925 was an agreement reached which permitted French ships in American territorial waters to carry alcoholic beverages so long as they were kept under lock and key.[25]

In the French discussion of Prohibition, two apparently contradictory images of America were presented to the reading public. The traditional view of a puritanical America which attempted to outlaw pleasure was juxtaposed against the portrait of a violent society given to illegality and the pursuit of pleasure. These two views could be reconciled by the image of an extremist America; puritanism and sensationalism were, then, two different sides of the same coin. As Marcel Braunschvig explained, Prohibition and the speakeasy symbolized both kinds of extremism. "We have difficulty in France understanding both the rigor of this law and the lack of rigor in its enforcement."[26] Paul Morand regarded New York City, which represented all of America, as another symbol of two-sided extremism:

New York is extreme. Its climate is violent and freakish. In April this year [1929] they were picking up people dying from heat stroke . . . a town of contrasts, puritan and libertine; the two-sided picture of a well-policed America and a savage continent of east and west; a few yards from the luxury of Fifth Avenue and one is in a battered and dirty Eighth Avenue. New York is the symbol of America and half of its population is foreign.[27]

The impression of extremism was strengthened, as Morand implied, by the existence of a large "foreign" population in America, which created conflict, confusion, and, on occasion, violence. The new immigration laws, like Prohibition, could be explained by the desire of Anglo-Saxons to preserve their hegemony in America. They too ran counter to the values of French visitors. This was evident in Jean Ferrandi's complaint that "the United States no longer wants to admit immigrants, especially if they are labeled with a certain scorn 'Mediterranean.' " This was absurd, according to Ferrandi, because the Mediterranean area "was the crad e of human civilization, whether they [the Americans] like it or not."[28] André Siegfried feared the laws were only a first step toward racial purification. Siegfried suspected that in such an undertaking, Latins, as well as other racial groups, would be stigmatized as inferior. "In the hands of a people conscious of its superiority, systematic eugenicism would ultimately relegate to the past the outdated struggle for the rights of man. It would encourage the sterilization of blacks, yellows, and 'inferiors,' which might include us."[29] Anglo-Saxon prejudice against Latins had always been objectionable to Frenchmen. In the twenties, such feelings were considered more dangerous because they had the sanction of official policy.

No French travelers could experience directly the force of these new immigration laws, but the process of obtaining visas to enter the United States and the cumbersome customs inspection confirmed French impressions that America was no longer the open country it had been in the nineteenth century. Georges Duhamel acquired special notoriety for his strong objections to lengthy interrogation by United States officials with regard to his political and medical history.[30] Marcel Braunschvig discussed the significance of this policy. He called it a "complete change: America, formerly so hospitable, is today the one country in the whole world which is the most difficult for a foreigner to enter. How many formalities already exist in order to obtain a visa through the United States Consulate?"[31]

The passage of the immigration laws produced similar reflections among French observers. In André Siegfried's view, "Perhaps no more important event has occurred in the period since the Civil War."[32] The decision to pass the law restricting immigration marked the rising determination of the Anglo-Saxon majority to retain its domination in America. In this sense, the nation had at last reached maturity. It had officially proclaimed its ethnic identity. Marcel Braunschvig accordingly labeled immigration restriction "the first measure of defense" taken by the old Anglo-Saxon population to assure its domination over recent immigrants.[33]

The historic implications of the new policy became evident to Paul Morand while he was visiting the empty buildings on Ellis Island. "Today, America purifies herself. She is closed to Orientals just like a large club. In these early years of the twentieth century, peoples who were formerly received have become undesirables." A glimpse of the Statue of Liberty confirmed Morand's impression at Ellis Island. It was symbolic that the statue had been "exiled to sea on a little island; are they [the Americans] afraid that with her torch she will light a fire while the wind is blowing?"[34] Restricting the immigration of undesirable races was also a way of reducing the diversity of political and cultural ideas in the country. The new policy was the first step toward the isolation of America from Europe, according to Marcel Braunschvig:

> While immigration, year in and year out, brought successive waves of European immigrants, the memory of Europe and the interest in her were sustained in the American population by the newcomers. However, since the law has limited the possibility of European settlement on American soil, the Americans have less reason to take an interest in the old continent.[35]

While the primary focus of French discussion was on the cultural motivation for immigration restriction, there was some interest in economic aspects of the new policy. Travelers agreed that unions were interested in the new measures primarily to decrease the labor supply and, as a consequence, increase salaries. To replace the immigrants, American industry would use machines.[36]

From the perspective of French observers, the new legislation was an admission of failure; if America had lived up to her promise by producing a new race through the melting pot, immigration restriction would not have been necessary. Instead, as French critics constantly reiterated, the United States remained a polyglot society characterized by racial conflict. In André Siegfried's view, there was "no real American race." Siegfried found in its place "a juxtaposition of peoples," most of whom retained their original racial characteristics.[37] The same conclusion was reached by other contemporary travelers. Lucien Romier contended that "the United States is not at all the famous melting pot it has been said to be, and in which racial characteristics are completely fused. On the contrary, there has hardly ever been a more striking demonstration of the permanence of racial character."[38] Ethnic conflict might be somewhat diminished by the pursuit of common economic goals in America, but ethnic differences had by no means disappeared. André Tardieu claimed that each American village acted as a melting pot. However, the process of racial fusion must have been extreme y slow because Tardieu had no idea how long it would take for immigrants to become "exclusively and spontaneously American."[39]

Travelers were able to verify the failure of the melting pot by examining the situation of different minority groups in the United States. The separation of blacks and whites was clear to all. In the words of André Tardieu, blacks were "inassimilable."[40] Marcel Braunschvig lumped blacks with orientals. Both races "had shown themselves to be completely inassimilable."[41] Luc Durtain made the same point more graphically. He regarded blacks as "a kind of large foreign element, stuck in the throat of America, which she can neither swallow nor get rid of."[42]

In reality, there was little difference between America's colored population and some of her more recent immigrants. As Siegfried pointed out, fusion within the white race itself between different ethnic groups "was far from complete."[43] On the basis of his visit to the Bowery where Hungarians, Italians, and Jews lived in the same neighborhood, Paul Morand agreed. Not a word of English was spoken in the area, confirming the failure of Anglo-Saxon culture to penetrate the lives of these immigrants. What was more, there was little contact between the different "foreign" groups. "Nothing separates these races who live several yards from each other, but there is no way of mixing them. One street is Russian Jewish, another is Sicilian."[44] The failure of the melting pot was also confirmed by André Lafond. He was able to recognize by the "deep marks of the original race" the ethnic differences between the men he met on the streets of New York.[45]

Because the ethnic minorities were struggling to survive against a dominant Anglo-Saxon culture, their plight was treated sympathetically by French observers. Even blacks were no exception. Since French visitors in the twenties were preoccupied with American cities, especially New York, which now contained large black communities, blacks received more attention than they had at any time since the Reconstruction period. Some travelers were also drawn to the South where they could witness the more blatant discrimination against blacks. After visiting Tuskegee Institute, Durtain protested that the present state of race relations in the United States was "injurious, painful, and unjust" to the black man. He documented this point by describing an old black woman who was afraid to die because she could not face God whom she hated for making her black. Fair treatment for the colored races was far more likely to occur in a Latin society such as Cuba, according to Durtain.[46]

Georges Duhamel, who also visited Tuskegee, was impressed with black educational achievement, but dismayed that even educated blacks were regarded as inferior by whites. The treatment of a mulatto schoolmistress in New Orleans was a case in point. Duhamel described her as

an old woman still very alert and even gracious. She wears a long dress of shiny brown material. Like the pure Cevennol villager who was my wife's mother, she has tender and beautiful blue eyes and thin white headbands. Her hands are refined and frail with slightly mauve nails. Her face is paler than that of a Provençal.[47]

After a tour of her school, Duhamel invited the schoolmistress to join him for lunch. Her embarrassment in accepting the invitation brought the author to the conclusion that "in all of New Orleans there is not a single member of society who would shake hands in public with this honorable lady." It is evident that the persecution of the schoolmistress was considered by Duhamel an affront to his own identity as a Latin.

Persecution of other ethnic e ements in America was also vigorous-ly condemned by French travelers. André Siegfried deplored the fact that "the individual of Latin origin suffers in the United States from constant persecution of his personality."[48] This discrimination was the inevitable result of the crusade of Anglo-Saxons who, as Lucien Romier remarked, "hold Latin irony in horror."[49] It was not surprising, then, that French travelers should applaud the survival of these groups. Siegfried noted that "when you see a sparkling eye or a nimble mind it often belongs to an Italian, a Jew, or a Russian."[50] Paul Morand denounced the discrimination against Jews in large Ameri-can hotels, which he contrasted with egalitarian trends in Europe. "While Europe lowers social barriers, America raises them."[51] The sympathy for Jews and Italians was consistent with a feeling of attachment to the Irish. André Siegfried described their contribution to the American scene:

The Irish swarmed in the cities, where they supplied their spirit of unrest, injecting that element of devilry and charm so typical of the Celt. Without their love of amusement, mischief, and disorder, the American atmosphere might have been too heavy to breathe.[52]

French travelers were so impressed by the gravity of the ethnic crisis that they treated only sporadically the special problems of Americans of French origin. Georges Duhamel was among the minority of observers who noted the situation of the French population in New Orleans. He described one Richard Lionel, who

is what they call in this country a Creole, which means that he is the descendant of French settlers without the least blend of colored blood. He belongs to this old Louisiana society which still calls blocks "islands" and speaks eighteenth-century French in the family, but which will soon be submerged by the ponderous Anglo-Saxon wave.

The plight of French elements in New Orleans had clearly worsened since the prewar visits of Jules Huret and Paul Adam. They, like other ethnic elements, suffered from Anglo-Saxon domination. In the face of this debacle, Duhamel's discouragement was evident. He invited his readers to "come see the old cemeteries of New Orleans, the cemetery of French memories . . . the cemetery of a people and a civilization."[53]

It was not only the mistreatment of racial minorities, however, which offended Frenchmen. Racial divisions in the United States also were frightening, because they destroyed any real basis for a national community. Duhamel summed up the reactions of his fellow travelers when he asked: "How is it possible for people to trust anybody, anything, or even themselves in this great impure America where the races confront but do not understand or enjoy each other?"[54] Because of the relative homogeneity of France, observers were especially sensitive to ethnic conflict in the United States, which, even by American standards, was extensive in the twenties.

In the process of criticizing Anglo-Saxon treatment of minorities, French critics gave the erroneous impression that they themselves believed in the basic equality of all races. Stereotypes of blacks, Jews, and other groups in the travel literature, however, indicated that Frenchmen held views quite similar to their Anglo-Saxon counterparts. Georges Duhamel was typical in this regard. He criticized American prejudices against black men, particularly educated ones, but he noted the anthropoid features of some black students at Tuskegee. During a lecture at a northern college, Duhamel was embarrassed by a question from a black student regarding his reference to the Malagaches people as "savages." In response, he insisted he was telling the truth. He said the Malagaches had earned that label by their behavior, as, indeed, some whites had done.[55] Other travelers, like Paul Achard, were more blatant than Duhamel in stereotyping blacks. After a visit to Harlem, Achard concluded that "the black man is the most comic of beings when he wants to be. The funniest men in the whole world can be found in Harlem. . . . [The black man] is a born musician and a remarkable dancer, whose mystical atavism has given him a kind of congenital genius."[56]

Considerable attention was paid to the problems of American Jews in the twenties. Although most French travelers were highly critical of Anglo-Saxon discrimination against Jews, they nonetheless spiced their discussion with derogatory stereotypes of Jews. Siegfried claimed that New York was an "oriental city," because its Jewish population reminded him of "the human waves of Asiatic cities."[57] Paul Morand, who observed similar throngs in the Lower East Side, argued that "Orchard and Rivington are the most beautiful streets, because they are invaded in Oriental style, disordered like a Hebrew cemetery, like the ideas of a Jewish brain." He added, "I am reminded of the splendid expression of Heine's, which Nerval liked to recall: 'great swarms of Jews.'"[58] Such stereotypes rendered the Jewish population more exotic and, in the process, considerably less attractive to a French audience.

Similar stereotypes or derogatory remarks about other races can be found in the travel literature. While André Siegfried condemned American prejudices against Latins and Slavs, he could agree that "Europe, in the last half century, has not sent to the other side of the Atlantic her best elements." As a result, it is true that "for the American child, the Italian is a small-scale profiteer, the Greek a shady restauranteur, the Frenchman a low-class hairdresser." Americans had correctly judged the human worth of their immigrants, according to Siegfried, but they had been wrong in stereotyping Greeks, Italians, and Frenchmen who remained in Europe on the basis of the achievement of their compatriots in the United States. For the same reason, Siegfried sympathized strongly with the members of elite social clubs in America who excluded from their organizations certain ethnic groups. With regard to the distaste of the club members for inferior races, he remarked, "And how we understand them!"[59]

The French approach to the American racial problem in the twenties was in some respects a continuation of a traditional view of the United States, and in other ways a departure from that approach. The historic hostility to Anglo-Saxons was heightened by the rise of Prohibition and the restriction of immigration which stressed the conflict between Latin and Anglo-Saxon values even more strongly than before the war.

A second source of anti-Americanism in the twenties derived from the increasing strength of foreign racial elements in the American population. The prospect that the United States as a nation might be unable to fuse its diverse racial elements into a new American race was profoundly disquieting for French travelers. Although they could sympathize with ethnic minorities who were persecuted by the Anglo-Saxons, critics could not themselves envision a successful multiracial society. Moreover, the possibility of the eventual domination of America by exotic races was as abhorrent to Frenchmen as the triumph of Anglo-Saxon elements. Such a victory would help to fortify the position of the colored races in the world against their European opponents. In the minds of French observers, an America dominated by Anglo-Saxons, the colored races, or polyglot elements was equally distasteful.

## NOTES

1. *The American Experiment* (New York, 1929), 227. *Who Will Be Master, Europe or America?* (New York, 1928), 145.

2. *Les Etats-Unis d'aujourd'hui* (Paris, 1927), 18.

3. *Les Etats-Unis d'aujourd'hui*, 3. The concept "foreign blood" is applied here and in the rest of the chapter to nonwhite Americans as well as to recent immigrants from southern and eastern Europe. The "original American stock" is understood to include not only Anglo-Saxons, but also "other northern and western European elements" including Scandinavians, Germans, and usually the Irish.

4. At a number of points, this chapter draws on information and views

presented in Part I, chapter 3. Any reference to pre-World War I attitudes of French travelers to the racial situation in the United States may be explored in more detail in that chapter.

5. In the year 1927, the American Ambassador to France, Myron Herrick, reported receiving a delegation of Radical-Socialist members of the French Assembly who protested the coming execution of Sacco and Vanzetti. After the execution, a protest march, led by left-wing parties, was organized in Paris. For several months it was necessary to "station a platoon of 50 policemen" before the doors of the American Embassy. "Then interest in the case seemed to die out." This account is from Colonel T. Bentley Mott, *Myron T. Herrick, Friend of France* (Garden City, 1929), 291.

6. André Siegfried cited the influence of Stoddard's *The Rising Tide of Color*, along with Madison Grant's *The Passing of the Great Race*. *Les Etats-Unis d'aujourd'hui*, 104. The theme of the rising tide of color was explored in greater depth by Maurice Muret, *Le crépuscule des nations blancs* (Paris, 1925), who also cited Stoddard's work (p. 12). See Part II, chapter 5, for a more complete development of this issue. The concern for racial divisions within the United States among French observers may be seen in part as a projection of French problems onto the United States. As Theodore Zeldin points out, the number of foreign-born residents of France had risen rapidly after 1900 and would attain 4.4 million by 1940. *France, 1848-1945*: Vol. 2. *Intellect, Taste and Anxiety* (Oxford, 1977), 16.

7. *New-York flamboie* (Paris, 1931), 80-81.

8. *La vie américaine* (Paris, 1931), 123.

9. *Les Etats-Unis d'aujourd'hui*, 69.

10. *Ce qu'il faut connaître de l'âme américaine* (Paris, 1929), 85.

11. *Scènes de la vie future* (Paris, 1930), 79. Silenus, a figure in Greek mythology, was a drunken attendant of Bacchus and closely allied to the Satyrs, 50.

12. *Quelques notes d'U.S.A.* (Paris, 1928), 50.

13. *Ibid.*, 52.

14. *New-York* (Paris, 1930), 151; *New-York flamboie*, 65.

15. *Quelques notes d'U.S.A.*, 52.

16. *Un oeil neuf sur l'Amérique* (Paris, 1930), 248.

17. *New-York '28* (Paris, 1929), 22-23.

18. *New-York flamboie*, 64-65.

19. *Les Etats-Unis d'aujourd'hui*, 70, 85.

20. *Who Will Be Master*, 194.

21. *Scènes de la vie future*, 85.

22. *Un oeil neuf sur l'Amérique*, 252.

23. See, for example, André Siegfried, *Les Etats-Unis d'aujourd'hui*, 72.

24. "La Prohibition aux Etats-Unis," *Revue de Paris* (October 1, 1922), 625.

25. Paul Bastid, "La convention franco-américaine relative à la contrabande des boissons énivrantes," *Europe Nouvelle* (May 9, 1925), 612. *New York Times* (June 29, 1923), 2.

26. *La vie américaine*, 123.

27. *New-York*, 274.

28. *Chez nos frères d'armes d'Amérique* (Paris, 1931), 15.

29. *Les Etats-Unis d'aujourd'hui*, 113. Siegfried's claim that sterilization was a popular idea in the United States was based largely on his belief that Grant and Stoddard had a substantial following among Americans. Aside from Siegfried, Luc Durtain mentioned the fear of some blacks that castration or massacre might be the solution to the black problem in America. *Quelques notes d'U.S.A.*, 80.

30. *Scènes de la vie future*, 33.

31. *La vie américaine*, 21.

32. *Les Etats-Unis d'aujourd'hui*, 114.

33. *La vie américaine*, 20.

34. *New-York*, 32-33.

35. *La vie américaine*, 368.

36. See Siegfried, *Les Etats-Unis d'aujourd'hui*, 120.

37. *Ibid.*, 3.

38. *Who Will Be Master*, 145.

39. *Devant l'obstacle*, 29-30.

40. *Ibid.*, 29.

41. *La vie américaine*, 14.

42. *Quelques notes d'U.S.A.*, 79.

43. *Les Etats-Unis d'aujourd'hui*, 3.

44. *New-York*, 78.

45. *New-York '28*, 40.

46. *Quelques notes d'U.S.A.*, 81, 80.

47. *Scènes de la vie future*, 172, 164-166.

48. *Les Etats-Unis d'aujourd'hui*, 113.

49. *Who Will Be Master*, 201.

50. *Les Etats-Unis d'aujourd'hui*, 140.

51. *New-York*, 218.

52. *Les Etats-Unis d'aujourd'hui*, 5.

53. *Scènes de la vie future*, 166, 169.

54. *Ibid.*, 174.

55. *Scènes de la vie future*, 171, 175. Duhamel's discussion of the Malagaches occurs in his Goncourt Prize-winning volume entitled *Civilisation, 1914-1917* (Paris, 1918).

56. *Un oeil neuf sur l'Amérique*, 260. The most striking use of the stereotyped black occurs in a series of short novels by Paul Morand: *Baton-Rouge, Charleston*, and *Syracuse*, all written in 1928. In each of these works, black men in the United States succumb to their primitive instincts.

57. *Les Etats-Unis d'aujourd'hui*, 16.

58. *New-York*, 86-87.

59. *Les Etats-Unis d'aujourd'hui*, 137-138.

# chapter 11

# The Second Industrial Revolution: The Assembly Line and Mass Society

> I am horrified by her [America's] jazz, her shattering advertisements, her brutality, her cult of Mammon, the falsest of false gods, and I defend the grace, the order and the taste of Latin culture, within me and without, against these horrors.
>
> —Camille Mauclair, 1931

After American entry into World War I, the widespread use of the moving assembly line in American factories was frequently reported and praised in France. In the early twenties, the advocates of mass production persisted in their campaign and encountered little opposition within France. Suddenly in 1927, hostility to the assembly line became the central feature of the literature on the United States and the principal subject of other books and articles. This change in attitude was produced by several developments which were more or less directly related to the assembly line. Frenchmen who had ignored or tolerated this device now reconsidered their view at least in part in response to the deterioration of Franco-American relations. The end of the war and the consequent decline in the demand for armaments as well as the completion of reconstruction in the devastated areas made productivity somewhat less critical and less attractive. Even more important was the changing connotation of the assembly line. In the early twenties, it was regarded primarily as an efficient means of producing goods. Little attention was paid to its broader implications for society. After 1927, the assembly line ceased to be considered primarily as an efficient industrial process and was seen increasingly as one aspect of mass society. As such, it raised serious questions about the future of the individual in his role as worker, consumer, and citizen. Finally, the claim that mass production was only one of a number of aspects of American society no longer convinced most French observers after 1927. America came to be characterized as a system in which mass production was the central feature (see Part V, chapter 13).

The new perspective on mass production fitted remarkably well with an older approach to American society. French students of the United States in the late twenties were particularly concerned about the preference for material over spiritual values in America and the emphasis on collectivity at the expense of the individual. These two characteristics of American life had also been subjected to criticism by prewar French observers of American society. They too had expressed the belief that the new industrial system would generate materialism and conformity among the American people, although they continued to note the survival of certain mitigating spiritual concerns in the United States (see Part I of this study). By 1927, French observers were convinced that the old values had no place in the new system. The autonomous individual had disappeared from American life, a victim of the assembly line and other related aspects of the system including standardized products, advertising, mass production of ideas, and the film. The American citizen was now incapable of escaping from the all-encompassing tyranny of a mass society.

From the perspective of the French intellectual, committed to the value of individual autonomy, craftsmanship, and spiritual life, the new developments were both dangerous and distasteful. The campaign against mass society in France was evidence of their views. As Leau de Roncins remarked, "The defenders of mass production are rather hesitant in their arguments. . . . The opponents of mass production, on the contrary, are more numerous and much more convinced."[1] Despite the unpopularity of their position, the defenders of mass production persisted in airing their views in the midst of the predominant anti-Americanism of the late twenties. J. L. Duplan, Hyacinthe Dubreuil, and Madeline Cazamian, to name only the most eminent pro-Americans, continued to defend the assembly line;

their work, however, assumed a defensive cast which was not apparent in the books of their predecessors in the early twenties. Duplan's study, for example, was introduced by the philosopher Louis Rougier, who attacked mass production as harmful to the individual. Duplan was then compelled to undo the damage done by Rougier.[2] Hyacinthe Dubreuil used his second study of the American factory to refute the opinions of Georges Duhamel, thus confirming that Duhamel's views were widely accepted.[3] In addition to denouncing their opponents' opinions, the pro-Americans adopted two strategies for convincing readers of the validity of their own position. They argued that the assembly line would not necessarily destroy individualism or spiritual concerns. Some then proceeded to deny that America was a mass society, pointing to such attractive features of American life as universities and national parks. Others confessed that the United States had succumbed to materialism and conformity, but insisted that the American character rather than mass production was responsible for this development. In France, they argued, the assembly line would never lead to the demise of individualism.[4]

The critics of mass society, although they feared the spread of that system, agreed with some of America's defenders that the development of the new institutions had to be understood in terms of the American character and American society. They saw the rise of mass society as the culmination of old habits and values. Paul Achard, for example, regarded the adoption of the assembly line in the United States as part of the normal course of events. "Of course, there is mass production. Would any other system have been possible in such a country? The people who have introduced this system, with its peculiar countenance, into the life of this people, knew them admirably well."[5] The success of mass production clearly rested on the abundance of resources in America. Their availability was a prerequisite both for obtaining the power to run the assembly line and the raw materials which could be transformed by it. In this respect, the United States was in a far better position than the European nations which would have to depend on foreign trade for some of their resources. The adoption of mass production was also favored by the relative shortage of labor in America, especially after the postwar restrictions on immigration. To combat the high price of labor, American factory owners turned to the relatively economical moving assembly line.[6]

The American character, as well as New World resources, was an essential ingredient in the development of mass society. Critics were convinced that the collectivist impulses of American citizens had prepared them for the advent of standardization. Count de Keyserling proclaimed that "the Americans are the only true socialists in the western world."[7] He was referring, in particular, to the conformity of American tastes and ideas. In no other country was there such an interest in sacrificing personal differences in order to collaborate in achieving national prosperity. Keyserling believed that American capitalism, with its concern for the community rather than the individual, was primarily responsible for collectivism. Léon Ragot agreed with Keyserling. He attributed the acceptance of the Taylor System among American capitalists to "the Yankee mentality which believes that the worker must adapt to necessities."[8] Although Lucien Romier considered "individualism" to be an American value, he gave the term a special meaning. Americans, he argued, developed "those qualities in individuals which would offer the greatest advantage, the best chances for all." This cooperative instinct was directly linked to materialism. Romier believed that all Americans were "proletarians" because they were subservient to "the merciless law of economic return."[9] Thus, in the eyes of French observers a new system had been established in America, but it was one built upon and, in turn, reinforcing certain elements of the American character which persisted from the past.

The second industrial revolution was, despite its antecedents, truly revolutionary in its effects on the lives of American citizens. French observers were specially concerned about the future of the working man, the freedom of the consumer, and the autonomy of the citizen under the new system. The worker was, of course, most directly affected by the advent of the assembly line, which accentuated the specialization and division of labor characteristic of all industrial systems. The need for skilled laborers was substantially reduced, and the work itself provided little or no outlet for the creative instincts of the worker. These features of the assembly line were reinforced by the Taylor System, which was not always clearly distinguished from it by French critics.[10] By attempting to render the motions of individual workers more efficient through time-and-motion studies, the Taylor System contributed to the impression that the American factory was an oppressive place for workers. So did the rise of personnel management which applied new psychological techniques to workers in an effort to make them more efficient in their jobs.

These new institutions were greeted by most French observers with scepticism and hostility, because they appeared to increase productivity by sacrificing the worker's enjoyment of his job. Jean Ferrandi believed that the assembly line "enslaved workers more completely than any plantation boss had done in the nineteenth century."[11] After a careful study of American workers, André Philip came to a similar conclusion. He admitted that the workers were well paid, but claimed that the work routine "kills them."[12] André Siegfried deplored "the exhaustion which results from the extremely intense rhythm of work" in factories where the new methods were used. The workers appeared "worn out" by the excessive concern for efficiency.[13] A slightly different objection was raised by Marcel Braunschvig, who regretted that specialization would narrow the intellectual horizons of the worker.[14]

If the worker's freedom of movement was confined by the speed of the assembly line, his thoughts were also controlled by the new system of personnel management. As André Philip pointed out, some psychologists employed by industrial concerns deliberately discussed the private lives of workers as well as their activities in the factory.[15] The manipulation of the worker might also result from the increased use of aptitude tests. André Siegfried complained that an individual's score on a test could determine his choice of profession.[16] The fact that Americans placed such a high value on efficiency led Georges Duhamel to suppose that they might take the ultimate step by resorting to eugenicism:

If the machine made of iron is incapable of producing more profitably, the only alternative is to go back to man, to change the human machine. . . . Wouldn't it be possible to manage scientifically human growth and selection? . . . Is it impossible . . . to imitate the bees and ants, to develop a population of asexual workers, who are passionless, devoted exclusively to the building, feeding, and defense of the city?[17]

Duhamel's imagination only embroidered on the reality which other Frenchmen perceived. They agreed that the new industrial methods already infringed on the physical and psychological freedom of the worker.

The advent of mass production had effects which could not be confined to workers on the assembly line. The ability to finance the machines, for example, depended on the existence of a market to absorb mass-produced items. The United States, with its population of 120,000,000 people, would provide such a market, but only if Americans could afford the new products. The market was, in part, assured by paying workers high enough salaries to enable them to consume the products they turned out. The installment system also helped to stimulate buying. However, the development of a market depended on psychological as well as economic factors. Before the age of standardization, consumers could choose from a variety of sizes, shapes, and colors which appeared on store counters. With the rise of mass production, the activity of the artisan who designed his own product had been eliminated in favor of a uniform design which could be executed by the machine.[18] The consumer would have to forego variety in favor of the standardized product. Changing ingrained habits was a difficult process which could only be accomplished through education. Advertising, as André Siegfried pointed out, was designed to sell products, but it was also useful in promoting the concept of standardization.[19] The effect of advertising was to subject the American consumer to the same kind of coercion endured by workers on the assembly line. Régis Michaud claimed that advertising was a new kind of tyranny which forced people to buy products they did not want. Such coercion debased men.[20] Georges Duhamel complained that "modern advertising treats the public with insulting scorn. It assumes that man is the most obtuse of the inferior animals."[21]

Advertising was used by Americans to market ideas as well as goods. Bernard Faÿ decried the fact that "magazine literature is sold like a food product. Its circulation and the demand for it are identical with the market for shaving cream."[22] The advertising process contaminated ideas as well as the magazines and books which contained them. Georges Duhamel pointed out, through an American spokesman, Thomas Baker, that selling ideas often injured their creators:

The processes of the manufacturer are extended to the realm of letters and journalism and, thanks to the prodigious art of the American advertisement and to the efforts of salesmen working under extreme pressure, insignificant personalities are exploited as cleverly and sometimes just as profitably as pharmaceutical specialities by men who could be called literary merchants.[23]

The new system, however, posed its greatest threat to the survival of the autonomous individual. The educational process, which occurred in a limited fashion through advertising, was undertaken more systematically by the entire society. As a result, American citizens were brainwashed to accept identical values, precisely the ones which would enable the system to function most effectively. Lucien Romier pointed to the education in service and profit which Americans received, while André Siegfried claimed that service had surpassed profit as the most important American goal. In either case, the individual's needs were secondary to those of the economy. As André Siegfried explained, "Standardizing the individual in order to more completely standardize the product is to lose sight of the fact that things are made for man and not man for possessions."[24] A similar charge was phrased somewhat more carefully by Marcel Braunschvig:

For Americans, the most serious threat—one which is already a reality—is that standardization is applied not only to material objects but also to matters of the spirit. In different areas of thought, the press has the role of spreading ideas which are already developed, ideas moreover which change with time, like manufactured goods themselves (because custom dictates one as much as the other); but these are ideas which are always accepted without a discussion and which tend to make robots of individuals and of society a blind mechanism.[25]

Braunschvig's charge was more serious than Siegfried's. He not only foresaw the destruction of the individual by the social system, but claimed that the system itself was essentially aimless and out of control. What was needed in America was the revival of the critical spirit. Unfortunately, the technique of brainwashing, of which advertising was one aspect, had weakened the capacity for making rational choices.

Other observers joined Siegfried and Braunschvig in deploring the disappearance of the autonomous individual. Gerard de Catalogne, introducing his survey of the opinions of French intellectuals about American life, described the United States as "the kingdom of excessive production, which results in the creation of a single type, in the appearance of one social truth, and in the disappearance of essential differences."[26] Régis Michaud complained that people were treated like products. "There is a standardization of the human element equivalent to that of products." He added, "The individual has abandoned his most private individuality. He has become an automat."[27]

The standardization of the individual and the debasement of human values were advanced most radically, according to French observers, by the development of the American cinema in the twenties. The cinema made use of the new technology to produce an art form for the masses. Like advertising, it educated the tastes of the American public. Indeed, the cinema was among those devices which were most responsible for destroying the critical intellect in America. As Marcel Braunschvig explained, movies provided entertainment without "great intellectual effort." They were geared to the intellectual level of the masses.[28]

Braunschvig's argument was extended by Georges Duhamel from American films to all films. He called the cinema "a pastime of illiterates." It is "a spectacle which demands no effort, which assumes no continuity in ideas, raises no questions, and deals seriously with no problems." In short, the cinema was totally devoid of intellectual content. From Duhamel's point of view, this absence of ideas was at least partly the result of the technology of the film. "The very dynamism of the cinema tears from us the images on which we would like to meditate." Duhamel predicted that a steady diet of films over a period of fifty years would destroy the intellect of the American people. Already in 1930, the Americans, as Duhamel portrayed them, were operating a mindless civilization.[29]

The American movie theater was nearly as good an index of the state of American civilization as the film. Like other mass-produced items, it had no aesthetic quality. Marcel Braunschvig criticized the "illusion of luxury" created by New York theaters. They were comfortable, but excessively adorned with decorative marble and mirrors. Georges Duhamel was appalled by the fake oriental rugs, the reproductions of famous European pictures, and the plastic statues illuminated from within by electric lights. The romantic atmosphere of the theater contributed to the similar effect of the film, creating an escape from reality for the movie-goer.[30] For Duhamel, viewing an American film was a frightening experience:

Here, all is false. The life of the shadows on the screen is false. The ridiculous music broadcast among us by I know not what impetuous, mechanical instruments is false. And who knows? even this crowd, which seems to dream of what it watches and silently shifts with the movements of someone asleep, may be false. Everything is false. The world is false. I myself am only a semblance of a man, an imitation of Duhamel.[31]

Unlike great art, the movie debased the individual. It prevented him from understanding the world, and alienated him from himself. This experience was consistent with Duhamel's expectations. After all, the movie and the theater had been mass-produced for a mass audience. Inevitably their quality would suffer. Moreover, the movie had become one of the most powerful instruments for creating mass society. Its escapist tendencies reduced the power of the critical faculties and brought about a submissive attitude on the part of the spectators. This, in turn, would lead them to accept the new institutions.

The development of mass society in America, like the assertion of Anglo-Saxon control, offended Frenchmen because it challenged their most cherished values. The very basis for the critique of mass society was the belief in the primacy of the individual. As Marcel Braunschvig pointed out, "A society materially and intellectually standardized is most repugnant to our obstinate individualism."[32] This was an opinion which was expressed in some fashion by almost every French critic of American society. Lucien Romier argued that the Latin masses would resist the goals of service and profit because they "are bred in the spirit of individual questioning, free criticism, and disputes over first principles."[33] Individualism would also be an obstacle to the acceptance of the assembly line. André Siegfried explained that "as a result of experience, they [French laborers] have worked out their own particular culture which depends less on social ideas like 'credit' and 'service' than on professional pride in work well done." Siegfried also asserted that the behavior of American consumers conflicted strongly with the standards of their French counterparts:

In older civilizations, where tastes vary according to local customs and refinements of culture, industry is obliged to furnish a great range of models and cannot specialize in a limited number of articles. On the other hand, the 100,000,000 [*sic*] individuals in the U.S.A. are astonishingly alike.[34]

The uniform tastes of the American consumer conflicted with the greater material and human variety of the European continent.

Frenchmen were also extremely critical of the lack of balance between industry and agriculture in the American economy. The predominance of industry was an index for some critics of widespread indifference to individualism. In this regard, André Siegfried found French society a more attractive model:

As for the races that are individuals in their work—the Frenchman who insists on thinking for himself and by himself; the Mediterranean with his genius for gardening and love of the soil . . . they all aggressively assert their individuality as if they could not fit into the American machine.[35]

For Siegfried, Romier, and other Frenchmen, the peasant and the artisan were not just outdated remnants of a less efficient economic past. They personified the virtues of European humanity and provided a perspective from which to judge the new system arising in America. The United States had always been a progressive society. Americans, in the eyes of French observers, had always erred in their preference for material over spiritual concerns. However, the twenties marked a radical departure from New World precedents. Production and consumption had now become obsessive. Americans had sacrificed the individual to their new system. In the process, the New World had created a dehumanized man whose life had no elements of transcendence.

## NOTES

1. "Méchanisme et civilisation," *Mercure de France* (November 15, 1934), 7.

2. *Sa majesté la machine* (Paris, 1930).

3. Dubreuil denounced the views of those aristocrats who "are firmly convinced that our land is the mother of all perfections and modestly persuaded that they are themselves the flower of these." *Nouveaux standards* (Paris, 1931), 44-47, 78.

4. The first strategy was adopted by Madeleine Cazamian in her *L'autre Amérique* (Paris, 1931), while Dubreuil was the chief proponent of the second position.

5. *Un oeil neuf sur l'Amérique* (Paris, 1930), 52.

6. The effect of the abundance of resources and the scarcity of labor on the growth of mass production in America was analyzed in Siegfried, *Les Etats-Unis d'aujourd'hui* (Paris, 1927), 143, 154-156; and Braunschvig, *La vie américaine* (Paris, 1931), 198-199.

7. *Psychanalyse de l'Amérique* (Paris, 1930), 207.

8. Quoted in Jean Bonnefon-Craponne, *La pénétration économique et financière des capitaux américains en Europe* (Paris, 1930), 10.

9. *Who Will Be Master, Europe or America?* (New York, 1928), 165, 273.

10. Hyacinthe Dubreuil complained bitterly that French critics of the American system could not distinguish between these two elements of industrialism. *Nouveaux standards*, 44-45.

11. *Chez nos frères d'armes d'Amérique* (Paris, 1931), 78.

12. *Le problème ouvrier aux Etats-Unis* (Paris, 1927), 86.

13. *Les Etats-Unis d'aujourd'hui*, 171.

14. *La vie américaine*, 204-205.

15. *Le problème ouvrier*, 157.

16. *Les Etats-Unis d'aujourd'hui*, 172.

17. *Scènes de la vie future* (Paris, 1930), 226. A classic illustration of worker degradation is presented by Louis-Ferdinand Céline in the novel *Voyage au bout de la nuit*. His hero, Bardamu, is warned at the Ford factory that "you have not come here to think, but to make the motions you will be ordered to execute. . . . We don't need imagination in our firm. It's just chimpanzees we need" (Paris, 1932), 287.

18. Louis Gillet, "Littératures étrangères," *Revue des Deux Mondes* (September 1, 1924), 216.

19. *Les Etats-Unis d'aujourd'hui*, 165. Marcel Braunschvig devoted an entire chapter to the effects of advertising in the United States. *La vie américaine*, 179-188.

20. *Ce qu'il faut connaître de l'âme américaine* (Paris, 1929), 92.

21. *Scènes de la vie future*, 159.

22. *The American Experiment* (New York, 1929), 186.

23. *Scènes de la vie future*, 161.

24. *Who Will Be Master*, 27. *Les Etats-Unis d'aujourd'hui*, 175-176, 166.

25. *La vie américaine*, 213.

26. *Dialogue entre deux mondes* (Paris, 1931), 22.

27. *Ce qu'il faut connaître de l'âme américaine*, 43-44.

28. *La vie américaine*, 357-358.

29. *Scènes de la vie future*, 58-59. Duhamel argued that a steady diet of American films in France would reduce Frenchmen to such a state of numbness that they would be unable to govern themselves.

30. Braunschvig, *La vie américaine*, 359; Duhamel, *Scènes de la vie future*, 49.

31. *Scènes de la vie future*, 51.

32. *La vie américaine*, 213.

33. *Who Will Be Master*, 27.

34. *Les Etats-Unis d'aujourd'hui*, 180, 164.

35. *Ibid.*, 23. André Tardieu also praised the traditional character of French peasant life. He admired "the indestructible love of man for the soil" in French villages "which, unchanged, have seen twenty generations handing down the torch." He contrasted the sedentary quality of French peasants to the restlessness of the American pioneer. The United States was "a land unretentive of man which but witnessed his passing." *Devant l'obstacle*, 99, 14.

# chapter 12

## American Authors

There is more to America than "bootleggers" and "Babbitts."
—H. C. de Courcy-May, 1931

In 1930, the Swedish Academy for the first time gave the Nobel Prize for Literature to an American author; the award recognized not only the work of Sinclair Lewis, but also the achievements of a whole generation of American writers. In choosing Lewis for the prize, the academy, like French critics in the three preceding years, called attention to the wholesale assault on American culture which these writers had undertaken since World War I.[1] The work of H. L. Mencken, Sinclair Lewis, Waldo Frank, and to a lesser extent Dreiser, Dos Passos, and Sherwood Anderson, naturally appealed to French observers of the United States who were themselves distressed with American materialism, standardization, and the rise of racial conflict. The opinions of these native Americans reassured Frenchmen that their own views were not merely the product of cultural chauvinism. As Georges Lecomte, a member of the French Academy, explained, "Mr. Sinclair Lewis thinks and speaks exactly like our own Georges Duhamel." Indeed, the *Figaro* poll of French intellectuals specifically directed respondants to evaluate the views of Mencken, Lewis, Frank, and other American authors.[2]

The correlation between the reliance on America's social critics and the acceptance of anti-American beliefs in France can be established in several ways. It is important to note that Mencken, Lewis, Frank, and company were rarely cited by French observers before 1927, and their comprehensive indictment of American society was ignored in France.[3] After 1927, while the authoritative French observers were applauding the opinions of these same American authors, the pro-American minority explicitly repudiated their work as a basis for judging American society. Charles Cestre, for example, argued that the American spirit was more accurately represented by the idealism of Emerson and Whitman than it was by *Main Street* or *Winesburg, Ohio*.[4] Hyacinthe Dubreuil and Madeleine Cazamian were troubled by the failure of French critics to place the views of American writers in proper perspective. Contrary to the usual interpretation, they denied that American writers meant to portray American life as devoid of spiritual elements. Cazamian and Dubreuil also urged French critics to remember the similar critiques directed against middle-class materialism in Europe by Flaubert and Zola. In effect, France was just as guilty as America of indifference to matters of the intellect and the soul.[5]

The apparent coincidence between the views of American authors and their French counterparts might imply that in origin and substance anti-Americanism was an American rather than a French doctrine. Certainly, the publication of *Babbitt*, *Main Street*, *Our America*, and the *American Mercury* provided an impetus to anti-Americanism in France. However, it is equally evident that the conflicts over the war debt, security, and disarmament and the decline of Europe's position were important in stimulating anti-American reaction in France. Moreover, it would be misleading to suggest that French intellectuals needed Lewis, Mencken, or Frank to awaken in them a sensitivity to Anglo-Saxon domination, materialism, conformity, and American power. All of these issues had been raised by French observers in the prewar years. The developments of the twenties, which brought them to the fore again, would certainly have attracted the attention of French commentators even without the provocation of American authors.

Not only the timing and source, but also the content of anti-Americanism had distinctive features in the two countries. American critics and French observers agreed on the aspects of American life they opposed, but the intensity of their opposition and the perspective from which it occurred were substantially different. The conflict between their views was evident when the *Figaro* asked American intellectuals to respond to the poll on American civilization in 1931.

John Dos Passos proceeded to denounce Georges Duhamel's attitudes as unduly nostalgic. Mencken and Sherwood Anderson protested that their own critique of American life applied equally well to France.[6] The two responses suggested that, on the one hand, American writers did not necessarily endorse the traditional way of life which many French observers were advocating, while, on the other, they were uncomfortable with the nationalistic tone of French criticism.

The conflict in perspective was also apparent in the French reaction to Waldo Frank's critique of America. Both Frank and his French readers opposed Anglo-Saxon domination of American life. However, Frank's vision of a new culture which would blend the heritage of all immigrants was anathema to conservative Frenchmen who accepted the traditional nation-state under the control of a single ethnic group.[7] A similar conflict arose over the avant-garde theater in America. While George Jean Nathan, the drama critic of Mencken's *American Mercury*, praised the new plays of Eugene O'Neill, Paul Morand voiced the fear that they would undermine the traditional theater.[8]

The conflict between American and French anti-Americanism reflected the differences in perspective from which the critique of the United States emerged. Frenchmen were chiefly concerned about the protection of their own national identity during a period of crisis. American intellectuals were largely interested in redirecting the energies of their compatriots toward more constructive goals. The work of Lewis, Mencken, and company was clearly intended for an American public which was complacent and chauvinistic. Intense anti-Americanism from the pens of American authors was a device for deflating American pride. In the French context, however, the same views could be taken to prove the superiority of French to American civilization, or of the traditional to the modern way of life. The reactions of the American critics in the *Figaro* poll indicate their dissatisfaction with such an interpretation of their work.

The uniqueness of the French perspective is also clear from the selectivity of their approach to American literature. Such important writers as Hemingway, Fitzgerald, and Faulkner, who were living in Paris in the twenties, were totally ignored by French observers. Only occasional references were made to the work of Robert Frost, Carl

Sandburg, or Edgar Lee Masters.⁹ In part, the exclusion of these
authors was a product of the language barrier. In part, it was an
expression of the preference for literature primarily concerned with
the assessment of the typical features of American life.

Even the best-known contemporary American authors were read
selectively and infrequently by French observers. Again, the language barrier played a negative role. *Babbitt*, the first Sinclair Lewis
novel to be translated, did not appear in French until 1930.¹⁰ Waldo
Frank's work fared much better. *Our America* was published in
French in 1920, while *Rediscovery of America* was translated in
1930. Many French intellectuals, of course, read American works in
the original. How many did so and to what effect is difficult to
establish. However, certain patterns do appear to characterize the
use of American works by French observers. For the most part,
French authors restricted themselves to a few choice passages from
their favorite American authors. These passages were either quoted
or paraphrased. In the travel literature of the twenties, H.L. Mencken's *American Mercury* was cited on only one occasion.¹¹ Only one
passage appears from *Arrowsmith*, although it is cited by three
different French observers. Two of the authors (Gerard de Catalogne
and André Lafond) had both read the third author (André Siegfried)
and relied heavily on his judgment in other matters.¹² It is possible
that they and others depended on their authoritative predecessors
for an indirect acquaintance with the new American literature as well
as for judgments about American civilization.

The tension between the views of French and American critics of
the United States was largely obscured during the late twenties by
virtue of their common opposition to puritanism and mechanization.
French critics regarded their American counterparts as courageous
allies in a common crusade against evil. Since the Americans were
struggling from within, their plight was viewed with special sympathy. As Robert Brasillach explained, "The whole American tragedy
is contained in this alternative: revolt, with all the drawbacks of
romanticism, or purely mechanical conformity, a submission to the
civilization of the 'monneymaker' [*sic*] and the Puritan."¹³

American writers were approached by French observers as students of American society rather than as creators of literary works.
Because French observers were primarily concerned about the dan-

gers of American civilization, they tended to disregard the differences in tone and approach between their various American counterparts. Lewis, Mencken, and company constituted in the eyes of French observers a single force for the achievement of superior values in American life. Bernard Faÿ and Marcel Braunschvig, for example, identified the social realists as a basically anti-Anglo-Saxon school of authors which was devoted to protecting ethnic minorities against the tyranny of the Puritans.[14] For Firmin Roz, the outstanding feature of the new writers was their opposition to the provincial ways of American life.[15] In either case, the values of American writers seemed to coincide with those of the French critic.

French observers turned more frequently to the work of Sinclair Lewis than to any other American writer, and there were more references to *Babbitt* than to any other American book in the twenties. The reasons for this preference are obvious. *Babbitt* provided a ready formula for characterizing the typical American. Indeed, by 1930, the word had entered the French language. An article in the *Revue Universelle* was entitled "In the Land of Babbitt," while Dante Bellesgarde coined the term "Babittisation [*sic*]."[16]

In most cases, Babbitt was a convenient label by which Frenchmen could identify the overwhelming conformity of Americans, itself the result of the standardization of the personality. Count de Keyserling accordingly referred to Babbitt as the representative American, a citizen of a mechanized society who was unable to put down roots. Babbitt had not experienced the tradition of any particular locale. His character was abstract, in vivid contrast to the individuality and vitality of the average European.[17]

Babbitt was blamed by other writers for a wide variety of ills which beset the American character. Aron and Dandieu pointed to the bland optimism of American life which stemmed from Babbitt's contentment with the status quo, and his refusal to tolerate the critical spirit in America.[18] Other observers blamed American commercialism on Babbitt's exclusive concern for material possessions. Marcel Braunschvig believed that Americans would be much happier if they were not always hurrying; the pace of American life was determined by the hunger for profits.[19] André Siegfried condemned the hypocrisy of Babbitt's belief that individual profit-seeking was perfectly compatible with the welfare of American society. Babbitt was also blamed by Siegfried for the crusade of the fundamentalists and the Klan. His bigotry was a direct heritage from America's Puritan past.[20]

When French critics wanted to stigmatize the American environment, social or natural, they most often turned to *Main Street*. As Babbitt came to stand for the uniformity of the American character, Main Street represented the monotony and provincialism of American small-town life. The dull character of the American landscape and the similar appearance of all towns was described by André Siegfried and Marcel Braunschvig. They, like Lewis, criticized the uniform plans of each town, the boxlike form of houses, the similarity of the products in the stores, and the identical layouts of the newspapers, reflecting the influence of the trusts which owned them. The boredom of Main Street was relieved by two institutions, the railroad and the Catholic church. The latter, with its ritual, created the only mystery in the American environment.[21] The provincial spirit of these small towns very often held sway in the United States during the twenties, despite the rise of great cosmopolitan centers. One such occasion was the election of Herbert Hoover in 1928, which *Europe Nouvelle* regarded as the triumph of "the spirit of Main Street which inspired the very cruel satire of Sinclair Lewis."[22]

The only passage which interested French observers in *Arrowsmith* was the ironic description of the hero's "Anglo-Saxon heritage." Frenchmen were amused by the variety of ethnic groups which had contributed to the so-called Anglo-Saxon stock. The mixed racial heritage of the original Americans suggested that their claim to racial purity was a myth. The fact that they insisted on making the claim, however, showed the rise of ethnic conflict in the United States. In contrast to *Babbitt* and *Main Street*, which provided evidence of the uniformity of American life, *Arrowsmith* was used by French observers to demonstrate the heterogeneity of the American people.

References to H. L. Mencken by French critics were somewhat less frequent and far vaguer than those to Sinclair Lewis. Observers were generally aware of the tone and substance of Mencken's work, but rarely quoted him directly. Particularly surprising is the absence of any reference to Mencken's attacks on American puritanism or fundamentalism. No doubt French critics would have used this excellent ammunition if Mencken's work had been more readily available to them. André Siegfried did cite James Cain's critique of service which appeared in the *American Mercury*. Cain pointed with amusement to the fact that the concept was generally associated with profitable occupations, while nonservice professions such as writing, prostitution, and baseball were far less remunerative.[23] Other French critics, like Lucien Lehmen, used Mencken in a more general way to criticize the commercialism of American life.[24]

More than any other writer, Mencken stood out as a symbol to Frenchmen of resistance to the tyranny of American life. While French intellectuals sympathized with the general plight of American writers, Mencken, by deliberately defying the American public, seemed to merit special praise. Georges Duhamel singled out Mencken for his ardent defense of individual liberty. Duhamel's special interest in the preservation of individual rights and Mencken's concern for the protection of eccentricity created an obvious bond between them.[25]

The French interest in Waldo Frank was explained in part by special factors. Frank had met the publisher Gallimard and the theater director Copeau during their wartime visits to the United States. It was they who had urged Frank to write an essay explaining the sources of American culture.[26] Gallimard responded by publishing *Our America* in French even before the English version appeared. It is not surprising, then, that Frank's critique of puritanism and materialism should appeal to French observers, particularly after 1927. The analysis of the failure of the melting pot in *Our America* provided evidence of the rise of racial conflict in the United States. *Our America* also helped critics to corroborate Georges Duhamel's polemic against the materialism of American life.[27]

Other American writers were mentioned with less frequency and cited even more vaguely than Mencken, Lewis, and Frank. Nonetheless, it is clear that the testimony of Dos Passos, Dreiser, and Sherwood Anderson carried some weight with French critics. Dreiser and Dos Passos, for example, were mentioned along with Paul Morand for offering the best portraits of New York City in their work.[28] Dreiser was also cited as one example of the revolt against Anglo-Saxon values in America.[29] Charles Cestre must have felt that Anderson's *Winesburg, Ohio* was important, because he attempted to refute it on two occasions, while Madeleine Cazamian noted that

Dreiser, Dos Passos, and Anderson were three of the most potent critics of American life.[30] It is significant that the three novelists, like Mencken, Lewis, and Waldo Frank, were selected by French observers because they gave a fairly comprehensive view of the contemporary American scene. French critics had little use for other American writers of the decade.

There is little question, then, that the work of American writers gave aid and comfort to their French counterparts, although it is unlikely that Americans were the cause of French hostility to American life. Even before American works were translated, they were known in France through the reviews in elite journals or the citations of such authorities as André Siegfried and Luc Durtain. Despite certain conflicts in goals, the substance and tone of American criticisms meshed well with French views and contributed significantly to the anti-American campaign at the end of the decade.

## NOTES

1. *Europe Nouvelle* expressed the belief that the Nobel Prize was awarded to Lewis as an expression of support for Lewis's attack on American civilization. "Sinclair Lewis, Prix Nobel 1930" (November 22, 1930), 1691.

2. Gerard de Catalogne, ed., *Dialogue entre deux mondes* (Paris, 1931), 111, 77.

3. Henri Hauser offered *Main Street* and *Babbitt* as evidence of the prevalence of hypocrisy in American life, but he refused to discuss Lewis's comprehensive indictment of American civilization. *L'Amérique vivant* (Paris, 1924), 10. The French reaction to *Our America* before 1927 was similar. Charles Le Verrier gave Frank credit for introducing the French to American civilization, but he said little about the major themes of Frank's work. "Un nouveau livre de M. Waldo Frank," *Europe Nouvelle* (June 3, 1922), 679. Francois Crucy, correspondent for *Le Petit Parisien*, remarked merely that *Our America* provided the best images of Chicago. "En voyage aux Etats-Unis," *Europe Nouvelle* (March 3, 1923), 273.

4. *Les Etats-Unis* (Paris, 1927), 335, 232.

5. *L'autre Amérique* (Paris, 1931), 290. *Nouveaux standards* (Paris, 1931), 74-76.

6. *Dialogue entre deux mondes*, 259, 268, 269.

7. André Siegfried, *Les Etats-Unis d'aujourd'hui* (Paris, 1927), 140;

Robert Cahan Salsberry, "Waldo Frank et le nouvel idéal américain," *Mercure de France* (April 15, 1930), 354.

8. *New-York* (Paris, 1930), 175.

9. Even Eugene O'Neill was mentioned only once by French observers in the twenties. *Ibid.*, 175.

10. André Gide commented that he was "unable to get interested in *Babbitt.*" *The Journals of André Gide*, trans. by Justin O'Brien (New York, 1961), III, 112. The fact that Gide tried to read *Babbitt* suggests that it was an item on the agenda of many French intellectuals in 1930.

11. André Siegfried, *Les Etats-Unis d'aujourd'hui*, 176. It is also possible that Lucien Romier borrowed his ideas on "service" from the *American Mercury*, although he did not cite any specific source. *Who Will Be Master, Europe or America?* (New York, 1928), 27.

12. *New-York '28* (Rouen, 1928), 39; *Dialogue entre deux mondes*, 7; *Les Etats-Unis d'aujourd'hui*, 9.

13. "Figures américaines par André Levinson," *Revue Universelle* (November 15, 1930), 499.

14. *The American Experiment* (New York, 1929), 188. *La vie américaine* (Paris, 1931), 29.

15. "L'esprit nouveau du roman américain," *Revue des Deux Mondes* (October 15, 1925), 886.

16. André Rousseaux (April 15, 1930); *Dialogue entre deux mondes*, 86.

17. *Psychanalyse de l'Amérique* (Paris, 1930), 56, 81, 85.

18. *Le cancer américain* (Paris, 1931), 96.

19. *La vie américaine*, 146.

20. *Les Etats-Unis d'aujourd'hui*, 44, 47.

21. *La vie américaine*, 212; *Les Etats-Unis d'aujourd'hui*, 46, 165.

22. "L'élection de M. Herbert Hoover" (November 10, 1928), 1528.

23. *Les Etats-Unis d'aujourd'hui*, 176.

24. *Le grand mirage: U.S.A.* (Paris, 1929), 243.

25. *Scènes de la vie future* (Paris, 1930), 73.

26. *Notre Amérique* (Paris, 1920), 9. The translation was the work of H. Boussinesq.

27. Gabriel Brunet, "Georges Duhamel et la 'civilisation' américaine," *Mercure de France* (January 1, 1931), 10-17.

28. André Chaumeix, "Revue littéraire—Images de l'Amérique," *Revue des Deux Mondes* (June 15, 1930), 931.

29. Firmin Roz, "L'esprit nouveau du roman américain," *Revue des Deux Mondes* (October 15, 1925), 886.

30. *Les Etats-Unis*, 39, 232; *L'autre Amérique*, 290.

# PART V:

# From Entente
# to Opposition, 1917–1932

# chapter 13

# Opposition Renewed _____

> In 1917, we thought that the American responded only to higher
> ideals. We considered them "knights," "crusaders," and "saviors of
> civilization." . . . Several years later, we considered Americans a
> race which hungered after profits, wallowing in comfort, and deaf
> to nobility.
>
> —Robert de Saint-Jean, 1934

The hostility of French observers to developments in American
society and foreign policy inevitably influenced their judgments
about the culture as a whole. However, it would be misleading to
assume that Frenchmen sought to define American civilization by
combining their impressions of the particular events of the twenties.
The formation of the new image was a selective process. French
observers recognized Prohibition, immigration restriction, and the
rise of the Klan as important developments in the United States, but
their conception of American civilization was based almost entirely
on the various elements of mass culture. It was the assembly line
rather than racial intolerance, urban life rather than the Main Street
of Sinclair Lewis which characterized America for most Frenchmen
in the late twenties.

There is no doubt that French observers were correct in assessing
the rise of mass culture to be the most important development in
American life after World War I. However, their insistence on
defining the civilization of the United States in such narrow terms
was a reflection of their own concerns as well. The movie and the
assembly line were making their debuts in France. Moreover, it was
especially disconcerting to Frenchmen that these cultural changes

should be so closely associated with the dynamism of American corporations and the policy of the United States government.[1] The interplay between aggressive American policy and the development of a new French image of American civilization was suggested by Lucien Romier:

From a borrower full of promise, the uncle had become a creditor full of demands. It was essential to have a close look at the causes of such a change. Believing that we would meet an old miser, we found a civilization.[2]

America's role as debt collector helped to feed the image of American materialism which was confirmed in the discovery of mass culture. That discovery, however, did not await the Mellon-Bérenger agreement of 1926. As Romier himself argued, "in the evolution of morals and tastes" American influence was already perceptible in Europe. "One could draw quite an amazing picture of 'Americanism' to be witnessed in the oldest capitals of Europe: London, Paris, and Rome."[3]

America's cultural presence in France not only provided the elements out of which emerged a new definition of American civilization, but contributed as well to a reformulation of the concept of relations between the two countries.[4] The entente image reflected the common participation in a war supposedly fought for democratic ideals. The American doughboy, offering his life to help save France from Germany, was the primary material out of which the image was constructed. After the doughboys were replaced by American corporations seeking to install new methods of production, it was natural that Frenchmen should regard profits rather than ideals as the essential goal of American civilization. This materialism they rejected because it was incompatible with their own values. The rise of conflict at the cultural level undermined the entente image, while conflict in the diplomatic realm stimulated the reformulation of the American image in France.

The antithesis accurately reflected the feelings of French intellectuals, but it made little sense as a description of social and economic trends on the two sides of the Atlantic. After all, mass culture was developing at different rates in both France and the United States. Since the two countries were experiencing the same, rather than

opposite social forces, the rejection of the entente must be understood as a measure of the cultural and political situation of the French
elite. Once intellectuals began to perceive the assembly line as a
threat to their own way of life, they were anxious to discourage the
rise of the new technology. The antithesis helped to accomplish this
goal.

Although the terms of the opposition were labeled "Europe" and
"America," they identified principles as well as geographical entities.
"America" referred to a set of values and institutions which were
increasingly visible in the Old World. "Europe" represented the
quasi-feudal or traditional economic system which was rapidly disap-
pearing even in France. The opposition of these terms provided
Frenchmen with a dramatic way of presenting the problems associated with modernization.

The belief in the opposition between Europe and America, however, reflected more than an abstract cultural clash. It is quite clear that
the repudiation of mass culture or "Americanism" took place in the
context of rising American power. Regardless of their feelings about
modernization, Frenchmen were convinced that their country and
continent must be preserved as independent political entities. The
antithesis dramatized the conflict between Europe and America in
the political—as well as the cultural—realm and implied that the
desirable outcome was the continued independence of the Old
World.

Since American technology and power were inseparable in the
minds of Frenchmen, the opposition to the latter generated resistance to the former. This confusion between diplomatic and cultural
developments also helps to explain the extreme and swift change in
the French image of America.[5] The exaggeration of American idealism during the war years and the effort to link the spread of new
methods to the entente helped to generate anti-Americanism. The
benign image of America was bound to produce a feeling of deception
among Frenchmen when American practices did not measure up to
the high expectations created by the image. To counter this excessively favorable view Frenchmen would exaggerate the defects of
America, thus contributing to the extreme shift from pro- to anti-
American feeling. The link between cultural and diplomatic matters
worked to the same effect. The development of conflict in either

realm naturally affected perceptions in both areas. Doubts about American culture fed the belief in diplomatic conflict and vice versa.[6] Just ten years after the establishment of the entente, Frenchmen were prepared to reassert the validity of an old conception of relations, which lay dormant during the war.

The battle against "Americanism" in France took shape in 1927. The year of Lindbergh's flight across the Atlantic also witnessed the publication of three major studies of America by Frenchmen. While Lindbergh's flight seemed to bring together the two continents, travelers were proclaiming uniformly that America was establishing her independence from Europe and that the two civilizations were growing farther apart in a cultural sense. This was evident in Lucien Romier's comment that "Europe and America no longer represent the same type of civilization. America no longer leans upon Europe. America is accentuating her points of difference on essential matters."[7] As at the turn of the century, the independence of American civilization from Europe was noted just as America emerged as an independent power in the world. As in 1900, so in 1927, America's desertion from the ranks of the European way of life was deplored by spokesmen for the European tradition. This was especially true of Georges Duhamel:

If I thought that this civilization [American] was the prolongation of the one which for 30 or 40 centuries, despite many errors, has enriched, adorned, and ennobled the heritage of the race, I would sing its praises from the bottom of my heart. But where others see an extension, I sense a deviation which amounts to a rupture.[8]

Most French observers of America after 1927 took special care to explain that the differences between America and Europe were not geographic in character, although the physical distance between the two continents became a useful metaphor. André Tardieu saw "a chasm wider than the Atlantic" separating France and America,[9] while in the same year, André Siegfried wrote that "the chief contrast between Europe and America is not so much one of geography as a fundamental difference between two epochs in the history of mankind."[10] The conflict which they described was between a civilization devoted exclusively to mechanization and another which featured a peasant and artisan economy.

The confrontation with the civilization of the future produced a strong reaction on the part of French visitors. They were sufficiently overwhelmed by the differences between new and traditional institutions, as to suggest that all traditional societies were relatively similar. Georges Duhamel explained:

We are uprooted by certain voyages because we feel uprooted in time even more than in space. The past is less disconcerting than the future: a normal, educated, adult westerner finds himself less uprooted in the land of the Troglodytes of Matmata than in certain streets of Chicago.[11]

A similar revulsion against American power in the early twentieth century had helped Jules Huret to perceive that, in the face of the American system, the differences between European nations were relatively minor, and that European civilization was a reality.[12] Now, French critics were insisting that the institutions of the future were so distasteful and so different that traditional societies, whether primitive or European, were at least united against the new way of life.

The tacit accord between Europe and other traditional societies, all of which rejected the principle of modernization, was articulated most explicitly in the widely quoted conclusion of André Siegfried's major study of American life. After asserting the fundamental contrast between American and European civilizations, he noted from the perspective of the American continent "certain traits that are common to the psychology of both Europe and the Orient. So the discussion broadens until it becomes, as it were, a dialogue between Ford and Gandhi."[13] The accord in values between Europe and the Orient became evident only in contrast to the pervasive mechanization of American society.

Contrary to the impression given by Duhamel and Siegfried, however, the trip to America was only incidental to the formulation of the antithesis between America and Europe; it was merely an occasion for entering the current debate in Europe over the future of European civilization. Critics such as René Guénon and Romain Rolland were invoking the Orient to condemn Europe's own preoccupation with materialism. Siegfried's antithesis was a useful way of protesting the conclusions of the critics. Compared to the United

States, Siegfried claimed, Europe was still preoccupied with matters of the spirit.

Siegfried's antithesis did more than reassure his countrymen that Europe had not succumbed to materialism. It also served to clarify the French image of America. In one stroke, Siegfried managed to identify America exclusively with a process. Once, it had been considered a continent of diverse human and natural resources; the country now became, in the eyes of literate Frenchmen, a moving assembly line devoted exclusively to production and consumption. This narrow view of American life was widely accepted by critics after 1927. Georges Duhamel remarked that "no nation up to this moment has addicted itself more deliberately than the United States to the excesses of industrial civilization."[14] Such an addiction, moreover, was not a result of superficial aspects of the American character. It arose from the fact that "in physical composition, moral trend, rhythm of growth, volume of production . . . the world offers no analogy to the United States, but if antithesis be sought, France provides it."[15]

After 1927, Frenchmen increasingly represented American civilization as a system which had no regard for human concerns. Aron and Dandieu, for example, argued that "America is not a country; it is certainly not a fatherland. . . . If it is a structure, America is no longer a territorial structure, but a system of thought and action. America is a method, a technique, a disease of the spirit."[16] Not all critics agreed with Aron and Dandieu that the American system was a "cancer," as they labeled it in the title of their book, but they were now persuaded that America, once a territory, was now a way of life.

It was less the purposes of the system than its power and complexity which disturbed Georges Duhamel. The net effect, however, was the same: the human element was obscured if not destroyed.

America hides the Americans from me. . . . Between the American citizen and me rises I know not what monstrous phantom, an ensemble of laws, institutions, prejudices, and even myths, a social apparatus unequalled in the world and without analogy in history. Rather than a people, I see a system.[17]

Of course, people still lived in America, but they were shaped by the process of mass production, just as objects were.

Some critics did protest that the United States should not be considered a system exclusively devoted to the production of material goods. Luc Durtain, Duhamel's friend, criticized this narrow conception of the United States:

The crude practices believed to be essentially American, such as the reign of the machine, the standardization of luxury, the disdain of intellectual elements, constitute for the Old World a superficial Americanism perfectly false as an image of the U.S.A., but peculiarly forceful as propaganda and powerfully contagious.[18]

Whether or not certain critics were misrepresenting America, it is clear from Durtain's assertion that the dominant conception of America was in terms of advanced industrialism.

Contrary to Durtain's view, it was not the advocates of mass production who were responsible for the new image of the United States. They had been careful to establish the diversity of life in the New World. It was the critics of mass production, including Durtain himself, who insisted upon the uniformity of life in the New World. This focus was reflected in the organization of their studies of American life. They lacked the interest of prewar travelers in aspects of the continent including scenic wonders, factories, and encounters with people. In place of these observations, the travelers stressed certain broad themes which would help to explain the nature of the American system. The effects of mass production and the consumer society on the individual, racial conflict in American society, and voting patterns of Americans were major topics in the new travel literature. If the natural beauty of the continent was not ignored, its existence was denied. Régis Michaud saw in America "a geographic mass without harmony, a country of contrasts and disparities on a grand scale with a violent climate."[19] As it turned out, the characteristics which Michaud discovered in the landscape of the New World matched perfectly the characteristics of American urban life.

For the most part, travelers came to visit American cities rather than to enjoy the scenery of the continent. As a result, the old image of America as a land of cowboys and Indians was rapidly replaced by a picture of a superurban land of skyscrapers.[20] While it was true that cities, and even very large cities, came to play an increasingly important role in American life in the twenties, the overemphasis of this aspect of the United States tended to distort its image in France. Indeed, French critics had a veritable obsession with New York City. Between 1928 and 1931, no less than seven volumes were devoted primarily or exclusively to reporting on life in that city.[21] Such an obsession was perfectly consistent with the effort to identify America exclusively with the moving assembly line. It suggested a homogeneous landscape just at the moment when French travelers were insisting that all objects and individuals had been standardized by the assembly line. It also followed that a nation exclusively concerned with assembly-line production would have to house its factories in large urban centers. The equation of the American system with the assembly line was followed logically by the equation of the American landscape with the city of New York.

The effort to characterize all of the United States through a study of New York was most explicitly avowed by Paul Morand. He proclaimed that

Manhattan is the microcosm of the U.S. All American life is machinery for sensation—and there is more sensation to be got in one day on Broadway than in all the forty-eight states of the Union put together.[22]

In addition to its capacity for producing sensations, Manhattan shared other attributes of American life:

New York is big, New York is new; but big and new as all America is . . . New York's supreme beauty, its truly unique quality, is its violence. Violence gives it nobility, excuses it, makes its vulgarity forgettable. For New York is vulgar; it is stronger, richer, newer than anything you like, but it is common. The town's violence is in its rhythm.[23]

Morand's obvious pleasure in experiencing the sensations of New York life should not be construed as evidence of pro-Americanism. New York's violence, size, and vulgarity were interesting, but they were later rejected as a model for French life (see Part V, chapter 14). Almost all French critics preferred the aesthetic charm of their own cities to the vulgarity of American urban life, a preference which dated from the reports of Paul de Rousiers and Paul Bourget at the turn of the century. As Régis Michaud explained in discussing American cities, "Neither art nor harmony preceded their birth. . . . One can hardly believe that civilized beings have been able to pile up so many dreadful spectacles."[24]

The aesthetic failures of American cities were even more strikingly apparent when contrasted with the pastoral qualities of the French countryside. Georges Duhamel depicted the differences between a Chicago hotel and his own home:

Let me escape from my tattered recollection for a minute. Let Chicago retreat behind its poisonous fog. As I write these lines, here I am in my home, in our home, in my Isle de France garden, fondled for yet some time by the smile of an ancient, noble and learned civilization. . . . However, the frantic impressions pursue me even here. I am sometimes visited by the hideous desire to be once again at the window of the monstrous hotel building where one can change rooms every night for seven years without sleeping twice in the same one. To be high up there for even an instant, as on the balcony of death, and stare with all my strength to try to understand this miserable and demented world, this world without a witness, this hell without Alighieri.[25]

The discovery and condemnation of a mechanized urban world on the American continent was the major task of French travelers. Their preoccupation with this world, however, did not prevent them from recognizing, on occasion, other more attractive aspects of American life. As in the prewar period, the travelers explained the existence of these places and individuals as European enclaves in the New World. They were imperiled by the new system, but found sustenance in the European tradition. These same elements had proved attractive to Frenchmen in the immediate postwar period as well. Then, they could be understood as genuinely rooted in the New World which supported a wide variety of behavior and activities. Now that America was considered a system, these elements were assumed to be in opposition to the dominant ways.

The criticism of the new technology by American intellectuals made it evident to travelers that the intellectuals were alien to the system. Their open embrace of European ways further clarified their relation to America and reinforced the conception of opposition. There was, for example, the Chicago writer who wanted "to buy a little old stone house in France on the Mediterranean shore where he will spend his vacations and later die in peace." This intelligent

"American" had already divorced himself from the United States in
favor of Europe. So, in fact, had all the other intellectuals of consequence:

North America has inspired no painters, kindled no sculptors, brought forth
no songs from its musicians, except for the monotone Negroes. This same
America, however, whose ferociously industrial architecture seems indifferent to the future, has produced poets and writers. Almost all of them, oh
mockery! turn away from their native soil with bitterness.[26]

In addition to their persistent attachment to American intellectuals, the travelers preferred certain regions to others. Condemning
most Americans for provincialism and a missionary impulse, André
Siegfried excepted "the Atlantic states, old California, and here and
there some university towns [which] contain a cultivated and refined
society, capable of irony, and susceptible under certain circumstances of admiration for Europe."[27]

In the course of their lecture tours, French travelers had ample
occasion to visit American universities, and enjoy their campuses. It
seemed strange, however, that in an urban industrial country like
America there should be a place for such lovely rural settings. Luc
Durtain, after admiring the Smith campus, concluded that "this is no
longer the American atmosphere. We seem to be in England, at
Cambridge."[28] Even a building like the Boston library in which
Georges Duhamel found a moment of solace could not be an outgrowth of modern American life. Duhamel described the library as

rich, hospitable, and orderly. A man with a friendly look guides me through
while speaking in a whisper like a priest before the altar. Millions of shadows
worked there with a religious fervor. A soft living warmth comforts the
traveler. How nice it feels. Oh fatherland![29]

There were other remnants of Europe scattered about the United
States, all of which were nourished by the spirit of the Old World,
and survived in opposition to the power of mass society. Mount
Vernon, Salem, and New Orleans were examples of European influence in the New World. Their beauty could never have been produced in the era of mass society.[30] Count de Keyserling made this

clear when he attributed the exceptional quality of life in New Orleans to the ethnic origins of the population:

The French are the most tenacious of all the races. The reign of beauty in certain American markets proves that the French sense of quality, stimulated by American mass production, seems more than ever determined to survive. Isn't it marvelous that America contains a great city possessing such an innate culture?[31]

The major exception to the domination of the new civilization was the existence of non-Anglo-Saxon racial groups in the New World. While these groups were seriously threatened by the process of assimilation, their appeal remained a real force in the twenties for French travelers. André Siegfried was especially vigilant in applauding the achievements of the non-Anglo-Saxon groups (see Part IV, chapter 10). Count de Keyserling also looked with favor on the immigrant who "cultivates in himself a very strong counter-tradition opposed to that of the 100 percent American."[32]

For the most part, French critics of America in the early twenties saw evidence of cultural achievement as the result of a rebellion against the new American civilization, which sought nourishment in the rich soil of Europe. Only infrequently did travelers speak of American cultural achievements as an integral part of the civilization. The exception to the rule was Marcel Braunschvig's fairly detailed remarks on American schools, museums, and libraries. He was particularly enthusiastic about such progressive schools as Lincoln and Dalton in New York City. Yet, Braunschvig insisted in his conclusion on the "profound opposition [between America] and the civilizations which preceded it."[33] The existence of a specifically American culture did not lead him to challenge the conclusions of those critics who believed there was no culture at all in the United States.

After 1927, Frenchmen succeeded in portraying American culture as narrowly materialistic and urban in character. Such an orientation, of course, conflicted with the pastoral idealism which was espoused by many French intellectuals. The resulting confrontation between Americanism and French values was particularly sharp because of the dynamic character of American civilization and the sensitivity of French intellectuals. In responding to this threat, Frenchmen began to reformulate their vision of the world. They were assisted by the discovery that other European countries were also experiencing the impact of American culture. The realization that France and her neighbors had common problems encouraged the development of a common program for resisting American hegemony.

## NOTES

1. The American presence in Europe was also augmented in the twenties by the hordes of tourists who crossed the Atlantic during the decade. In 1927 alone, 300,000 Americans visited Paris. *New York Times* (May 16, 1928), 7.

2. André Lafond, *New York '28* (Rouen, 1929), xiii.

3. *Who Will Be Master, Europe or America?* (New York, 1928), 148.

4. The impact of American culture in France during the twenties was described in vivid terms by the French Ambassador to the United States, Paul Claudel. "The place in French life and culture formerly held by Spain and Italy and in the nineteenth century by England, now belongs to America. More and more, we are following America." *New York Times* (February 7, 1930), 20.

5. Such sweeping and rapid changes in the image are not without precedent in the history of Franco-American relations. Professor René Rémond has noted two occasions, one in 1790 and the other in 1830, when a similar repudiation of pro-American views occurred in France. "La France regarde les Etats-Unis (1815-1852)," *Bulletin de la Société d'Histoire Moderne*, douzième série (1960), 15.

6. Professor Echeverria has observed that American influence in France was generated by factors other than a favorable image in the nineteenth century. In pro-American periods, the United States had almost no influence on France. "L'Amérique devant l'opinion française, 1734-1870: Questions de méthode et d'interprétation," *Revue d'Histoire Moderne et Contemporaine* (1961), 57-58.

7. *Who Will Be Master*, 41.

8. *Scènes de la vie future* (Paris, 1930), 247.

9. *Devant l'obstacle* (Paris, 1927), 18.

10. *Les Etats-Unis d'aujourd'hui* (Paris, 1927), 351.

11. *Scènes de la vie future*, 18. The Troglodytes were a cave-dwelling people of prehistoric Turkey. Montesquieu's *Lettres persanes* used an imaginary account of Troglodyte life as a critique of French society in the eighteenth century. Colonel Jean Ferrandi chose a different primitive society to make the same point as Duhamel. "This is truly a New World which we

see; it is a way of life, even a civilization, which breaks deliberately with the past. I was certainly less surprised at the age of twenty when I saw the first encampment of nomadic tribesmen of Banzires on the banks of the Ouban-gui." *Chez nes frères d'armes d'Amérique* (Paris, 1931), 20-21.

12. *En Amérique*, II, 209.

13. *Les Etats-Unis d'aujourd'hui*, 351. Marcel Braunschvig, *La vie américaine* (Paris, 1931), 361, remarked, "We understand how André Siegfried could declare that the opposition between the civilization of the new world and that of the old becomes a dialogue between Ford and Gandhi." Kadmi-Cohen, *L'abomination américaine* (Paris, 1930), v, noted that "it is the phrase 'dialogue between Ford and Gandhi' which concludes the best book written on the United States."

14. *Scènes de la vie future*, 18.

15. André Tardieu, *Devant l'obstacle*, 13.

16. *Le cancer américain* (Paris, 1931), 79.

17. *Scènes de la vie future*, 67.

18. *Quelques notes d'U.S.A.* (Paris, 1928), 27.

19. *Ce qu'il faut connaître de l'âme américaine* (Paris, 1929), 29.

20. *New York Times* (May 19, 1929), X, 2.

21. J. Villani, *Paris, New-York, Paris* (Paris, 1928); A. Lafond, *New-York '28* (Paris, 1929); L. Cazamian, *L'humour de New-York* (Paris, 1929); F. Debat, *New-York: images mouvantes* (Paris, 1929); Y. Lapaquellerie, *New-York aux sept couleurs* (Paris, 1930); P. Morand, *New-York* (Paris, 1930); and J. Joseph Renaud, *New-York flamboie* (Paris, 1931).

22. *New-York*, 118.

23. *Ibid.*, 116.

24. *Ce qu'il faut connaître de l'âme américaine*, 31.

25. *Scènes de la vie future*, 109.

26. *Ibid.*, 108, 116.

27. *Les Etats-Unis d'aujourd'hui*, 139.

28. *Quelques notes d'U.S.A.*, 86.

29. *Scènes de la vie future*, 218.

30. *Who Will Be Master*, 142.

31. *Psychanalyse de l'Amérique* (Paris, 1930), 67.

32. *Ibid.*, 116.

33. *La vie américaine*, 302-307, 280. Madeleine Cazamian, *L'autre Amérique* (Paris, 1931), also considered parks, libraries, and schools an integral part of American civilization.

# chapter 14

# The Defense of Europe _____

> Europe will be punished for her policy; she will be deprived of wines, beer, and liqueurs. And other things. . . .
>
> Europe clearly aspires to be governed by an American commission. Her whole policy is oriented toward that end.
>
> —Paul Valéry, 1919

"The trip to America taught me more about Europe than long years spent on our continent," remarked André Siegfried. "We become conscious of a reality which escapes us here: that there exists a European spirit of which the American spirit is often the perfect antithesis."[1] The discovery of a European spirit did not, of course, await André Siegfried's trip to the United States. In the early postwar period, as Valéry, Demangeon, and others reflected on the destruction of the war years and the rise of extra-European powers, they came to the realization that the nations which had so recently fought each other belonged to a common civilization. The bitter hatred of the postwar years, however, provided a poor climate in which to nourish the concept of a European consciousness. As Albert Thibaudet explained in 1925,

At the time of the Armistice, the words "Europe" and "European" had a bad connotation in France. Anyone who accepted them as political and moral rather than geographic expressions was suspected of a lukewarm feeling toward his country. The dilemma—France or Europe—was a difficult one.[2]

The preoccupation with the war and the belief that it was necessary to use force in dealing with Germany persisted until 1924. As late as

1922, it was possible to assert that "the [public] state of mind was very close to what it was during the war; people were constantly reminded of the war."[3]

The quest for security against a future attack by Germany remained the basic goal of French foreign policy through the whole interwar period; however, after the failure of the Ruhr occupation, the French public became disenchanted with the coercive approach to security which the Poincaré administration had practiced. In 1925, Herriot and Briand shifted from a policy of confrontation in dealing with Germany, to one of negotiation. The Locarno Pact, the major product of this new strategy, helped to ease tensions between the European powers by guaranteeing the status quo in western Europe. At the same time, it gave some substance to the claim that there existed a European civilization which was united by the acceptance of certain common values. The diplomatic climate in the late twenties helped to nourish this conviction in the minds of many intellectuals in France and elsewhere.

Moreover, the rapprochement between France and Germany coincided with the implementation of the American policies on debts and reparations. The antithetical aims of the French and American governments suggested to Frenchmen the enormous difference in values between the two countries. By comparison, France's European neighbors seemed relatively compatible. After 1925, the obsession with Germanism[4] was replaced by a concern for the rise of Americanism and other extra-European forces;[5] the problems of Frenchmen, like those of other Europeans, now appeared to have a common origin outside of the Continent. In 1928, Luc Durtain suggested:

Contacts and antagonisms among peoples developed formerly between cities, then between nations. Today the real problems arise between continents. Disagreements are less numerous, but perhaps more profound.[6]

Five years earlier, this reflection would have seemed far less appropriate than it did in the midst of Durtain's discussion of American civilization. It not only implied an interlude in hostilities between European countries, but also suggested what was more explicitly argued by Paul Morand: that despite Europe's apparent divisions, she had the potential to become a focus for the common loyalties of her inhabitants:

Europe [is] egotistical, envious, democratic and dispersed, like all the old peninsulas; a curious and miniscule spectacle seen from without, at a time when the world belongs to massive continents: Africa, China, Asia, and North America, shaped like a club. Europe is dismantled by modern explosives, the taste for money and the spirit of revolt. Europe has become so ugly, but she is our mother. . . .[7]

Morand's perspective, consistent with Valéry's, recognized the paradox of a divided Europe which nonetheless was the locus of common values.

Of course, the emergence of the United States as a world power was only a part of a more general problem. Europe was also being challenged by the rise of other peoples and continents. In the eyes of Maurice Muret, for example, the greatest danger to Europe arose from the rise of the colored races. The danger from such a threat would have to be met with "a spirit of defense" on the part of members of the white race.[8] For Henri Massis, on the other hand, the menace to Europe's future came from the East. However, the solution to the problem was similar. As the title of his volume suggested, the *Défense de l'Occident* would require a coordination of efforts of the European peoples.

As French spokesmen came increasingly to focus on threats from outside of Europe, whether from the United States or elsewhere, they recognized that their own problems were indistinguishable from those of other European countries. The American assault was as clearly directed against Germany and Britain as it was against France. "The American viewpoint," claimed Luc Durtain, "spreads like a religion, or rather . . . conquers whole continents like a simplistic and abbreviated Islam."[9] It was, of course, the future of the European continent which most intensely concerned Durtain. "In our refined European countries," he observed, individuals and couples "are seduced by the American example."[10] The transnational character of Americanization also struck André Siegfried, who regarded its growth as "the great problem of the present generation in Europe."[11] Georges Duhamel expressed this continental perspective in its most urgent form. "We can no longer doubt that this civilization

[America] has the capacity for and is in the process of conquering the Old World."[12]

The American threat not only stimulated the rise of European consciousness, but it helped to bring about the movement for the unification of Europe. Indeed, there was considerable overlap between the advocates of unification and the opponents of Americanization. Herriot, Briand, Valéry, Romier, and Jules Romains all supported the efforts to achieve unification, and all were concerned about the rising influence of Americanism. This parallel development was logical enough. If, indeed, Europe was suffering from extra-European influences, then the power to resist them could be found in the unification of the Continent.

The movement for unification, like the development of the belief in a common European consciousness, awaited the partial healing of wounds inflicted by the war. As Albert Thibaudet remarked in 1925, "It is just now that the idea of Europe appears timidly like a flag half unsheathed."[13] In reality, the idea was already two years old. It was first developed by a Viennese citizen, Count Coudenhove-Kalergi, who published his Manifesto for Pan-Europe in 1923, but it took a year or two for the idea to spread. Like his French followers, Coudenhove-Kalergi based his argument for a united Europe on the existence of impressive extra-European forces which must be contained if Europe was to survive as a center of power in the world. In his "Open Letter to French Parliamentarians," the count argued that European hegemony was being undermined by three major forces: the Soviet Union, the British Empire, and the United States. The connection between the rising European movement and the perception of an American threat was evident in January of 1925 when Herriot shouted before the French Parliament, "My greatest desire is one day to witness the appearance of a United States of Europe";[14] his speech followed by only a few days Senator Marin's denunciation of American efforts to collect the war debt.

The parallel development of anti-Americanism and the movement for European unity continued through the late twenties. In October of 1926, just six months after the signing of the Mellon-Bérenger agreement, a Pan-Europe Congress assembled in Vienna, bringing together statesmen and men of letters who had demonstrated a concern for the future of Europe. In 1929, the movement for unification reached its climax with Aristide Briand's proposal for a "kind of federal link" between the European nations. Briand later explained that his proposal was consistent with the maintenance of national sovereignty; nonetheless, it marked the first time a government official had publicly embraced the concept of European unification.[15] Briand's appeal preceded by just a few months the publication of Duhamel's *Scènes de la vie future*, which brought to a climax the anti-American campaign in France. The summer of 1929 was also the occasion for the signing of the Young Plan, the culmination of the Franco-German rapprochement.

In the discussion of rising American influence in Europe, the idea of European unity played an important role. There were a variety of strategies which could be applied to remedy Europe's problem, and all of them involved some form of unification. At one end of the spectrum, there were advocates of a European federation which would resist the United States by making over Europe in the image of America. At the other end were the supporters of an all-out resistance to modernization, based on a recognition of the superiority of European, that is, traditional culture. In between were those who favored the acceptance of some of the new technology as long as it could be reconciled with the cultural ideals of Europe. All of the strategists found themselves trying to delineate the values which were distinctively European, and therefore basic to the European community.

The vision of the new Europe which emerged from the work of André Siegfried and Lucien Romier attempted to strike a balance between the traditional European economy and the new American methods. As Romier suggested in his discussion of the conflict between European and American ways, the new machines had their place in the world, but it had to be clearly defined:

The master of the world will be the "civilized" man who knows how to employ the machine to his own ends, and not the "proletarian" seeking within the machine the secret of civilization.

With these considerations in mind the issue of the contest is still open either to Europe or America.

It will be decided and won by the mother of the family and the school. The future belongs to the best school and the best family which will be capable, despite the machine, of furnishing human energy with a purpose and a justification other than that merely of eating and drinking.[16]

The real danger which Romier saw in the machine was the stimulus it gave to the growth of materialism. In the concern for producing more and better goods, man might forget that life was endowed with a higher purpose. Romier therefore recommended that the adoption of American methods be severely limited in order to prevent them from destroying European values. "It is necessary to limit [American influence] not out of hostility to others, but to affirm a common respect for the same laws of reason, the same hierarchy of values, the same methods in the search for knowledge and in judgment."[17] The ultimate guide to the extent of Americanization for Romier was the European tradition. As long as old values were not undermined, American methods could be tolerated. Beyond a certain point, however, Americanism would inevitably subvert these values.

André Siegfried approached the problem of Americanization in a similar vein. He warned against the unrestrained imitation of American methods, which was advocated by some of his compatriots:

Some who are eager to rejuvenate industrial Europe look to America for inspiration and guidance; but others hold back, deeming the past superior and preferable. . . . In the light of the American contrast we see that material pursuits have not entirely absorbed the soul of Europe and that it can still appreciate free and disinterested thought and spiritual joys which can often be obtained only by renouncing comfort and fortune.[18]

Siegfried here noted with approval the traditional institutions which helped to combat materialism. Nonetheless, he made it clear elsewhere that the proper mix of modernism with traditional ways was not only necessary but desirable. Indeed, the genius of Europe consisted in its capacity for adapting new ways to old. The best solution to the present dilemma was to adopt "an intermediary position between the extreme Orient and the extreme Occident."[19] Couched in geographer's language, this statement articulated a set of values for the European community. Europe would adopt a moderate position, accepting progress as long as it could be reconciled with spiritual and intellectual concerns.

The opposition to Americanism in the work of Siegfried and

Romier was designed to combat the results of these methods in the United States rather than the methods per se. Siegfried and Romier might have accepted an unlimited adherence to mass production if this system had not produced unfortunate effects in other areas. The individual and the family were most severely affected, in their judgment. While Romier claimed that there was a contest under way between Europe and America to see which could endow the machine with a purpose, he made it quite clear that America was already overwhelmed by materialism. If the family and the school were the standards by which the success of a civilization in turning its energies toward higher purposes was to be judged, then America had already lost the contest. As Romier remarked, "The family is indeed the moot question; it is verily the exposed flank of American civilization."[20] In effect, Europe remained the only contestant which had not yet succumbed to materialism. To avoid the pitfalls of the new methods, Europe would have to permit its elite to assume leadership.[21] Only then would the demands of the great masses for material satisfaction be resisted.

Siegfried's condemnation of Americanism was focused on the same areas as Romier's. He argued that "Americanization in the ong run tends to atrophy the family and reduce the individual's originality."[22] Because of this tendency, it would be necessary to adopt the new methods slowly and integrate them into the culture. Fortunately, Europe and France were better equipped than the United States to maintain humane values. "Among the European peoples, the French are the most conscious of the nature of the individual and of men. . . . It is still our function in the debate on the rise of the new humanity to defend man considered as an individual."[23]

While both Siegfried and Romier placed considerable importance on the existence of a European consciousness, neither was prepared to advocate the creation of a political union of European countries. Their restraint in this regard was consistent with their belief that Europe might selectively adopt American ways without endangering basic values. What was needed was not radical political solutions, but certain changes in the European economy, which would help European businessmen compete with their American counterparts. The two authors agreed that the cartel movement, designed to concentrate production in a given industry in the hands of a small number of corporations without regard to national boundaries, was a logical first step.[24] It might ultimately lead to "a political federation or tariff union," but that was, in Siegfried's view, "a solution for the future which is still utopian."[25] In the meantime, the most important task was for Europeans to achieve intellectual unity by defining their own values against those which emerged from the American experience.

The solution to Europe's spiritual problems could not be achieved without the guidance of an elite. By its very nature, however, mass society undermined the traditional elite which was the guardian of Europe's cultural achievements. Unless this elite could be protected against the ravages of the new system, European culture was obviously threatened. The natural response of French critics was to defend the value of an elite, particularly an intellectual elite. Gaston Riou maintained that "the presence of a clergy, spontaneous or organized, free or official, capable of maintaining within the body of the citizens the spirit of fraternity is essential for a legitimate democracy because of its spiritual character."[26] To strengthen the elite against the power of the masses, solidarity within national boundaries was necessary but not sufficient. Many critics urged the unity of elites across national boundaries, consistent with the newly discovered unity of the European spirit.[27] Even then, according to Lucien Romier, the elites could only protect spiritual values if they understood the operation of the new technology. This paradox reflected Romier's conviction that the consumer society was inevitable. The only question was the goals which it would serve. In an age of growing economic equality, French critics preached the salvation of European society through the leadership of a social elite committed to spiritual values.

A far more negative response to Americanism was articulated in the work of Georges Duhamel, Luc Durtain, and Paul Morand. It was accompanied by a more fervent defense of traditional values than either Siegfried or Romier could muster and by a stronger expression of allegiance to the whole European continent. The rejection of all aspects of Americanism was urged without qualification by Georges Duhamel. "At this point in the debate, let each of us denounce the American items which he finds in his house, in his wardrobe, and in his soul."[28] The systematic opposition to modernization was followed logically by an endorsement of the traditional aspects of

French life. Duhamel began by praising the diversity of French agriculture:

I was born in a country whose soul, inhabitants, and products are diverse, motley, changing, and ingenious. From milk, this simple and elementary food, we Frenchmen know how to make more than 100 kinds of cheese. All are good, healthy, strong, substantial, and amusing. All have their history, character, and role. In this feature alone, I recognize the genius of my country, in it I understand that she has produced so many great men in all professions.

I belong to a peasant people which has cultivated lovingly for centuries 50 different plums and which finds in each one a deliciously incomparable taste.[29]

The diversity of French agriculture reminded Duhamel of the corresponding variety of the human landscape in France. It was this precious heritage which was threatened with annihilation if American methods were introduced in France. While Siegfried and Romier supposed that the machine could be adapted to European as well as American values, Duhamel assumed that technology would destroy individual differences in Europe, as it had already done in the United States.

The new methods were not only devastating to products of the soil, but they threatened important social institutions as well. Duhamel feared that the French café might succumb to the requirements of efficiency, if France should accept modernization:

Will you disappear some day, little bistros of our land, little low rooms, warm and smoky, where three chaps, shoulder to shoulder, around a low iron table, gorge themselves on Burgundy beef, tell each other stories, and laugh by thunder! while swilling wine?[30]

The survival of the bistro and of French agricultural life were, in turn, dependent on the future of the French peasant. Duhamel's appreciation of this element of the French population was immeasurably enhanced by his stay in America. After an exhausting day in which Duhamel did battle with the noise and speed of life in Philadelphia, he retired to his hotel room. In rebellion against the urban experience, he announced his allegiance to the peasantry:

Inspire me, French peasants, you whose virtues resemble defects, whom I have often scoffed at, whose history is composed entirely of patience, reserve, economy, and finesse. Inspire me, because I am alone among these foreigners. Fathers, come to my aid![31]

Comforted in his hour of need by the memory of a more attractive way of life, Duhamel, with his day's misery apparently behind him, lay down to sleep. In the middle of the night, he awoke with a start, bathed in perspiration. He had been dreaming of the standardized manufacture of flowers, the next step in the application of American methods.

Duhamel's systematic aversion to modernization was shared by Paul Morand and Luc Durtain, although the tone which they adopted was somewhat less hysterical than Duhamel's. Durtain appeared to leave the door open to limited use of the machine when he argued that "French society ought to be the last to accept universal mechanization."[32] In fact, his invitation to readers to search out American influences in their own homes suggested that he too was uncompromising in his rejection of the new technology.

The case of Paul Morand is even more deceptive. His enthusiasm for the newness and vulgarity of New York might very well be taken for an endorsement of modernism. In reality, he rejected New York as a model for French life, and he refused to accept the view that "France has no alternative [but] to become American or Bolshevik." Indeed, he urged his compatriots to "exert all our strength to avoid these abysses." The proper model for Frenchmen to adopt in charting their future course could be found at home. It was "the spirit of Paris, which is precisely that of a meticulous artist."[33]

While these bitter critics of American civilization were also adamant spokesmen of a European consciousness, they were not particularly interested in a European political union. In certain respects, such a union would have contradicted their basic values, especially the belief in a diversity of cultures. Against the monotony of modern American life, the extreme critics of modernization could propose the example of a European continent which had a variety of cultures, all of which, nonetheless, respected certain underlying principles. To create a political union was to raise the specter of homogenizing this diversity, after the fashion of the Americans. Aron and Dandieu argued that the best way to combat modernization was to urge "the diversity of countries and cultures which have slowly promoted to the rank of supreme value the power of the specifically human creative spirit against the will of the states and diplomats."[34] Only by avoiding a strong central authority could Europe save itself from the fate of America.

It was precisely this position which Edouard Herriot and Charles Pomaret were attempting to refute by proposing a European political union. In their view, the only way for Europe to resist the United States was to beat the Americans at their own game. Pomaret explained that "Europe is a continent in decline. Before her very eyes lies a prosperous continent. Instead of accusing or scoffing at our triumphant rival America, why don't we seek, through her example, the instrument of our recovery—and our revenge?"[35] America could serve as a model for France in several respects. At the political level, Europeans would do well to imitate the federalist principle which created a unified nation out of quarreling states. At the economic level, the vast American market should become a model for a Europe-wide customs union. With tariff barriers eliminated, European manufacturers could sell their products to a larger population than American corporations served. The European common market would also encourage the movement toward the concentration of industries and the adoption of American methods. In this regard, the American multinational corporation would serve as a model.[36] Both developments were essential if European corporations were to compete with their American counterparts. These changes in European social, economic, and political institutions were to be accomplished, however, without succumbing to American values. Europe, said Herriot, "will defend a concept of life different from what was, until now at least, the American ideal."[37] In short, Herriot believed that Europe could undertake these momentous changes without falling prey to American materialism and conformity.

On the surface, at least, the position adopted by Herriot and Pomaret was remarkably pro-American in character. The imitation of American ways in so many areas seemed to offer an implicit endorsement of the American experience. Yet, both authors defended themselves carefully against such a charge. Their ultimate aim was the preservation of Europe as an independent political system, free from American control. Moreover, they were both convinced that this revolutionary enterprise could be undertaken while still preserving the allegiance to certain values which were peculiarly European.

Despite important disagreements on the vision of a European future, critics in all three camps shared a common fear of the decline of Europe based in large part on the rise of extra-European powers. Central to their work was the conviction that there existed a common European consciousness which could be defined in contrast to the American experience. As a counterpart of the campaign against Americanism in Europe, they asserted the necessity of preserving the unique European values. They could agree with Gaston Riou that "Europe should not Americanize, Britainize, or Russify herself. Europe must remain Europe."[38] Some authors placed greater stress on political unity, others on the affirmation of a European culture. For many, political and cultural independence were related issues.

The movement for European unity rose along with the Franco-German rapprochement and the fear of extra-European threats. It is hardly surprising that when these conditions changed abruptly after 1929, the impetus for a European political union should be radically undercut. After 1931, it became clear that America was too preoccupied with her own economic crisis to be able to dominate the European economy. In the same year, the proposed Austro-German customs union, and the consequent agitation in France, ended any prospect of continued collaboration between the two countries. In the wake of these changes, the talk of a common European consciousness and the need for unity continued, but on a far more limited scale.

In 1934, looking back over the period since the war, Georges Duhamel spoke for many individuals of his generation when he said, "It was during the war that we developed a strong consciousness of Europe. With my friends, with Jules Romains, I shouted, 'Europe, in this frenzy [the war] you must not die,' and when the war was over, we devoted ourselves to the destiny, to the salvation of Europe."[39] For Duhamel and others, the struggle against American methods was an important phase of their effort to preserve European culture. By 1933, however, with the United States in the midst of a full-scale depression and the Nazis in power, anti-Americanism no longer seemed an appropriate strategy for saving Europe. The struggle for Europe would continue, but on a different basis.

## NOTES

1. André Philip, *Le problème ouvrier aux Etats-Unis* (Paris, 1927), ix.

2. "L'Europe de demain," *Europe Nouvelle* (August 1, 1925), 1016. Nonetheless, three periodicals were founded in the immediate postwar period with the word "Europe" as part of their titles. In addition to *Europe Nouvelle*, there was Romain Rolland's *Europe* and *La Revue Européene*.

3. Jean Prévost, *Histoire de France depuis la guerre* (Paris, 1932), 177.

4. "Germanism" referred to the spirit of aggression which was supposed to be a fundamental aspect of German culture. According to French critics, the philosophy of Nietzsche and Wagner, both popular in Germany, was responsible for the preoccupation with conquest. The change in the French view of Germany after 1924 can be seen in the expression of concern about the predominance of American finance in Germany by J. L. Chastanet, *L'Oncle Shylock* (Paris, 1927), 112, and by Charles Pomaret, who believed the Americans were "prepared to buy" Germany, *L'Amérique à la conquête de l'Europe* (Paris, 1931), 135. As early as 1924, a few French industrialists even professed a desire for marketing agreements with their German counterparts in the steel industry. Stephen Schuker, *The End of French Predominance in Europe* (Chapel Hill, 1976), 233-234; and Charles Maier, *Recasting Bourgeois Europe* (Princeton, 1975), 406-411.

5. Two respondents to the *Figaro* poll which explored the rise of Americanism in Europe, Robert Valéry-Radot and Georges de Cardonnel, pointed out that the new threat from the United States was not perceived in France until Germanism had declined as the focus of French fears. Gerard de Catalogne, *Dialogue entre Deux Mondes* (Paris, 1931), 126, 209.

6. *Quelques notes d'U.S.A.* (Paris, 1928), 17. Maurice Muret argued that because nationalism was outdated, "one must think by continents." *Le crépuscule des nations blancs* (Paris, 1925), 223.

7. Quoted in André Siegfried, *Qu'est-ce que l'Amérique* (Paris, 1938), 7.

8. *Le crépuscule des nations blancs*, 223.

9. *Quelques notes d'U.S.A.*, 108.

10. *Ibid.*, 109.

11. "L'Europe devant la civilisation américaine," *Revue des Deux Mondes* (April 15, 1930), 757.

12. *Scènes de la vie future* (Paris, 1930), 19.

13. "L'Europe de demain," *Europe Nouvelle* (August 1, 1925), 1016. The

founding of *La Revue de l'Allemagne* in 1927 by leading intellectuals on both sides of the Rhine was an important symbol of improving relations between the two countries. Jules Romains, Jean Giraudoux, Ernst Curtius, and Thomas Mann all contributed to the new journal.

14. J. B. Duroselle, *L'Idée de l'Europe dans l'histoire* (Paris, 1965), 274.

15. The Briand proposal was presented to other governments in the form of an official memorandum, which received equivocal responses. The Assembly of the league created a committee to study European unification in 1930. In the next two years, the league committee met six times, but its work was seriously hampered by the depression as well as deteriorating relations between the European powers. Its last meeting was held in September of 1932.

While the movement for the unification of Europe at the political level has received much attention, there were serious efforts to promote economic unity as well. In addition to the efforts of businessmen to further the cartel movement, Gaston Riou and others formed the Comité d'action pour une Union Douanière Européene in 1926 in pursuit of a common market on the Continent. Francis Delaisi also led a movement to promote a common agricultural policy for Europe.

16. *Who Will Be Master, Europe or America?* (New York, 1928), 299.

17. *Nation et civilisation* (Paris, 1926), 104.

18. *Les Etats-Unis d'aujourd'hui* (Paris, 1927), 351.

19. *La crise de l'Europe* (Paris, 1935), 116.

20. *Who Will Be Master*, 210.

21. *Nation et civilisation*, 104.

22. *Les Etats-Unis d'aujourd'hui*, 22.

23. André Philip, *Le problème ouvrier*, xi.

24. *Nation et civilisation*, 98.

25. "L'Europe devant la civilisation américaine," *Revue des Deux Mondes* (April 15, 1930), 765.

26. *Europe, ma patrie* (Paris, 1928), 41.

27. The first and foremost spokesman for the new role of a European elite was Lucien Romier. In both *Explication de notre temps* (Paris, 1925), 286, and *Nation et civilisation*, 165-167, he argued the case for the elite. His arguments were cited by other writers including Maurice Muret, *Le crépuscule des nations blancs*, 231; and Henri Massis, *Défense de l'Occident* (Paris, 1927), 257.

28. *Scènes de la vie future*, 19.

29. *Ibid.*, 231.

30. *Ibid.*, 210.

31. *Ibid.*, 216.

32. *Quelques notes d'U.S.A.*, 109.

33. *New-York* (Paris, 1930), 122, 116.

34. *Le cancer américain* (Paris, 1931), 244-245.

35. *L'Amérique à la conquête de l'Europe* (Paris, 1932), 213. Pomaret's argument bears a striking resemblance to the ideas of Jean-Jacques Servan-Schreiber in *Le défi américain* (Paris, 1968). Both writers sought to stem the American tide by exploiting American technology.

36. It is interesting to note that one of the leading French proponents of this view was Ernest Mercier, a French businessman, who came to the United States in 1925 as the guest of General Electric. After returning to France, he became president of the French Pan-Europe committee and an advocate of American technology under European control.

A Europe-wide strategy to prevent American domination was promoted by Jean Allary as a solution to the economic problems of the French and European film industries. He maintained that "the dispersion of capital in Europe, and the struggle between the various jealous and hostile national markets prolongs the inferiority of the old continent." "Hollywood menaçant, ou le problème du contingentement," *Europe Nouvelle* (May 11, 1929), 603.

37. *Europe* (Paris, 1930), 221-222.

38. *Europe, ma patrie*, 24.

39. *Entretiens: L'avenir de l'esprit Européen* (Librairie Stock, 1934), 128.

# PART VI:

## And After, 1933–1976

# chapter 15

# The Roosevelt Revolution: French Observers and the New Deal

> During the decade following World War I, a careful observer might well have feared the spiritual secession of America from European civilization. Certain New World countries, after establishing their political independence and reasonable autonomy in the economic sphere, apparently dreamed of abandoning completely western civilization in order to seek a new destiny. . . . Since the onset of economic disorder, this threat has lost much of its force.
> —Georges Duhamel, 1937

"The stereotypes which nourished opinion up to 1940 and which condition the whole process of later Americanization," remarked Cyrille Arnavon, can be attributed to "the writings of French travelers returning from America" between the wars.[1] Indeed, the influence of the anti-American views of the twenties on French observers of the New Deal and post-World War II America was decisive. The work of Georges Duhamel, André Siegfried, and other authorities of the twenties provided an orientation to America for French travelers during the next twenty years.

The new observers of America, however, lacked the conviction of their predecessors. The clarity and emphasis which had been given to the American image by critics in the twenties seemed inappropriate to the new travelers. They were particularly uneasy about the unqualified opposition which their predecessors had perceived between the American and French ways of life. As Pierre Lyautey, a French observer of the thirties, put it, "The mistake of our reporters was to insist on finding in America the Americanism which was also spreading in Europe. . . . The French public was thus sometimes deceived about America. . . . A legend was created which could be summarized as follows: America is the country of standardization."[2]

The desire of French observers from 1933 to 1947 to maintain the old image of America and at the same time to qualify, if not to repudiate, the opposition between French and American civilizations may be explained by the contradictory nature of developments in the thirties and forties, as they were interpreted by observers. Among the most important "events" was the established image of America which was inherited from the twenties. The clarity and emphasis of that image helped to sustain it amidst the confusing events of the next two decades. At the same time, the clarity of the image posed problems. It was virtually impossible to reconcile certain events with such a narrowly defined conception of America. In fact, French critics found themselves simultaneously accepting the old image and rejecting it out of hand.

Among the events which, from the perspective of French observers, threatened the old image of America was the depression. French critics of the twenties had placed great weight on the materialism of the American people in a period of enormous prosperity. They took a particularly jaundiced view of this prosperity because it elevated the American nation to a position of power at the very moment that France, in the aftermath of the war, was losing her own status as a world power. The depression modified this situation considerably. The material prosperity of individual Americans suffered while American power on the international scene declined. Americans withdrew some of their investments from Europe. As the nation became preoccupied with curing the depression at home, less attention was paid to international affairs. The issues of debts and disarmament, which had created such acrimonious feeling between the two countries in the twenties, were raised infrequently after 1933. No settlement had been found for either of these questions, but American pressure on France to fulfill her obligations lessened substantially after 1933.

One event over which Americans had little or no control also challenged the French image of America. Hitler's rise to power in 1933 ended the belief that a united Europe in some form could be

achieved in the near future. The period of Franco-German rapprochement which lasted from Locarno to the depression coincided
with the rise of anti-Americanism. During that period, America
replaced Germany to some degree as the focus of French hostility.
After 1933, such a conception had to be revised. With the approach of
World War II, it became clear that if France was to defend herself
against German aggression, American aid would be essential. The
actual American entry into the war in 1941 brought the relationship
between France and America almost full circle to the entente of
1917. The major difference was that there were two French governments each of which claimed to be the legitimate representative of
the French people, thereby complicating the American task of supporting one or the other or both. In any event, the fact that France
and America again had a common enemy could not help but cast
doubts on the conception of America as a power diametrically opposed to the interests and values of France—DeGaulle's claims to the
contrary, notwithstanding.

Of course, none of these developments directly affected either the
development of mass society in the United States or the puritan
character of American civilization. American factories did not abandon mass production, nor did American citizens cease to attend
movies. To a certain degree, it could even be argued that the New
Deal reinforced the collectivist instincts of the American people by
encouraging large organization as a way of dealing with the depression. Of course, mass society in the context of the depression appeared less materialistic to French observers than it did during
prosperity.

French critics wavered somewhat in their belief that American
civilization was under Anglo-Saxon control. The repeal of Prohibition
helped to blur the old image. The passage of time served to diminish
French concern over immigration restriction. In addition, the belief
in Anglo-Saxon domination was weakened by the greater recognition
given to ethnic minorities in the Roosevelt administration. Nonetheless, most French observers continued to assert that the ethos of both
Roosevelt and the country at large remained essentially Anglo-Saxon.
Frenchmen still pointed to the innocence of the American character,
the anti-intellectual inclinations of Americans, and their ethnic
prejudices. Here was ample evidence of continuity between the

United States of the twenties and America in the depression and the period after the war.

The early observers of the New Deal, then, found evidence to support the anti-American views of their predecessors in the twenties as well as evidence which refuted those views. To resolve the apparent conflict in the evidence, they adopted two strategies. On the one hand, they continued to argue that America was a mass society under Anglo-Saxon control. On the other, they attempted to repudiate the image of the twenties and to contend that the New Deal was a revolutionary development which returned the United States to the idealism of its earlier years. The tension between these two claims was never fully resolved in the thirties.

Among French observers who came to investigate the future of Americanism were a number of professional journalists: Pierre Lyautey of *Le Matin* and Raymond Recouly of *Le Temps*, both large conservative Paris dailies, and three correspondents of liberal dailies—Georges Boris of *Le Quotidien*, Robert de Saint-Jean of Paris *Soir*, and Emmanuel Bourcier of *l'Intransigeant*. All collected their observations into book-length studies.

The most prestigious Frenchmen to witness and describe the New Deal were three future members of the French Academy: André Maurois, Jules Romains, and André Siegfried. Maurois's visit to the United States in 1933 was his third in five years, while Romains, who taught at Mills College in the summer of 1936, had seen America in silent dismay twelve years earlier. André Siegfried persisted in his long-standing interest in the United States as did Bernard Faÿ, who visited America for the twenty-second time in 1935.

There were three other observers of the New Deal who had traveled extensively in America before the depression. Two advocates of mass production and the assembly line, Hyacinthe Dubreuil and Emile Schreiber,[3] returned to see how the depression had affected modern technology, while Bertrand de Jouvenel, who was later to become an enthusiastic defender of modernization, witnessed the end of Hoover's administration and the early days of the New Deal.

Taken as a group, these observers practiced a variety of occupations including journalism, writing novels and biography, teaching, and labor organizing. Various positions on the political spectrum, ranging from moderate socialism on the left to conservative republicanism on the right, were represented. Moreover, conditions and timing of the visits were also diverse. The duration of the trips to America varied from a month to a year; some observers came as early as 1933, while others arrived only in 1936. Some came to teach, others as tourists, and still others as reporters.

Despite these differences of circumstances, predispositions, and interests, however, certain patterns emerged from the discussion of the New Deal. All of the travelers agreed that it constituted a major change in the American system. No less than three authors proclaimed the Roosevelt administration "revolutionary" in their titles. Pierre Lyautey discovered *La révolution américaine*; Georges Boris reported on *La révolution Roosevelt*;[4] and Robert de Saint-Jean considered *La vraie révolution de Roosevelt*.[5] In addition, Bertrand de Jouvenel entitled two of his chapters devoted to the New Deal "La révolution des idées," and "La révolution des faits."[6] Moreover, the contents, if not the titles, of other French reports on the New Deal indicated that their authors regarded the Roosevelt administration as an important departure from the American tradition.

For French observers, the change wrought by the New Deal was not to be measured in the number and scope of legislative enactments. The passage of laws was only the outward manifestation of significant changes of a less tangible nature which were occurring in the realm of American values. Robert de Saint-Jean argued:

The real revolution of Mr. Roosevelt, the one which he has pushed farther than the others, is of a psychological order. This revolution would be complete if people no longer waited for the golden age, if Americans stopped dreaming of fabulous fortunes, and coveted only honest comfort. . . . In any case, no one thinks of denying that the President has awakened American idealism; he has denounced in his compatriots what we French designate simply and sometimes wrongly with the pejorative term of Americanism.[7]

From Saint-Jean's point of view, the most significant feature of the New Deal was its deliberate effort to reform American values. President Roosevelt was in apparent accord with the campaign against Americanism, which French critics had begun in the twenties.

Saint-Jean's conception of the struggle waged by Roosevelt against "Americanism" was cast in the terms which Roosevelt had chosen in his first inaugural speech. Christ was driving the money changers from the temple. The American people, who once accepted the "promises of the sovereign tempter, the Satan of Wall Street, who strews at the feet of the skyscrapers the treasures of the World" were now prepared to join Roosevelt in a holy war against materialism.[8] This was evident in other facets of public life in the United States. Saint-Jean devoted a chapter of his book to the struggle of "Savonarole contre Morgan" in which he applauded the radio campaign of Father Coughlin against the leading figures of American capitalism, with special focus on J. P. Morgan, Jr. For Saint-Jean, the New Deal was a modern version of the Christian revolt against pagan values.

Saint-Jean's view of the Roosevelt administration was corroborated by the reports of other observers in somewhat different terms. This was evident in Bernard Faÿ's remarks on the significance of the election of 1932. "After the intoxication of prosperity, happiness, science, and expansion in all directions, the United States enters a difficult period where she must learn to appreciate more fully the pleasures of intelligence, discipline, and choice. The election of 1932 is not simply a defeat for Mr. Hoover, or Wall Street, or optimism *à la Ford*, but also for the machine and science."[9] The political and economic aspects of the election seemed far less important to Faÿ than the apparent repudiation of old values. Faÿ's endorsement of this change was made clear by his selection of chapter titles. The twenties were described in a unit called "l'Amérique perdue," while the chapter on the New Deal was entitled "l'Amérique se retrouve." Faÿ was particularly impressed by the willingness of the United States to devalue the dollar. Although the Roosevelt administration certainly hoped that this measure would stimulate the economy and return the country to a condition of prosperity, Faÿ applauded devaluation because it proved that Americans were now indifferent to material possessions.[10] Human needs took precedence over property.

In Bertrand de Jouvenel's opinion, the revolution which the New Deal had brought about consisted largely in the newfound concern among Americans for the public as opposed to the private domain:

For a Frenchman, the most astonishing characteristic of America in 1931 was the absence of any patriotism in the ruling classes. Bankers, professors, and politicians all appeared to feel no responsibility for the destinies of the nation. This indifference was not caused by egotism, but rather by a universal timidity. . . . Roosevelt has created a national mentality, a civic spirit transcending local borders.[11]

Unlike Faÿ and Saint-Jean, Jouvenel did not maintain that materialism had been overcome by the New Deal, but he did agree that the selfish concern of individuals for their own interests had been diminished. In this sense, Jouvenel was also describing a change in values.

Another way of characterizing the revolution was to speak of the shift in power from Wall Street to Washington. Jouvenel dramatized this development in his description of the hearings of the Senate Banking and Currency Committee. Ironically, these hearings had been instituted with the blessing of President Hoover, but their findings reached the public just as Roosevelt was taking office. The most dramatic revelation at the hearings was the fact that J. P. Morgan, Jr., had paid no income tax in the United States between 1929 and 1933. This information was elicited from Morgan by the committee counsel, Ferdinand Pecora, a Sicilian immigrant, which seemed to establish symbolically the shift in power from Wall Street bankers to the new rulers in Washington representing the lower and lower-middle classes.[12]

Other observers remarked on the emergence of Washington as a new center of power in the American system. Pierre Lyautey entitled one of his chapters "Qui sera le maître: Washington ou New-York?" After examining the question in the light of the events of 1933, Lyautey concluded that Wall Street's domination of American life was at an end.[13] The same issue was raised in other terms by Robert de Saint-Jean. He contrasted the indifference among Americans to the whole political process in the twenties with the new interest in the activities in Washington. It was evident to him that the exclusive concern for the pursuit of wealth was a thing of the past.[14]

Bernard Faÿ called attention to still another aspect of the shift in power which occurred in 1933. The struggle between Morgan and Pecora, which Bertrand de Jouvenel had found so revealing, concealed a somewhat different lesson for Faÿ: "Mr. Pecora, a good Italian, was transplanted in his youth from the laughing shores of the Mediterranean to the frigid coasts of the Atlantic, but he is still gifted with the eloquence which formerly inspired Cicero and which still today gives distinction to Mussolini. Mr. Pecora began torturing Mr. Morgan. The Italian verb, the proletarian zeal, and the political skill" were all weapons designed to undermine Anglo-Saxon domination.[15] In effect, the struggle against materialism was heightened by the ethnic conflict. The victory of Washington over Wall Street, of Pecora over Morgan, of idealism over materialism was also the beginning of the decline of Anglo-Saxon control in America.

The revolutionary character of the New Deal was confirmed as well by the creation of the Brain Trust. Most French observers were delighted and surprised by the role of the intellectual in Roosevelt's administration. Once again, the contrast of the present with the twenties was enlightening. The former dominance of businessmen was attributed by Bernard Faÿ to the nation's value system; Americans preferred action to thought. The collapse of the economy, however, destroyed the prestige of the business classes. Their inability to find a solution to the depression forced Americans to seek help from other quarters. The Brain Trust, according to Faÿ, provided the President with new ideas without restricting his freedom of movement. More important, "the underhanded blow which the upper bourgeoisie hoped to strike against him [Roosevelt] was parried by a few small professors."[16] They not only strengthened the impression that the new administration was creating a moral revolution against the reign of materialism, but also increased the power of the New Deal to curb big business.

The ideological alliance of the Brain Trust with the little man was also praised by Pierre Lyautey, who accordingly characterized the Roosevelt government as "popular and intellectual." Lyautey, like Faÿ, saw the intellectuals as an instrument to attack the interests of big business. The new power of the Brain Trust suggested the commitment of the nation to intellectual rather than material concerns.[17]

A few travelers expressed mild reservations about the role of intellectuals in the New Deal. André Maurois was somewhat dubious about the efforts of professors—as opposed to more practical men— to seek solutions for complex economic problems.[18] Nonetheless, Maurois and other French observers, who were themselves "intellectuals," identified with an administration which gave both power and prestige to Americans of similar professional backgrounds. The Brain Trust was just one of a number of factors which convinced French travelers that Roosevelt had brought about a revolution in American life.

The New Deal affected not only the character of the government in Washington and the business classes, but made its deepest mark on the attitudes of ordinary Americans. These attitudes could be measured, as Jules Romains suggested, by attempting to describe "the human atmosphere, or—to borrow an expression that Maurois has brought into fashion—the change in the moral and social climate."[19] In the twenties, Frenchmen had identified the typical American as a Babbitt. Now, according to Luc Durtain, America had entered the age of Roosevelt.[20] Smugness and optimism were no longer the trademarks of the American character. André Siegfried noted the same transition. "Babbitt appeared to be the definitive American type just after the great war. Today, he has gone out of fashion. The jobless wanderer and the distressed student in search of a job will no doubt be antiquated in the future."[21] Siegfried tended to regard the depression as an untypical period, but admitted that it had made at least temporary marks on the national character.

André Maurois also hailed the end of the age of Babbitt and the emergence of a new America. During his first visit to the United States in 1927, Maurois strongly criticized the absence of family life and the rigid conformity of individuals to social norms. In Maurois's view, Americans were far too concerned with the acquisition of material goods, a condition which bred bland optimism among the American people.

When Maurois returned to the United States in 1931 to teach at Princeton, he claimed that the emphasis on material values, characteristic of the twenties, had disappeared; Americans now understood suffering, which made them more sympathetic to the problems of Europe.[22] Maurois also noted the development of a more reflective atmosphere among ordinary Americans, the counterpart of the Brain Trust at higher levels. In the twenties, Americans "posed no problems. Thinking was suspect, dangerous, unhealthy." The depression had forced Americans to think as well as suffer. The economic crisis, however, had not created a morose atmosphere. On the contrary, with the repeal of Prohibition, America had become a more lively place. Maurois remarked with enthusiasm that "Puritanism is in retreat."[23]

It was this same decline of puritanism, related to the rise of non-Anglo-Saxon ethnic elements, which pleased Jules Romains. He thoroughly enjoyed the less refined aspects of New York including the crowds in Times Square and Coney Island. Their air of gaiety caused Romains to speak of a pervasive meridional atmosphere in Manhattan. The city had an electric climate like Nice. It could boast of a population of Mediterranean origin including Jews and Italians. "[Even] if the Irish are geographically of northern origin, their character traits and their religious and moral culture are unmarked by their origin."[24] French observers in the twenties had found Celts and Latins in the United States, but they were confronted by the overwhelming domination of the Anglo-Saxons. By 1935, the Nordic elements no longer established the tone of American life. The demise of Morgan before Pecora's onslaught found its counterpart in the American streets.

The retreat of puritanism was a logical counterpart of the decline of Anglo-Saxon influence. Romains, like Maurois, rejoiced at the repeal of Prohibition and the decline of materialism during the depression. He deplored the negative effects of Prohibition. "This absurd system had managed to destroy the daily savor of life. . . . impregnate the atmosphere with constraint and a subtle and polymorphous hypocrisy, create suspicion in the eyes of perfectly honest people and in their expression a recess of fraud." The end of Prohibition had a special importance for Frenchmen. Its enactment had indicated the hostility of Americans to French values. With its repeal, the French could once again believe in the compatibility between French and American values.

Romains was equally harsh in his condemnation of the materialism of the twenties, and for similar reasons:

The period of rising prosperity and smugness permitted no gaiety in the appearance of New York. . . . Neither a man nor a people can enjoy life if every minute of leisure granted to them is experienced as a missed opportunity to earn money. Americans, since the Crash, have lost neither their confidence nor their optimism. However, they realize that they have made mistakes and will make them again. They take themselves less seriously. They have learned the nuances of doubt and of smiling.[25]

The paradoxical assertion by French visitors that the depression was a happy era reflects their own distaste for mass production and Prohibition. Now that Americans had apparently repudiated these social constraints, they seemed to be both freer and happier as a result. So concerned were travelers with the themes of technology and race that little was said about the feelings or the condition of the millions of unemployed Americans.

The conviction of French critics that there was a decisive change in the human atmosphere in America forced them to restate their conception of the relationship between European and American civilizations. In the twenties, French critics had deplored the stress on materialism and puritanism in the United States. Now that these values were in decline, the cultural breach between the two continents seemed to disappear. As Pierre Lyautey explained, America "has built a way of life which was only known in Europe heretofore. . . . America used to be a factory. Art, Esthetics and the mind were the exclusive concerns of Europe. Now the United States is turning inward, and, in a few years, the former pupils will have developed an autonomous spiritual life requiring only exchanges with Europe."[26]

In attempting to assess the change in the American character wrought by the New Deal, French observers naturally looked to President Roosevelt himself. The personality of the president, especially in contrast to Hoover's, was striking evidence that the human atmosphere in the United States had indeed undergone a revolution. The French, of course, continued to nourish grievances against the former president for his opposition to their views on war debts as well as disarmament.[27] No doubt this disagreement accounted in part for the reaction to Hoover's defeat in 1932. "There is nobody in France who does not acclaim from the bottom of his heart the failure of Mr. Hoover. In our anguish, it is a smile, a ray of sunlight . . . the intoxicating odor of an enemy dead."[28]

Most observers focused their discussion on differences of personality between the two men. After meeting Roosevelt at a press conference, Raymond Recouly contrasted Roosevelt's warmth with Hoover's difficulties in communication. The contrast was strengthened in Recouly's mind by Roosevelt's ability to speak French. In comparison, Hoover seemed a provincial figure.[29] Even André Siegfried, who did not disguise his hostility to the inflationary objectives of the New Deal program, found Roosevelt personally attractive. "He gives the impression of a human being who understands you and wants to help you. He is extremely seductive; his smile is irresistible. When he tells you at a reception, 'I am happy to see you,' he gives the impression that he believes it, and you feel taken into his confidence."[30]

The press conference and the reception were not the only instruments by which Roosevelt conveyed to Frenchmen a sense of personal warmth. Hyacinthe Dubreuil argued that the Fireside Chat was an equally effective institution, especially because it enabled Roosevelt to appeal to the average citizen. "This is not the language of a statesman who delivers a solemn address from the top of a platform to the concentric seats of a Parliament. This is not the language of a European 'intellectual' who never forgets that he is a cultured man, and speaks a literary language which 'the man in the street' only understands in part. This is rather the calm conversation of a man speaking to his friends in some private meeting, in order to explain some difficulties, and invite them to help him to better understand them."[31]

While these judgments of individual personalities and the public mood were fundamental to the claim that a revolution was under way, Frenchmen did not entirely neglect the New Deal program itself. Indeed, a number of the bills supported by Roosevelt provided additional evidence for the French observer of the revolutionary character of the administration.

The New Deal which was described in the studies of French observers bears little resemblance to accounts of that movement by American historians. While considerable attention was given to certain phases of Roosevelt's program such as the NRA, the AAA, and monetary reforms, other developments including the CCC, TVA, and WPA were rarely mentioned.

Indeed, to many French critics the NRA was not only a central feature of the New Deal but it was considered the only important element in Roosevelt's program.[32] André Siegfried, for example, referred to the NRA as the economic solution of the thirties and contrasted it with Fordism which he regarded as the typical solution of the twenties. The NRA stressed high prices and limited production, precisely the contrary of Fordism. In analyzing the New Deal, Siegfried argued that a single policy could be identified and described as the essence of FDR's program.[33]

Other critics adopted his methods. Dubreuil entitled his volume *Les codes de Roosevelt*, and omitted most other efforts of the New Deal to solve the depression. One reason for the exaggerated importance given to the NRA is evident from Robert de Saint-Jean's chapter on "La campagne du NRA." He and others found it difficult to ignore the spectacular features of this operation, including the parades, the blue eagle, and, most of all, General Johnson and his pronouncements.[34]

French observers were quick to deny that the New Deal was tainted by any of the contemporary ideologies toward which Europeans were then turning for solutions to their problems. That Roosevelt occupied a middle ground somewhere between the extremes of communism and fascism was bound to be an attractive state of affairs for liberal and conservative observers, who admitted the necessity of reforms, but had little taste for totalitarian solutions. André Maurois saw the significance of the New Deal in precisely these terms. "For the first time, a non-revolutionary head of state has refused to tolerate the indefensible scandal by which abundance, accompanied by misery, becomes a necessary law of nature."[35]

Even those authors who considered the New Deal a revolution saw no link between the Roosevelt administration and European revolutionary movements. According to Georges Boris, all European theorists of a doctrinaire bent were bound to be hostile to the New Deal because of its experimental character. By European standards, even the members of the Brain Trust were empiricists. Boris especially cautioned his readers not to confuse Roosevelt with Hitler or Mussolini, who had no respect for the democratic tradition. The success of Roosevelt in achieving the passage of his program would not prevent the Congress from revising or eliminating parts of the New Deal.[36]

Boris's version of the nature and sources of the New Deal was accepted without qualification by Saint-Jean and Romains. According to Saint-Jean, the New Dealers' methods bore no resemblance to Cartesian rationalism, or any other European system. Both authors agreed that Roosevelt's program was rooted in the American tradition of pioneer empiricism.[37] Moreover, despite accusations to the contrary, Roosevelt was no totalitarian. Saint-Jean explained: "Mr. Roosevelt has strengthened the state without enslaving man. The blue eagle ought not to be confused with the swastika or the hammer and sickle."[38]

If most French critics were relieved that the Roosevelt "revolution" was being conducted in a democratic fashion, many were pleased to note that capitalism had survived the crisis. Indeed, Dubreuil believed that the NRA codes were designed to aid the recovery of the free enterprise system, rather than destroy it.[39] His fellow advocate of assembly-line techniques, Emile Schreiber, evidently agreed. Schreiber was particularly impressed by the absence of violence and class hatred in 1934, despite the upheaval which the American system was undergoing.[40]

Only one aspect of the New Deal program drew consistent criticism from French travelers. Almost all conservatives objected to the inflationary schemes of the administration. André Siegfried referred to the "mad policy of spending and government subsidies" undertaken by Roosevelt,[41] while André Maurois refused to believe that these policies helped the United States to recover from the depression.[42] Somewhat more extreme was Lucien Page, who devoted an entire volume to a critique of the devaluation of the dollar.[43] With the exception of Page and Siegfried, however, disapproval of particular reforms rarely led to a condemnation of the entire New Deal. As an alternative to communism and fascism, the Roosevelt administration elicited the sympathy of most French observers.

It is understandable that French critics would see in the New Deal a uniquely American phenomenon, rooted in the American tradition. In the early thirties, the contrast between the Roosevelt administration and Hitler and Stalin must have seemed striking indeed. What is far less clear is how the American tradition could have generated such a revolution, especially considering the French belief that American civilization before the New Deal had been synonymous with materialism. The supposed source of the revolution, pioneer empiricism, had been blamed by French critics for generating the exclusive interest in mass production which had characterized American life in the twenties. Either the account of American materialism was wrong, or else the New Deal stemmed from some other source.

Indeed, in the earlier discussion of a revolution in values, Frenchmen had implied at points, and stated explicitly elsewhere, that the new values which emerged in America during the depression had their source outside the country. Saint-Jean had pointed to the Christian inspiration for the New Deal, while Maurois and Romains, stressing the gaiety and intellectuality of Roosevelt's America, discovered Latin and Celtic influence in America. The sympathy of French critics for the United States in the thirties was based on the conviction that the new America had adopted European values. While French critics agreed that Americans were rebelling against their old values, they claimed that the source of the rebellion was at once within and outside of the American tradition. The tension might have been reconciled, but critics never addressed themselves to the issue.

To complicate matters further, French observers not only proclaimed the New Deal a revolution, but continued to argue that the old American system had survived intact. They were certain that the revolution had occurred, but it was equally clear that most of the old institutions were in place. The continuity between the twenties and the New Deal was especially evident in the work of André Siegfried. He was, of course, obliged to recognize the depression and the steps taken to remedy it. However, after admitting that the crisis might produce an aging effect on America, Siegfried confessed that "certain things which persist below the surface, could well reappear. . . . It sometimes happens that the conviction of youth survives youth itself."⁴⁴ According to Siegfried, the depression had produced no lasting effect on the United States. The country remained optimistic, and was still the land of prosperity.

Other critics agreed with Siegfried on the persistence of old traits. Although the architect of a revolution against earlier values, FDR was regarded by Saint-Jean as a typical American. His "infantile joy" suggested the youthfulness of the American character, in vivid contrast to the sophistication of the French character. The president's childish behavior was evident in his proposal to create a Children's Day as a counterpart to Mother's Day; it was also revealed when

Roosevelt made the carving of the turkey on Thanksgiving Day into a public ceremony.[45]

There was much evidence, as well, to support Siegfried's contention that, despite the depression, America remained the land of prosperity. Jules Romains observed in 1936 that the American worker was still two or three times better off than his French counterpart. Thanks to the machine, prices were low and salaries were high in the United States.[46] Even in 1933, Emile Schreiber was surprised to find the crowds of New York just as elegant, noisy, and active as before the war. The whole of New York, including Harlem, exhibited no signs of misery.[47] Although he recognized the existence of pockets of poverty in the South, André Maurois found the United States a flourishing land in comparison with Europe. The universities were full, the cinemas and popular restaurants heavily patronized. Despite the depression, the common man in the United States was far better off than the average European.[48]

A number of French observers, especially André Maurois and Jules Romains, argued that the suffering produced by the depression had radically changed America, thus diminishing the cultural gap between the Old World and the New. André Siegfried also considered these claims as the new French passenger ship, the *Normandy*, docked in New York harbor in 1935. "For several hours, I felt closer to Europe and France, and I was clearly aware of the link between continents which was established by putting such a boat into service." Improved transportation and communication did nothing, however, to alter the cultural gap between the continents. "The impression of distance and separation remains dominant in my mind. Europe's clamors reach here no doubt, but are confused, distant and softened. Europe and America form two continents, and the opposition would be more marked if we added: Old Europe and new continent."[49]

When Siegfried returned to America in 1938, it was evident that the cultural gap noted three years earlier had not diminished. He remarked, "When we speak of the New World, we often believe that we are employing simply a verbal expedient. In fact we are saying the most profound thing we can say about America." The geographic differences between two worlds were reflected in the rise of two radically different civilizations.[50] These differences were symbolized by the April 1933 encounter between Herriot and Roosevelt which Emmanuel Bourcier described in terms of "the Old World opposite the New."[51] The depression and the New Deal, which led some observers to the conclusion that the gap between the two worlds had decreased, merely confirmed in the minds of others the separation between the continents.

In other respects, as well, the America of the twenties escaped unscathed by poverty and the repeal of Prohibition, in the estimation of French critics. Despite setbacks in automobile production and heavy unemployment in Detroit, Siegfried proclaimed in 1935 that "America's heartbeat is in Detroit. I know of no American city which better reflects the development of postwar United States." He added, "If you haven't seen the assembly line at Ford, you haven't seen America."[52] Other reporters went to Washington to understand the United States in 1933, but Siegfried still regarded the assembly line as the single most noteworthy feature of American life. Here was major evidence of continuity between the twenties and the New Deal.

Other French observers were also impressed with the continued importance of new industrial methods in American life. Despite the *révolution américaine* accomplished by FDR, Pierre Lyautey insisted that America was still the land of factories.[53] Jules Romains did not hesitate to point up the similarities between American capitalism and Soviet communism. "Because of [America's] stress on machines and technology as well as the industrialized and rationalized atmosphere with which it surrounds man, an American would be less uprooted and disturbed by Communism than many Western Europeans."[54] The New Deal had done nothing to alter the enthusiasm of Americans for industrial progress.

The persistence of Americanism was especially obvious in the realm of agriculture. André Siegfried recommended that American farmers abandon the single crop and learn French peasant prudence.[55] He was joined by André Maurois, who found that "too many American farmers are businessmen." Maurois observed "not far from New York, a dairy farm which seems to emerge from your *Scènes de la vie future*, Duhamel."[56] To this standardization on the land, Maurois preferred the self-sufficient farmers of Perigord, where he spent his summers. Even Dubreuil, the persistent advocate of

American industrial methods, opposed commercial farming. In his opinion, the peasant class "is the only one which has assured the perenniality of nations."[57] All French reporters applauded New Deal measures to reconstitute small farms in America, but felt, as did André Maurois, that a greater effort was needed in this direction.

The standardization of agriculture and industry in the United States continued to have its effects on American communities and the American people. Robert de Saint-Jean regretted the absence of regional diversity in the nation, and André Siegfried continued to argue that all American towns resembled Main Street. It is not surprising that such a monotonous human environment should appear to discourage the development of individuality in the American character. Regarded by some Frenchmen as an outdated symbol of the American character, Babbitt remained for André Siegfried the typical American.[58]

If French critics were certain that the New Deal was a revolution, it nonetheless had not affected the American character, which remained basically childish and conformist. It had not altered the basic form of the economy, which was still oriented toward mass production. In these respects, critics agreed that American civilization continued to provide a vivid contrast to French and European life.

The contrast was reinforced by the persistent belief that the American experience was shaped by the Anglo-Saxon heritage. This belief was unaffected by the claim of French critics that the New Deal was evidence of a decline in Anglo-Saxon control of American life. Few critics disputed Pierre Lyautey's judgment that in spite of the Roosevelt administration, "Protestant America remains."[59]

Even President Roosevelt himself was unable to escape identification as a member of the dominant race. This was clear in Emmanuel Bourcier's description of the Roosevelt-Herriot meeting as a confrontation between "the American and the Latin."[60] Bernard Faÿ was more explicit. For Faÿ, the United States was still a cultural extension of England, and Roosevelt a typical representative of the American people. "Franklin Roosevelt is an Anglo-Saxon. With his Dutch name and his French blood, he is the descendant of a race in which the Anglo-Saxon element has been dominant. The American people elected him because he was an Anglo-Saxon." Like other Anglo-Saxon leaders such as Washington and Jefferson, Roosevelt, in Faÿ's view, was intellectually dull. This attribute of the race was a blessing, because it enabled Anglo-Saxons to avoid the interminable discussions which prevented Latin countries from achieving progress.[61] Such an analysis was especially puzzling, because Faÿ had previously seen the struggle between Pecora and Morgan as symbolizing the end of Anglo-Saxon control in America. Now he argued that the New Deal was itself the creation of the Anglo-Saxon mentality.

Other critics, like Pierre Lyautey, applied this theory of the Anglo-Saxon origins of the New Deal in somewhat modified form. Lyautey indicated that "the Roosevelts' Dutch origins have spared them the narrowness of New England Puritanism. Their Anglo-Saxonism has been rejuvenated by American battles."[62] At least one critic argued that Roosevelt's program, as well as his personality, derived from his Anglo-Saxon heritage. The adoption of an inflationary policy by FDR was regarded by Lucien Page as a typical response to economic problems by an Anglo-Saxon statesman.[63]

The claim that America remained under Anglo-Saxon domination was verified by numerous French observers. André Siegfried contrasted the American with the Latin attitude toward the law. "We Latins pass laws, but never enforce them 100 percent; that is why life in the Latin countries is always easy, charming, and human, although disordered."[64] This attitude toward the law helped to account for the greater individualism of Latin societies. On the other hand, the claim that Anglo-Saxons were individualists was only a "cliché," in the opinion of Jules Romains; moreover, like all Anglo-Saxons, Americans were conformists.[65] The constraints which ruled the society were especially apparent in aesthetic matters. Robert de Saint-Jean offered as evidence of the survival of puritanism an anecdote about a women's college in the Midwest which removed a Venus de Milo statue from the campus to avoid overstimulating male visitors.[66]

Other evidence of Anglo-Saxon domination of America was provided when French travelers discovered those enclaves in America which were still characterized by Latin behavior. André Siegfried contrasted French Canadian culture with the dominant Anglo-Saxon tradition. "In this America which we call the New World, it [French Canada] represents a tradition and is the symbol of stability. It, thus, maintains a philosophy of life which is similar to that of our peasants, in the midst of a continent where radically different cultural traditions are developing."[67] Other travelers looked to the United States proper for evidence of the survival of Latin behavior. Charleston and San Francisco were favorite spots for Frenchmen, along with the perennial Latin center of New Orleans. Raymond Recouly and Emile Schreiber recalled their visits with Huguenot families in Charleston.[68] Recouly also praised the French atmosphere of San Francisco, while Schreiber asked rhetorically: "Is it because the Spaniards and numerous Latins who live there have given it a character closer to our conceptions, that we enjoy San Francisco?"[69] The preferred behavior of Latins implied the existence of a dominant Anglo-Saxon culture which continued to exhibit features strongly distasteful to Frenchmen.

The preoccupation of French travelers with the two aspects of Americanism suggests the degree to which they were bound by the concerns of the twenties. While most Americans have seen the New Deal as a response to the problems of the depression, Frenchmen came seeking evidence that the United States had recognized her mistakes of the twenties and had adopted a higher set of goals. Given these preoccupations, Frenchmen placed special emphasis on certain developments which have seemed less important to Americans, such as the repeal of Prohibition, the rise of the Brain Trust, the NRA, and the personality of the president. While this selective attention tends to distort the New Deal taken as a political movement, it is perhaps fairer to consider French critics as commentators on American culture as a whole. In this regard, their perception of the central importance of ethnic and technological issues is more pertinent. However, even this perception is marred by the carelessness with which they considered the implications of some of the New Deal developments. Poverty and the repeal of Prohibition did not guarantee the fall of puritanism any more than the rise of the Brain Trust was proof of American conversion to intellectual values. Frenchmen were too quick to conclude that the New Deal was a revolution and, at the same time, too slow to abandon their narrow vision of the America of the twenties. They made no effort to reconcile the tension between their claim that the New Deal was a revolution and the belief that Americanism had survived the depression untarnished. In large part, this failure stemmed from the too rigid conception of the United States in the twenties. This conception was both carried over into the thirties and repudiated at the same time. Babbitt and Roosevelt managed to coexist in separate compartments of the French mind.

## NOTES

1. *L'américanisme et nous* (Paris, 1958), 14.
2. *La révolution américaine* (Paris, 1934), 215-216.
3. Schreiber's son, Jean-Jacques Servan-Schreiber, is the founder of the French weekly, *l'Express*.
4. (Paris, 1934).
5. (Paris, 1934).
6. *La crise du capitalisme américain* (Paris, 1933).
7. *La vraie révolution de Roosevelt*, 253.
8. *Ibid.*, 267.
9. *Roosevelt et son Amérique* (Paris, 1933), 284.
10. *Ibid.*, 266.
11. *La crise du capitalisme américain*, 343.
12. *Ibid.*, 318.
13. *La révolution américaine*, 101.
14. *La vraie révolution de Roosevelt*, 158.
15. *Roosevelt et son Amérique*, 280.
16. *Ibid.*, 233.
17. *La révolution américaine*, 232.
18. *Chantiers américains* (Paris, 1933), 81.
19. *Visite aux Américains* (Paris, 1936), 21.
20. Francois Drujon, *L'Amérique et l'avenir* (Paris, 1938), 13.
21. Didier Lazard, *Contrastes américaines* (Paris, 1940), 9.
22. *L'Amérique inattendue* (Paris, 1931), 99, 110.
23. *Chantiers américains*, 19, 181.
24. *Visite aux Américains*, 27.
25. *Ibid.*, 29, 32.
26. *La révolution américaine*, 241.
27. While Roosevelt's position on war debts was identical to Hoover's, this fact was obscured when the issue became dormant after 1933.
28. Quoted in Frances D. Pingeon, "French Opinion of Roosevelt and the New Deal" (master's essay, Columbia University, 1962), 3-4.
29. *L'Amérique pauvre* (Paris, 1933), 355, 357.
30. *Qu'est-ce que l'Amérique?* (Paris, 1938), 42.
31. *Les codes de Roosevelt* (Paris, 1934), 157.

32. In her study of the French press, Frances D. Pingeon found similar exaggeration of the role of the NRA. "French Opinion of the New Deal," 49.

33. *Qu'est-ce que l'Amérique?*, 41.

34. The exaggeration of the role of the NRA was compounded by misunderstandings. Emile Schreiber insisted that the NRA was a relief organization. *L'Amérique réagit* (Paris, 1934), 120. Louis Bonnichon suggested that the social aspects of the New Deal could be reduced exclusively to the NRA. *Des aspect sociaux de la "Réforme Roosevelt"* (Paris, 1934), 172.

35. *Chantiers américains*, 186.

36. *La révolution Roosevelt*, 8, 42, 203, 206.

37. *La vraie révolution de Roosevelt*, 9; *Visite aux Américains*, 200.

38. *La vraie révolution de Roosevelt*, 9.

39. *Les codes de Roosevelt*, 76.

40. *L'Amérique réagit*, 219.

41. *Etats-Unis, Canada, Mexique* (La Havre, 1935), 62.

42. *Etats-Unis 39* (Paris, 1939), 31-33.

43. *L'expérience Roosevelt* (Paris, 1934), 125.

44. *Qu'est-ce que l'Amérique?*, 48. French observers of the New Deal continued to praise Siegfried's study of America in the twenties, *Les Etats-Unis d'aujourd'hui* (Paris, 1927). Robert de Saint-Jean called it a "classic work" (*La vraie révolution de Roosevelt*, 157), while Pierre Lyautey considered it a "basic work" (*La révolution américaine*, 37). Other observers cited Siegfried's observations in support of their own.

45. *La vraie révolution de Roosevelt*, 37, 28.

46. *Visite aux Américains*, 238.

47. *L'Amérique réagit*, 23, 46.

48. *Chantiers américains*, 32; *Etats-Unis 39*, 119. Despite its title, Raymond Recouly's *L'Amérique pauvre* provided little evidence of the decline o, prosperity in America. The author recounted his visits with Vanderbilt in New York, Governor Lowden in Illinois, and a trip to the Hearst estate in California. There was much information about American gangsters, but very little about poverty.

49. *Etats-Unis, Canada, Mexique*, 3.

50. *Qu'est-ce que l'Amérique?*, 11, 14.

51. *U.S.A.—33* (Paris, 1934), 227.

52. *Etats-Unis, Canada, Mexique*, 13-14.

53. *La révolution américaine*, 172.

54. *Visite aux Américains*, 203.

55. *Etats-Unis, Canada, Mexique*, 24.

56. *Chantiers américains*, 49, 47.

57. *Les codes de Roosevelt*, 161.

58. *La vraie révolution de Roosevelt*, 34; *Etats-Unis, Canada, Mexique*, 10, 51, 42.

59. *La révolution américaine*, 121.

60. *U.S.A.—33*, 227.

61. *Roosevelt et son Amérique*, 13, 19.

62. *La révolution américaine*, 13.

63. *L'expérience Roosevelt*, 125.

64. *Etats-Unis, Canada, Mexique*, 60.

65. *Visite aux Américains*, 201.

66. *La vraie révolution de Roosevelt*, 44.

67. *Etats-Unis, Canada, Mexique*, 10.

68. *L'Amérique pauvre*, 290; *L'Amérique réagit*, 163.

69. *L'Amérique pauvre*, 199; *L'Amérique réagit*, 163.

# chapter 16

# Six French Resistants in the
# United States, 1945-1947 _____

> France, a civilization of individuals, is the very opposite of con-
> temporary America which is a conformist society oriented toward
> production.
> —André Siegfried, 1927
> In America, the individual is nothing.
> —Simone de Beauvoir, 1947

The development of the French image of America in the early
postwar years was strongly affected by the views of six important
figures in the French Resistance. Their travel accounts describing
American life are of special interest because, in the interwar period,
French visitors to the United States with few exceptions aligned
themselves with conservative republican parties. Only a scattering of
Socialists wrote book-length studies about the United States in that
period.[1] The observations of the Resistants in the early postwar years
provide the first occasion in the twentieth century for assessing
systematically the impact of leftist views on the representation of
American life.

The brief flurry of interest in the United States among French
Resistants must be seen as a product of the political situation at the
end of World War II. In 1945, the cold war was still in the future, and
even in left-wing circles, America was given credit for participating
in a war to defeat fascism. The overwhelming political and military
strength of the United States made it clear to all Frenchmen that
American culture would play a major role in French life in the
postwar period. An assessment of that culture was clearly an important motivation for visiting America.

The arrival of French Resistants was also stimulated by formal invitations from American authorities, private and public. University students and professors invited such new celebrities of the literary world as Simone de Beauvoir and Vercors to lecture at their institutions. Jean-Paul Sartre, strangely enough, visited America under the auspices of the Office of War Information with five other French journalists. The American government was obviously interested in spreading favorable views of the United States in France by displaying to influential Frenchmen the attractive elements of American life.

In attempting to assess the impact of political views on the travelers' image of the United States, some obvious difficulties arise. The six travelers under consideration represented at least three different political positions, even though all may be categorized as left wing. No less than three of the Resistants, Jean-Paul Sartre, Simone de Beauvoir, and Jacques-Laurent Bost, were existentialists.[2] They combined a Marxist approach to social problems with a philosophical perspective asserting the primacy of the individual. Pierre Schaeffer was a practicing Catholic who had participated in the Resistance and traveled in America as a journalist. He accepted the socially advanced views of some elements in the church. The only member of the Communist party among the travelers was Claude Roy. Roy too was a journalist who had contributed to the Communist Front review, *Les Lettres Françaises*, during the war. Classifying Vercors,[3] the leading literary figure of the Resistance, is considerably more difficult. He sympathized with many of the radical positions of the Communist and non-Communist left in the postwar period, but refused to join a political party.

Although the Resistants visited America under very special circumstances and held distinct political views, their approach to American life was remarkably like that of their predecessors in the interwar period. They saw in the United States the land of the future which they contrasted with the traditional culture of France. The technological wizardry of Americans was set off from the old-fashioned ways of Frenchmen. Of course, the Resistants experienced a sense of cultural distance from America because of their distaste for the oppression of blacks, workers, and tenant farmers in the United States. Nonetheless, the aspects of American life which they dis-

cussed and condemned most frequently were excessive urbaniza-
tion, advanced technology, and the overorganization of leisure—the
very conditions which offended their predecessors. Only occasionally did the Resistants protest against the American system of private
ownership of property; if they hoped to rescue the proletariat, their
observations indicate that it was not by giving workers control over
the assembly line, but by abolishing that institution altogether. The
six observers expressed a marked preference for the French character, the French landscape, and French buildings. In this respect, too,
they perpetuated the conservative attitudes of their predecessors in
the prewar period. Only a close examination of the Resistants' work
will enable us to understand why six progressives strongly committed
to social justice reacted to America as ardent French nationalists
wedded to a traditional way of life.

The tendency of the Resistants to cite the best-known French
observers of America in the twenties offers an important clue to
understanding their preference for older views. No less than five of
the six authors referred to Georges Duhamel's strictures against
American life. The postwar visitors, most of whom had come of age in
the twenties, were naturally familiar with Duhamel's work. However, their references to it indicate that the Resistants were anxious to
avoid Duhamel's polemical tone. His strictures against the American
methods of slaughtering animals drew the fire of Pierre Schaeffer
and Jacques-Laurent Bost. Both pointed to the similar processes
used in France. Bost went so far as to claim that any cow, given the
choice of dying in Chicago or La Villette (the Paris slaughterhouse)
would certainly prefer the former.[4] Simone de Beauvoir had no
objection to Duhamel's treatment of the stockyards, but she was
adamant in her defense of the American countryside. "Georges
Duhamel must have done very little traveling in America to have
dared to pretend that the countryside was hidden by advertising
billboards."[5] Vercors recommended that Duhamel change his title
from *Scènes de la vie future* to *Scènes de la vie précaire*, thus placing
the emphasis on the fast pace of American life.[6]

These minor disagreements with Duhamel reflected a more basic
reaction against the anti-American image of the twenties. Claude Roy
indicated his reservations with that image: "When I read Mr.
Duhamel, the French imprecations against the life of standardization

and the leveling of minds, I was tempted to agree. I am not so sure now. Certainly a gigantic machine is operating in America to force uniformity."[7] Nonetheless, Roy was convinced that Duhamel had exaggerated the faults of American life.

The effort to repudiate the errors of Duhamel was accompanied by a critique of certain themes of the literature of the twenties. Pierre Schaeffer warned Frenchmen not to equate the United States and materialism. He was especially critical of the tendency of French observers to conceive of American and French civilizations in opposition to each other. While noting the differences between two ways of life, he refuted the effort to oppose "a traditional French conception and Americanism."[8] Claude Roy was even more explicit. "Nothing is more ridiculous than those snails of the Old World who withdraw into their shells at the sight of the New World." If they had not concocted the antithesis, if they had not imagined that the individual in America was "devoured by the mob, cut off from all contact with nature by the machine and oppressed by the masses," they might have perceived the humanitarian influences in American life. Instead they insisted on depicting the "modern man, the mechanical man, . . . the robot, the man who has lost his soul, this poor little modern man, crushed, emptied, and rubbed out; flattened by the steamroller, the man preyed upon by the masses and devoured by myths." This fictitious character, whom Roy failed to encounter in America, was presented in opposition to an equally imaginary European in the accounts of ignorant French travelers. They portrayed the European as "the western man, this giant well installed on his gentle hillsides with his Christian, humanistic civilization, with his ox-cart, his Greco-Latin tradition, his kitchens without refrigerators, his respect for the individual and his sense of helleno-classic moderation."[9] Roy seemed to bid farewell here to the myth created by Duhamel in 1930. Humanism was no longer the sole possession of Europe, nor materialism a purely American disease.

The initial reluctance of French leftists to castigate American materialism and to oppose it to the virtues of a traditional way of life stemmed in part from their own reservations about that traditional way of life, and in part from their perception of recent American history. Certain developments of the past fifteen years justified a revision of the American image. The critics could not avoid the impression that the distance between Europe and America had been reduced by American participation in the war. Their own personal experience was evidence that the isolationism of the 1920s was no longer operative. The visitors had encountered American troops in France even before they had been invited to see the American continent for themselves.

The New Deal also helped to modify the anti-American image of the twenties. In that period, the United States appeared to many Frenchmen as an exclusively materialistic society and one indifferent to the hardships of impoverished minorities. The Resistants recognized that while the New Deal fell short of socialism, it was nonetheless concerned with the lot of the less fortunate elements in American society. The United States could no longer be considered a nation without a soul.[10]

The prominence of American intellectuals by 1945 also presented an obstacle to the renewal of the antithesis between a mindless America and an intelligent Europe. The intellectuals could no longer be ignored because French visitors were spending more time on American campuses and reading American books than had been the case in the twenties. The American novelist Nelson Algren achieved special notoriety by becoming one of the leading characters in Simone de Beauvoir's Goncourt prize-winning novel, *Les Mandarins*; his affair with the French author could be understood as a literal and symbolic union of intellectuals in the two countries.[11]

Despite these important changes, the Resistants were not prepared to abandon the old image of America. It soon became apparent that their objection to Duhamel and other predecessors revolved largely around the tone rather than the content of their work. America was indeed a mass society, as Duhamel had asserted, although this was no cause for hysteria. Claude Roy, for example, agreed with Duhamel on the pressure for conformity in American life. Vercors, who found *Scènes de la vie future* a misleading title, remarked that "on the whole, what Duhamel says is true. He has seen it; I have seen it too." Vercors added that life in America was "menaced, hurried and oppressed by monumental necessities."[12]

The Resistants followed the example of their predecessors in stressing the cultural and geographic distance between France and America, with only occasional qualifications. This was the case even though French visitors after 1945 frequently crossed the Atlantic by plane. Notwithstanding, Simone de Beauvoir was prepared to remark, before deplaning in New York, that "opposite old Europe, at the threshold of a continent of 160 million men, New York belongs to the future." The notion of geographical separation and cultural opposition was clarified immediately. "I not only landed in a foreign country, but in another world, separate and autonomous."[13]

Extreme differences amounting to opposition between two ways of life were acknowledged by other Resistants. They contrasted the density of Europe with the abundance of space in America. The size of the country explained the obsession with machines in the United States. Both in terms of geography and culture, Frenchmen felt justified in claiming, as Vercors did, that "America and Europe have no common measure." Indeed, in the West, where distances were greater, the sense of opposition might also be magnified. From the perspective of Nebraska, one visitor remarked: "[America] no longer seems like another continent, but really like another planet, almost inaccessible."[14]

The sense of distance which French leftists experienced may be explained in part by their opposition to a society which oppressed workers, racial minorities, and poor farmers. Jacques-Laurent Bost accurately expressed the feelings of all six travelers when he announced that "as a white European, even if you have always been indifferent to the Negroes, you automatically become a Negrophile after debarking in New York. The blacks are an oppressed minority and that is enough for you."[15] Simone de Beauvoir and Claude Roy discussed the plight of blacks at some length, finally arguing for a coalition between poor whites and blacks to ameliorate the situation of both groups.[16] The condition of unionized workers also received some attention. Jacques-Laurent Bost stayed with a working-class family in Detroit and attempted without success to convince striking automobile employees that Henry Ford had no right to profit from war contracts.[17]

The oppression which resulted from capitalist control and American racism was not, however, a major concern in the travel volumes of leftists. Neither Sartre nor Vercors dealt with the matter at all in their essays, and it was given only sporadic attention in the studies of other travelers.[18] For these reasons, neither racism nor capitalist oppression can be regarded as the principal factor in sustaining the antithesis among leftists. Their chief concern was the rise of mass society in America. For them, as for their predecessors in the twenties, the United States represented the future: that is, a new culture based on technological developments which had not yet taken root in Europe. Their insistence on contrasting modernism with the traditional way of life indicates the extent to which the leftists were apprehensive about many aspects of mass society.[19]

The Resistants made no pretense of presenting their readers with a new image of America. They were perfectly satisfied to rediscover the revolutionary United States of the twenties. Like their predecessors, they showed a disproportionate interest in New York, largely because it manifested in an extreme fashion the characteristics of mass society. As Jean-Paul Sartre confessed, "To the eyes of a Frenchman of my generation, [New York] possesses the melancholy of the past." The essential elements of the city had been discovered earlier and had not changed: "When we were 20, around 1925, we heard about the skyscrapers. They symbolized for us the fabulous American prosperity. We were dazzled by their appearance in the films. They were the architecture of the future, just as the cinema was the art and jazz the music of the future." The promise of these achievements had not been kept. Both jazz and the cinema had degenerated. "The skyscrapers then were living. Today, for a Frenchman who comes from Europe, they are no more than historical monuments, witnesses of a period that is over."[20] Regardless of Sartre's disillusionment, it is clear from this passage that he had come to America to see the wonders which he had first learned of in the twenties.

Sartre was not alone in confessing the formative effect of images prior to actual contact with America. Simone de Beauvoir feared that these images would overpower the impressions of contemporary New York which she was about to receive: "There is only one world and New York is a city in the world. But no. Despite all the books I have read, the films, the photographs, and the accounts, New York is a legendary city in my past: from reality to legend there is no road."[21]

The new observers paid special homage to their compatriots who had preceded them in the discovery of New York as a symbol of modernism. Sartre recalled Louis Céline's characterization of New

York as a "vertical city," while Jacques-Laurent Bost cited the paradoxical remark of Le Corbusier on the low level of New York's buildings despite its reputation as a city of skyscrapers.[22]

In addition to the literature of the twenties, travelers found a number of other guides from the past. Simone de Beauvoir remarked that "the friends whose travels in America I so envied pronounced the words: Sherry Netherland or Café Arnold with the pride of the initiated. I follow in their tracks. I have no past and I borrow theirs." Occasionally, the legend which had been created for her was contaminated by the reality of present-day New York. American streets and the drugstores, for example, lost their poetic luster when they were encountered directly. Simone de Beauvoir rectified this problem by returning to the movies on Forty-second Street. "By these black and white pictures, I first knew America and they still appear to me as its true substance."[23]

The image of an overly mechanized society, which was transmitted at least in part by the new medium of the cinema, was sustained by the Resistants' experience in New York. The American landscape, outside of the great cities, also offered the traveler opportunities to confirm the image. Once again, French literary antecedents played an important role in orienting postwar travelers. The natural beauty of the American countryside was frequently acknowledged, but the opportunities it offered for the imaginative use of technology were also stressed. Not far from Niagara Falls, Simone de Beauvoir discovered a beautiful lake. "As I have read in a Jules Verne novel, it would suffice to throw an ice cube into the lake in order to freeze all this moving surface. The lake is beautiful like a landscape from Jules Verne. It promises every adventure." The author, however, made no attempt to explore these promises, but hurried on across the continent. Her trip was a reenactment of science fiction, late nineteenth-century style:

The words Orient express and trans-Siberian have always made me dream. I wanted to take a train trip lasting several days; then, as in the Steam House of Jules Verne, the train becomes truly a home. . . . It is undoubtedly not by chance that, for the first time in twenty years, I remember the writing of Jules Verne and the recollection pursues me across America; it is a land of mechanical marvels where, on an adult scale, the childhood fancies of the "library of travels" are accomplished.[24]

The peculiarity of American life, as the French perceived it after World War II, owed much to their interest in experiencing the adventures which technology could offer.

The leftists' persistent search for adventure continued in the West. The great centers of mass entertainment were of special interest. Simone de Beauvoir, after observing Reno with its lights and gambling houses, remarked that "all America is a surprise box." Earlier, she announced her preference for Chicago and New York over Los Angeles. There were compensations, however. In Los Angeles, "one can enjoy oneself as with a kaleidoscope."[25]

The leftists, unlike the critics of the twenties, appeared to enjoy their encounter with technology. In reality, the playful approach obscured deep-seated fears. These emerged when the new observers contrasted an America defined exclusively in terms of the new technology with a traditional France in order to establish clearly their preference for the qualities of the latter. On his tour of Fontane, Tennessee, in the midst of the TVA project, Sartre denounced the antiseptic character of the prefabricated houses. He discovered in New York that American streets were "without mystery" and that he was "carried along like a package." He longed to replace the geometrical plan of American cities with European streets which were made for walking. "In the numerical anonymity of the streets and avenues, I am simply anyone anywhere."[26] The standardization of the American city threatened the survival of the individual. The human being was depersonalized by the environment.

On an excursion to the borough of Queens, Simone de Beauvoir paid her first visit to an American bowling alley. This encounter set her to musing about bowling conditions in France:

I recall a bowling match in the square of a French village on a July 14th afternoon; the uneven ground laid traps for the players. Gardens, country cabarets, and squares shaded by plane trees are all replaced in America by these great air-conditioned halls where they roll standardized balls on exactly measured alleys without arguments or laughter.[27]

The antiseptic character of the bowling alley was reflected in the actions of the players, while the more natural setting in France produced a happier reaction in the bowlers.

The American landscape, however, was not completely given over to standardized construction. Simone de Beauvoir had no difficulty in appreciating the Indian pueblos of New Mexico:

What we find here is the same rural civilization, several thousand years old, which is preserved in European country-sides and in the privileged American territories where they have not assassinated the past; on the other hand, the American town possesses to our eyes the unpleasing exotism of objects which are too new.[28]

The Indian village was considered antithetical in character to the typically urban, industrial civilization of the United States. It was identified with Europe on the grounds that traditional culture was predominant there.

The uniformity of American construction continued to produce a standardization of the personality which was deplored by all of the leftists. In contrast to these lamentable conditions, the visitors praised French diversity and individuality. For example, Jean-Paul Sartre explained that French individualism was the result of resistance to both the state and the rest of society. In America, however, the individual operated freely only in the economic sphere. Thus, individualism was equated in the United States with base materialism. "Conformism, rather than individualism, is basic" in Amerca. By Sartre's standards, the American was "a man devoid of individuality who has risen to a universal impersonality."[29] Americans were content to be directed from Washington or by their fellowmen.

The oppressive character of modern America was due not only to the rise of mass society, but also to the persistence of Anglo-Saxon, Puritan hegemony. Jean-Paul Sartre explained that the melting pot was an instrument for turning foreigners into Puritans. He witnessed a "European in the midst of melting." The results of this process were not encouraging. The individual "laughs but he is cold; Puritanism is not far off. I feel frozen." Sartre had a marked preference for the French character. He recognized that "the face of this man is yet too expressive; he has retained the slightly annoying appearance of intelligence which reveals a French head everywhere. Soon, however, he will turn into a tree or a rock."[30] According to this view, the Puritan lacked two essential qualities which the Frenchman possessed: intelligence and individuality.

French critics described the effects of puritanism as well as its origins; they maintained that it was responsible for American innocence, racism, and missionary zeal. Sartre, for example, attributed the effort to spread American culture to the Puritans' belief in the superiority of their way of life.[31] Simone de Beauvoir was distressed by the "armor of Puritan virtue" worn by white Americans. Their "stiff frigidity" was unfavorably contrasted with the physical charm of vibrant Negro women in New York. Her experience in Indian territory demonstrated that "American Puritanism" was frightened by "this lovely red blood." Finally, the Puritan heritage explained the inclination of Americans "to believe in virtue and in the good with a kind of sincerity."[32] Their innocence, according to Simone de Beauvoir, was revealed in the failure to remember German war crimes.

The observers' critique of puritanism and the Anglo-Saxon character was expressed indirectly in their preference for French people and customs during their stay in America. The case of Simone de Beauvoir was especially interesting. Just off the plane from Paris, she protested against her frequent contacts with compatriots living in New York. "I am not in a colonial country where the customs render it almost impossible to mix with the natives. On the contrary, we are the ones who form what they call a colony here." Her preference for foreigners stemmed from a tendency to associate Frenchmen with her parents, which, in turn, caused a certain deception. Contacts with Americans, however, produced deceptions of a different sort. At a cocktail party for American intellectuals, Simone de Beauvoir was distressed to hear her American counterparts gloat over the supplies of dried milk then being shipped by the government to France. In silent retaliation, she confessed her shock at the gaudy dresses worn by the American women at the party. No French woman of taste would have been seen in such outfits.[33]

After her stay in New York, Simone de Beauvoir left by bus for California where she picked up a French female traveling companion. By the time they reached New Mexico, two French architects had joined the party. They split up for daily visits to the pueblos, but met again at dinner. "And here we are: four French people gathered by chance around a table as in the old adventure stories where one sees the travelers fraternize at the inns. . . . we compare our impressions with a very French volubility; the Americans eat rapidly and silently as is their custom."[34] Apparently, Simone de Beauvoir had overestimated her capacity for mixing with the natives. Determined to avoid a French colony in New York, she had formed one of her own in New Mexico.

It should now be clear that the Resistants' image of America can only be understood in terms of the complex interaction between their own values and forces at work on the American scene. For a number of reasons, the reports of postwar visitors stressed the continuity between the America of the twenties and forties. This appearance of continuity was based, to some degree at least, on reality. The New Deal and World War II did not substantially alter mass society in the United States. Indeed, the Resistants' reliance on the testimony of their predecessors may be understood in one sense as evidence of the essential modernity of America in the twenties. While the reading of Duhamel, Morand, and others helped orient the Resistants, the emphasis on mass society would have emerged in any event. This was so because the process of modernization was already under way in France. Clearly, the exploration of American society, where that process was further advanced, offered French Resistants a useful opportunity to test the future.

This conclusion would be less troublesome if it were not for the circumstances of the postwar era and the identification of postwar travelers with the political left. The Resistants' commitment to social justice for oppressed groups everywhere and their recent engagement in a war against fascism would not have led us to anticipate their enraptured references to French individualism and rural life in France. Such views suggest a preference for a return to precapitalist society rather than progress toward socialism. Taken literally, these preferences do not make much sense. However, they may be understood in the postwar period as an almost instinctive effort on the part of Resistants to assert the independence and distinctive character of French culture in the face of what appeared to be the threat of American cultural and political hegemony. The continuity between Resistants and French critics of the twenties then becomes clear. Their strictures against America can be regarded as a strategy to save France. Only then would they turn to the matter of eliminating oppression.

It is also evident that political differences between citizens of one society do not necessarily preclude a broad agreement about cultural values. This often emerges with special clarity in an encounter with a foreign country. In the American context, the oppression of the proletariat was perceived as less threatening than the stifling of individual liberty. For Frenchmen of the right and the left, individualism was a sacred value; its defense was of highest priority.

Not only were French leftists moved to defend individual liberty by their adherence to an older tradition of individualism which transcended party lines, but their existentialism also predisposed them in this direction. That philosophy, of course, was fundamentally concerned with the necessity for individual choice. Life became meaningful only when a person attempted to shape his own destiny.

Moreover, the preoccupation of Sartre and his cohorts with individualism rather than the problems of oppressed minorities can be understood as a reflection of their priorities in the early postwar period. At that moment, they were more existentialist than Marxist.[35] Indeed, a systematic approach to the oppressed elements in society by existentialists would await the reformulation of the concepts of history, class conflict, and proleterian revolution. Even then, Marxism was fitted to existentialism rather than the reverse. The existentialists continued to view the situation of the oppressed groups as a particular, though dramatic, instance of the denial of freedom which was a universal problem.

Hence, reactions of the Resistants and critics in the twenties coincide nicely. The foreign character of the American environment, the fear of American power, and the commitment to individualism all served to minimize the differences between postwar leftists and their traditionalist predecessors in the prewar period.

## NOTES

1. Among the best known works about American life by Socialists in the interwar period were André Philip, *Le problème ouvrier aux Etats-Unis* (Paris, 1927); and Georges Boris, *La révolution Roosevelt* (Paris, 1934).

2. Some of Sartre's observations on the United States were published in *Le Figaro* during his visit, while others served to introduce the special issue of

his journal *Les Temps Modernes* which appeared in August of 1946 and was completely devoted to American life. The same impressions were republished in *Situations III* (Paris, 1949), dedicated to Jacques-Laurent Bost. Bost in turn dedicated his volume, *Trois mois aux Etats-Unis*, to two other existentialists, Albert Camus and Pascal Pia. Indeed, some of Bost's impressions had been published in Camus's daily, *Combat*, for which Bost was a reporter. Simone de Beauvoir's notes on America originally appeared in five issues of *Les Temps Modernes* (December 1947-April 1948).

3. Vercors was the pen name which Jean Bruhlers adopted during the Resistance. It was also the name of the region of the French Alps where Bruhlers was hiding. The author visited the United States in 1946, but his impressions were not published until 1954 in *Les pas dans le sable* (Paris).

4. *Amérique, nous t'ignorons* (Paris, 1946), 40; *Trois mois aux Etats-Unis*, 51.

5. *L'Amérique au jour le jour* (Paris, 1948), 128.

6. *Les pas dans le sable*, 41.

7. *Clefs pour l'Amérique* (Paris, 1949), 223.

8. *Amérique, nous t'ignorons*, 15, 223.

9. *Clefs pour l'Amérique*, 306.

10. The positive effect of the New Deal on the French image of America was suggested in Claude Roy's praise of FDR for saving America from the bankers. *Clefs pour l'Amérique*, 224.

11. Vercors also paid homage to the coming of age of American intellectuals, but he refused to talk with them about their own country in order to maintain a fresh and unbiased approach. *Les pas dans le sable*, 14.

12. *Ibid.*, 41.

13. *L'Amérique au jour le jour*, 21.

14. *Les pas dans le sable*, 38; *Trois mois aux Etats-Unis*, 63.

15. *Trois mois aux Etats-Unis*, 148.

16. *L'Amérique au jour le jour*, 209; *Clefs pour l'Amérique*, 283. Simone de Beauvoir dedicated her account of American life to Ellen and Richard Wright whom she and Sartre had known in Paris.

17. *Trois mois aux Etats-Unis*, 43.

18. Sartre reserved his treatment of the black problem for his play *La p . . . respectueuse*, which was written and produced in 1947.

19. Mary McCarthy pointed to the fear of the future as an important factor in understanding Simone de Beauvoir's reaction to America. "Mlle. Gulliver en Amérique," in *On the Contrary* (New York, 1961), 30-31.

20. *Situations III*, 122.

21. *L'Amérique au jour le jour*, 11.

22. *Situations III*, 115; *Trois mois aux Etats-Unis*, 135. The observations

of Jules Romains and Paul Morand on life in New York City were also cited by Sartre and Simone de Beauvoir, respectively. *Situations III*, 115; *L'Amérique au jour le jour*, 311.

23. *L'Amérique au jour le jour*, 24, 77.

24. *Ibid.*, 90, 107. Jacques-Laurent Bost fancied himself in the role of Phineas Fogg, a Jules Verne character. *Trois mois aux Etats-Unis*, 15. It would appear, however, that like the modern French leftists and despite his fascination with American technology, Jules Verne praised the traditional elements of French culture. Theodore Zeldin, *France, 1848-1945*: Vol. 2. *Intellect, Taste and Anxiety* (Oxford, 1977), 131.

25. *L'Amérique au jour le jour*, 14, 123.

26. *Situations III*, 105, 118. Jacques-Laurent Bost also experienced a feeling of "profound uprootedness" in New York. He much preferred the cities of the Old World. *Trois mois aux Etats-Unis*, 131, 98.

27. *L'Amérique au jour le jour*, 72.

28. *Ibid.*, 188.

29. *Situations III*, 91. After speaking at Oberlin College, Simone de Beauvoir reacted against the conformist behavior of American students. She remarked that "in America, the individual is nothing." *L'Amérique au jour le jour*, 96.

30. *Situations III*, 76-77.

31. *Ibid.*, 82.

32. *L'Amérique au jour le jour*, 42, 117, 68.

33. *Ibid.*, 24, 27.

34. *Ibid.*, 184. Vercors maintained his contact with France by visiting Charles Boyer in Los Angeles, while Claude Roy was entertained by Darius Milhaud at Mills College. *Les pas dans le sable*, 39; *Clefs pour l'Amérique*, 96.

35. The effort to reconcile existentialism with Marxism, which was spearheaded by Sartre's friend Merleau-Ponty, is discussed at length in the following studies: Michael-Antoine Burnier, *Choice of Action: The French Existentialists in Politics* (New York, 1968); H. Stuart Hughes, *The Obstructed Path: French Social Thought in the Years of Desperation, 1930-1960* (New York, 1966); and George Lichtheim, *Marxism in Modern France* (New York, 1966).

# chapter 17

# French Anti-Americanism Today ____

> The underlying cause of these opposite reflexes is the antagonism
> of two civilizations. The one—ours—is the daughter of pagan an-
> tiquity; the other the daughter of the Reformation. The one de-
> scended from Greece and Rome; the other from the Bible. We
> French represent two traditions, the ancient and the Catholic,
> which Protestant Anglo-Saxons must distrust.
> —André Tardieu, 1927

Two decades separate the appearance of Siegfried's *Les Etats-Unis
d'aujourd'hui* from the publication of Simone de Beauvoir's
*L'Amérique au jour le jour*. We are farther removed in time from her
work, therefore, than she was from Siegfried's. Have the events of
these three decades served to undermine the conception shared by
Siegfried and Simone de Beauvoir of a traditionalist France falling
prey to the power of a modernizing America? This durable conception of opposition survived the New Deal and the collaboration of
Americans and Europeans during World War II. Is it still a useful
device, and does it imply the necessity of French resistance to
America?

The events following World War II have done much to change the
conditions which encouraged the articulation of the antithesis by
French critics after World War I. The failure of the United States to
collaborate with France in the 1920s was an important reason for the
acceptance of the idea of opposition. If many Frenchmen agreed that
the appearance of American soldiers in Europe during World War II
was only an aberration, the Marshall Plan and NATO constituted
evidence that the Atlantic Ocean was not an unbridgeable gap.

Through the participation of American troops in an integrated military force and the opening of American bases in Europe, the United States maintained a tangible and official presence in the Old World. Political and military collaboration between the two countries was a routine matter—at least until the advent of General de Gaulle. His insistence that America could not be a reliable partner for France served to resurrect the idea of the Atlantic as a barrier between Old and New Worlds—an idea which appeared to have been discredited. In 1966, while France remained a member of NATO, she ceased to participate in the integrated military operations of the alliance, and American bases were closed down in France, thus reducing collaboration between the two countries.

Economic developments on both sides of the Atlantic have also affected the French view of America and Franco-American relations since the war. In the United States, the prewar trend toward a consumer society with mass production, mass consumption, and the proliferation of mass leisure activities has continued. The growth orientation of the American economy, so evident in the twenties, has been reaffirmed since 1945. Similar developments are strikingly evident in France. Modernization has proceeded rapidly in that country. The population has become increasingly urban and middle class. It now has available the amenities of the consumer society including the automobile. While the French standard of living falls below the American, the French government and people have made a clear commitment to the creation of economic abundance through technology and planning. In this respect, the two countries differ in degree, but not in kind.

Domestic politics, far more than diplomacy or economic development, provide some evidence of a gap between French and American practices. Both the ministerial instability of the Fourth Republic and the authoritarian aspects of the Fifth contrast with American-style democracy. The two-party system in the United States remains substantially different from the multiparty French system. There have also been sharp conflicts between the two countries over the conduct of foreign affairs. The French protested the American defense of South Vietnam, while Washington was sharply critical of French efforts to maintain control over Algeria. Each country has experienced a major political crisis arising in part out of the conduct of these imperial wars, but the responses to the crises have been strikingly different. Criticism of the conduct of the Algerian War helped cause the downfall of the Fourth Republic, while the war in Vietnam helped to provoke not only an antiwar movement but also broad-gauged reform activity intended to equalize treatment of blacks and women, as well as change the school system and reform the environment.

On balance, political, economic, and diplomatic trends have raised serious questions about the validity of opposition as a conception of relations between France and America. Nonetheless, it is also true that the antithesis, reiterated on many occasions since 1927, was well entrenched in the French mind by 1947. The last thirty years, then, might be regarded as a period in which events have operated, for the most part, in tension with the conventional wisdom. In examining some of the important French books on America in this period, it is evident that the conventional wisdom has, in fact, been challenged. Two distinct responses may be discerned. From 1947 to 1960, the conception of antithesis was criticized and, to some degree, replaced by the notion of convergence. After 1960, the antithesis emerged anew, but in a substantially different form and to serve somewhat different purposes.

The convergence theme is evident in the work of two important French authors: Daniel Guérin and Claude Julien. Both are leftists; both studied in the United States on fellowships after World War II. Julien made his reputation not only as an author of works on the United States, but also as an editor of the prestigious French daily, Le Monde. Both authors specialized in the study of labor movements.[1]

Like so many observers of postwar America, Julien and Guérin repudiated the classic studies of the 1920s by Duhamel and Siegfried.[2] The Resistants after World War II had done the same. The reasons, however, were different. The Resistants, while embarrassed by the extreme rhetoric of Duhamel and company, accepted traditional values.[3] Julien and Guérin were modernists who regarded the industrial revolution as a progressive development, which must, however, be directed to the benefit of the less fortunate classes.

The rejection of the antithesis between New and Old Worlds was most evident in Julien's conclusion that "in many respects, Europe is Americanizing. This is especially true because analogous problems, in spite of differences, confront the two continents."[4] In short, studying America was a way of coming to grips with the problems of Europe. The contrast theme was no longer a viable way of relating the two worlds.

While Sartre and company formally acknowledged the deficiencies of antithesis, they continued to operate under its influence. Their contribution was to rediscover the main elements of American culture—those values and institutions which were shared by all Americans—and to contrast these with the essential characteristics of French culture. Julien and Guérin adopted a different approach. They stressed the main components of American society, focusing on the divisions within the American social order. Since American groups had their counterparts in France, social conflict was revealed as a transatlantic matter.

As Marxist critics, it is hardly surprising that Julien and Guérin pointed to the existence of ruling elites with special emphasis on the business classes. Writing just after the publication of C. Wright Mills's *Power Elite*, Julien portrayed the business classes as collaborators of the military and political leaders in ruling American society, while Guérin, relying on older research, presented a more traditional Marxist analysis.[5] He maintained that corporate leaders exercised exclusive control of the United States. For both observers, then, the central feature of American life was the gap between the pretense of majority control and the reality of elite domination. The tyranny of the majority, so feared by French traditionalists, no longer appeared to threaten the American social order.

Neither Julien nor Guérin believed that minority control was permanent. It would be undermined, they agreed, by other interests which were organizing to challenge the dominant elites. Both authors had considerable confidence in the American labor movement, praising the Reuther as opposed to the Meany wing. In the struggle against the rich and wellborn, labor would be joined by black Americans. The two critics applauded the organization and activism of blacks, although Julien had considerably more to cheer about in 1960 than Guérin did in 1950. The coalition of progressive groups would be completed, according to Guérin, by the organization of farm workers, while Julien placed more hope in the rise of middle-class professors and clergymen.[6]

For traditionalists, the problem with the United States was the too rapid modernization of the country. Their basic impulse was to repeal progress. For Julien and Guérin, the essential question was whether the process of modernization could be pushed to its logical conclusion so that the fruits of progress could be more equally distributed. Whereas the traditionalists portrayed a homogeneous society immersed in unrelenting modernization, the two progressive authors discovered major cleavages within the society which would only disappear when power had been shifted to other groups.

While Guérin and Julien were not popular authors in France, their approach to American life reflected the increasing doubt about the cultural gap between France and America, which was experienced by many Frenchmen at the height of the NATO enterprise and reflected in such popular studies as Raymond Cartier's *Les 48 Amériques* and Pierre and Renée Gosset's *L'Amérique aux Américains*.[7] The discovery of cultural convergence coincided with the development of close diplomatic relations between the two countries in the 1950s. However, the liquidation of the Algerian War and the passing of the worst tensions of the cold war helped to encourage a more independent stance by French leaders. General de Gaulle, of course, was prepared to seize the opportunity to give a new direction to French foreign policy. In the early sixties, de Gaulle launched his strident attack on American political domination.

The development of an explicitly anti-American policy at the official level provided the context in which French intellectuals interpreted American civilization. The extent to which Gaullism affected the French view of American culture is difficult to determine because of the quantity of documentation available; moreover, it would be unfair to assume that influence flowed only from politics to culture, when, in fact, cultural anti-Americanism was a well-established phenomenon in France long before de Gaulle's rise to power. Indeed, de Gaulle, like Sartre, lived through the 1920s, and his *Mémoires* suggest that the claims of opposition between Europe and America, so popular at the time, made a deep and lasting impact.[8] Surely, one source of de Gaulle's anti-American policy was this cultural heritage.

An index to the French reaction to American culture in the Gaullist and post-Gaullist years may be found in three books which have been widely read and discussed in France. While the complexities of the French reaction cannot be gauged from an examination of only three works, they do suggest the main themes of the debate on American culture during this period. In all three volumes, the antithesis between a future-oriented America and a traditional France is dramatically revived. Once again, the theme of American power and French subservience is raised, and again Frenchmen are called upon to resist American hegemony, to accept it, or to be selective in their borrowing.

However, it would be dangerous to lump together these three recent studies of the United States which differ in approach and in the backgrounds of their authors. Jean-Jacques Servan-Schreiber and Jean-Francois Revel are professional journalists who have both written for and edited the French news weekly, *L'Express*. They have staked out a centrist position on the French political spectrum, equally critical of Gaullism and communism. René Etiemble, who spent five years in the United States before and during World War II, is professor of comparative literature at the Sorbonne. His concerns are more literary than political, but he has taken a stand for French independence and against French imperialists.

Etiemble's *Parlez-vous franglais?* was published in 1964, at the peak of de Gaulle's power and prestige, to record the author's dismay at the corruption of the French language; however, in the process of defending the language, Etiemble provided an explicit endorsement of Gaullism.[9] According to the author, the French language had been undermined by the penetration of American civilization in France, which, in turn, had been encouraged by fifth-column supporters. The defense of the language, however, was not a task which could be undertaken in isolation from the campaign against American cultural and political advances. According to Etiemble, both American imperialism and the demise of the French language had simultaneous origins in the era of World War I. France's collaboration with the Anglo-Saxon powers, which continued during World War II, brought her into a subservient relationship with both England and the United States, a position from which she never recovered. The dominance of the Anglo-Saxons reached crisis proportions with the signing of the NATO agreement.[10]

American control over the destinies of France was further enhanced by developments in the economic sphere. Etiemble devoted attention to the rising American investments in France. The control over French industries, he suggested, would permit American companies to make decisions about the hiring and firing of French workers exclusively in terms of profit margins and without regard for the French national interest. Meanwhile, France had opened her frontiers to American tourists and their dollars, thus introducing an additional element of American influence.[11]

This kind of political and economic control was both the cause of and caused by the corruption of the French language. The increasing interaction between subservient Frenchmen and Americans in positions of command had encouraged the borrowing of American words and, thus, the contamination of the language. The integration of the French army into NATO forces, for example, forced French officers to speak to their American counterparts in English. The French learned American military terms like "missile gap" and thereby acquired an American outlook on political and military questions. In this sequence, American power led to corruption of the language which, in turn, affected policy.[12]

French cultural life was also subject to contamination from Americans and once again the cause of the problem was the adoption of American words. For Etiemble, "the heritage of words is a heritage of ideas: with the 'twist' and 'segregation,' the Coca-Cola civilization and the American way of not living are going to contaminate and botch what we have left of cuisine, wine, love, and original thoughts."[13] The penetration of American terms paved the way for the development of a consumer society in France which would feature chewing gum and hamburgers. Equally dangerous, however, was the prospect of adopting American social practices such as segregation.

For Etiemble, France's social, political, and economic problems could be solved by attending exclusively to the purity of the French language.[14] The program for the defense of the language would be the work of the Ministries of Education, Culture, and Information. They would check the textbooks, the press, and television programs to make certain that no American words were used if there was an appropriate French equivalent; and, even in cases where no such equivalent existed, American words would be Gallicized.[15] The maintenance of the French language, of course, would assure the independence of French cultural and political life. In this sense, Etiemble's program was simply a form of Gaullism in the area of language.

Servan-Schreiber, like Etiemble, regarded America as the land of the future, but, in many respects, it was not a future to be rejected. Whereas Etiemble condemned the United States as a *"cauchemar climatisée,"* and looked upon the spread of American ways as a *"cancer yanqui,"*[16] Servan-Schreiber was enamored of the new technology which was rapidly bringing America into the postindustrial age of plenty. The consumer society, a childish and materialistic enterprise according to Etiemble, was judged to be a creative and imaginative world by Servan-Schreiber. He stressed the intellectual skills which were necessary to take advantage of the computer with its capacity for generating information and the managerial talents essential to run the new multinational firms. Moreover, the technological innovations, the foundations of the entire postindustrial system, were only feasible with the systematic collaboration between industry, government, and the universities in order to advance research and development.[17]

In all of these respects, the American system had progressed far beyond France and Europe. Indeed, it was this advance into the future which made America a model. However, while Servan-Schreiber advocated the adoption of American innovations in research, technology, and managerial techniques, he was as adamantly opposed to American control of the European system as was Etiemble. The great danger in the present situation was that new techniques were being introduced in Europe by American companies; moreover, with the benefit of these techniques, American firms were beginning to capture the new market created by the European economic community. If present trends continued, the key decisions about the European economy would soon be made by American corporate executives, and the control over European life would pass into the hands of Americans.[18]

Servan-Schreiber's solution to this dilemma was simple in the extreme. He would have Europe model herself after America. Politically, Europe would establish a federation. Once united, the European community would encourage the development of American-style firms under the control of European managers which would exploit the larger market and stress research and development. An industrially dynamic Europe, in Servan-Schreiber's view, would be capable of competing with both the United States and the Soviet Union. Moreover, regional cultures could survive this scheme for modernization, much as Japan had retained many of her traditions despite rapid industrialization.[19]

With Jean-Francois Revel, the contemporary French image of America comes full circle to its revolutionary origins. Once again, as in the days of the eighteenth-century philosophes, the United States emerges as a model for social change in France. Like Lafayette and Condorcet, Revel would have France imitate the political, economic, and cultural system of the United States.

For Revel, the protest activities of the late sixties in the United States constituted the beginning of a second world revolution; it was altogether appropriate that this revolution, like the first one, should begin in the most progressive country in the world. The second revolution was based on the political freedoms guaranteed by the events of 1776, as well as the economic growth which followed shortly thereafter, but it was chiefly concerned with certain social inequities which had arisen since 1776. In the area of international affairs, the first revolution failed to eliminate wars between nation-states; domestically, racial and sexual discrimination were still an integral part of the system. The new revolution had to begin in the most advanced country where the consciousness of these problems was most acute. Contrary to opinion in France, Revel maintained that the United States was far more revolutionary than the Soviet Union, China, Cuba, or any of the European countries.[20]

By the logic of history, Revel was persuaded that Europe would follow the United States in moving toward a revolution as modernization made her more acutely aware of unresolved problems. In preparation for that moment, he advocated the remodeling of the French left. Its doctrinal commitment to revolution was clear, but internal divisions prevented the development of revolutionary potential. A more pragmatic attitude was therefore essential. Moreover, the French political system would have to be altered so that freedom of speech and the press, as well as the diffusion of education to the masses, could be secured. In all of these respects, the United States would provide a model for French changes.[21]

Taken together, the works of Etiemble, Servan-Schreiber, and Revel suggest the vitality of the anti-American tradition in France in recent years. All three authors were persuaded that the American system was the wave of the future and that because of American power, the system could, indeed was, being exported to France. Like the anti-Americans of the twenties, then, these writers believed that the future of France (and Europe) was at stake in what transpired in America. However, their responses to American developments were more diverse than their predecessors. Certainly, no writer of the twenties went so far as Revel in recommending the acceptance of the American system. It is evident, however, that Revel's pro-Americanism was not widely shared in France. He himself devoted a chapter to attacking the anti-Americanism of both right and left, and his polemical tone suggests that he was speaking to a sceptical audience.[22]

Servan-Schreiber and Etiemble were anti-American, but in different ways. The former adopted the moderate anti-Americanism of the advanced radicals, Herriot and Pomaret, in the early thirties. Modernization was acceptable to all of them so long as it was not accompanied by American control. Etiemble went further, reviving the full-blown anti-Americanism of Duhamel. Persuaded that American civilization was fundamentally flawed, he advocated resistance to modernization and American control. Moreover, once again, the polemical tone suggests that Etiemble's position was more extreme than most Frenchmen were willing to accept. By 1960, the opposition to modernization, so intense in the 1920s, had been undercut by the strong commitment of the French government and people to economic growth. It was now more difficult to chastise the United States for a future orientation which so many Frenchmen shared.

While the antithesis proved to be a useful device for articulating an anti-American position even after 1960, anti-Americans found other ways of structuring their arguments. The works of Julien and Guérin provide interesting examples. Their anti-Americanism was only one aspect of a larger opposition to capitalist societies which would also include France and other western countries. Clearly, by the late 1960s, anti-Americans in France had begun to use a Marxist approach to criticize the American system. The intensity of their opposition to America, however, was diminished because they could no longer exploit the contrast between a culturally superior France and a materialistic America.[23]

Moreover, a more substantial current of pro-Americanism, drawing upon both the antithesis and the convergence theme, had also emerged. In effect, the response to America by Frenchmen in the early seventies was far less monolithic than it had been in 1930, although a healthy current of anti-Americanism survived. Moreover, there is no evidence to show that the disappearance of de Gaulle from the political scene has caused the demise of anti-Americanism. Obviously, his hostility toward the United States helped to encourage writers like Etiemble, but the anti-American tradition antedated de Gaulle, and it will certainly survive him.

The primary objective of this study has been to identify the sources of modern anti-Americanism in France, to understand how they came together at a particular moment in history, and to check their staying power in subsequent decades. Little has been said about the accuracy of the images of America which French intellectuals have created for themselves and their public. Yet this is an important subject if only because of the contradictory uses which historians have made of foreign opinions of America. Two basic positions have developed.[24] Some scholars maintain that foreigners looking at the United States are objective observers because, with the advantage of cultural distance, they can understand and reveal the basic assumptions and values which are frequently hidden from Americans. Others would argue that the foreign observer is partisan in at least one of two ways. First, he cannot escape the biases of his own culture. As a patriot, he is primarily concerned with upholding the national culture and the prestige of his nation in the world. Second, he is often the partisan of a particular political tradition within his country. His visit to a foreign country may frequently give him an opportunity to score points in a partisan debate in France. He may do this by portraying certain institutions, policies, or events in the foreign country so as to support claims which he wishes to make at home.

By identifying the image makers as "anti-Americans," this study has no doubt contributed to the view that the images they have created are inaccurate or partisan. However, it should be clear that anti-Americanism is not necessarily an irrational position. It is an ideology, sometimes articulated with passion; but, given the values which the anti-American wishes to defend, it may be an entirely appropriate strategy. Moreover, the articulation of an anti-American position is not necessarily incompatible with accurately portraying the values and institutions of the United States. It will be useful to review some of the charges made against French observers of America as a way of testing the validity of their images.

The presumed antithesis between Europe and America, which so many French critics have adopted, is, of course, a central issue in determining the accuracy of the French image. The persistent use of this device has led Annie Kriegel, for one, to argue that European observers are impervious to social realities. In her view, only a long-standing tradition can account for their acceptance of an "unbridgeable gap between the Old World and the New that cannot be closed by more and more rapid means of crossing the Atlantic." Such a position, according to Kriegel, misrepresents the actual relationship between America and France. "The French may no longer be the aristocratic society of the *ancien régime* nor a mass of peasants brandishing their pitchforks in the name of revolution." When they react to the United States, however, they assume the perspective of "sceptical, rural landholders, Latin and Catholic."[25] In this study, of course, such a perspective has been frequently encountered, most notably in the works of the Protestant André Siegfried and the atheist Simone de Beauvoir. However, it does not follow that the only source of the antithesis is the long-standing impulse to associate America with the future and France with the past. While Frenchmen frequently exaggerated the differences between France and America, it is nonetheless true that in the early nineteenth century, American political institutions were more progressive than their European counterparts, while, in the early twentieth century, economic modernization proceeded more rapidly in America than in Europe.

It is also important to note that the opposition has not been uniformly accepted over time. For a period of ten years from 1917 to 1927 it was held at least partially in abeyance, while the prospects of entente were still alive and the assembly line was regarded as viable.

Again, after World War II, a sense of cultural convergence between France and America emerged, as I have already noted. Of course, the challenge of both leftists and moderates to the antithesis has by no means laid to rest that concept, as I have also pointed out. This fluctuation suggests that French critics are not simply observing a ritual when they use the antithesis. At least to some degree, the acceptance or rejection of the concept of Franco-American opposition has depended upon the changing political, economic, and social forces which affect relations between the two countries.

One other persistent generalization about the sources of national images has been challenged in the findings of this study. The uniformity of the French reaction in the interwar period appears to contradict the claim that foreign images are a product of partisan differences and are generated in response to issues in the home country of the observers. Studies of the French image of the United States in the period 1760 to 1852 indicate clearly that French liberals portrayed America in substantially different terms than French conservatives.[26] Indeed, the image of America became a weapon in partisan struggles between the two groups.

The evidence presented here suggests that after 1917 America ceased for a time to serve as an instrument for partisan debate. The change came about for several reasons. First of all, the rise of political democracy in France made the American model irrelevant for partisan purposes after 1870. However, if American political institutions were no longer controversial, American culture and technology soon became important issues in France. A new division might have emerged between technological progressives and conservatives if the issue had not been distorted by political factors. The Americanist "party" was undermined by the fear of American power which was perceived as an integral part of American technology. In short, once the security of France appeared to be jeopardized by the rise of American empire, French conservatives and liberals found an issue on which they could stand together. Only when French security was threatened in the thirties by the Nazis and after World War II by the Soviet Union would some elements in France reconsider their adamant stand against Americanism.

Several other factors contributed to the virtual unanimity of French opinion in the twenties. First, the failure of the Communists to respond at length to the debate on technology eliminated the most extreme segment of opinion in France and decreased the likelihood of conflict. Second, the racial divisions of the twenties in America evoked a uniform response in France, because both Prohibition and immigration restriction could be perceived as "Anglo-Saxon" measures. Regardless of party, Frenchmen were prepared to identify with Latin values. In a similar fashion, American foreign policy in the twenties provoked a uniformly hostile reaction. The French rejected the American position on debts and disarmament largely because these policies appeared to undermine French hegemony. In other periods and on different issues, however, Frenchmen reacted to American policies along party lines. The Marshall Plan and NATO were treated sympathetically by anti-Communist elements in France who regarded the Soviet Union as a greater threat to France than the United States. Leftist elements, of course, reacted in an opposite fashion.[27]

Thus, partisan divisions as a factor in skewing the image of American civilization and even of America as a political entity were at least partially eliminated in the 1920s. Partisan divisions over American policies after World War II influenced but did not determine attitudes toward American culture. Even conservatives, who were pro-American on political issues, remained exceedingly wary of modernization. In this sense, there is no perfect fit between political and cultural anti-Americanism.

The French, of course, have been partisans in another sense. Most of the travelers, regardless of their political stance, were vigorous French nationalists who preferred the values of individualism and craftsmanship, and were jealous of the relative decline of the French position in foreign affairs. Clearly, this rendered them subjective in their judgments about American life, but it also gave them an ideal position from which to observe changes which were taking place in America. The acute reaction of the French to modernization, their sensitivity to the cultural direction of American life, was, no doubt, aided by their preference for traditional values. The agreement between their strictures against American empire, racism, and mass culture and subsequent judgments by American intellectuals suggests that French biases actually enabled them to anticipate more clearly than Americans the nature of the social and cultural revolution of the twenties; in this sense, the biases were helpful. French-men exaggerated some features of the system, including its dangers to the individual, but they accurately identified a major twentieth-century phenomenon.

The question of the objective basis of French views can be considered from another angle. After all, many other Europeans witnessed and wrote about American life in this period. It would be helpful to examine their views to determine how consistent they are with those of French observers. Of particular importance is to gauge the extent to which other Europeans developed an anti-American position in reaction to the United States. Of course, a systematic comparison is beyond the scope of this study, but the availability of secondary literature on Germany and England is helpful for my purposes.

Anti-Americanism was a European phenomenon which developed as a response to problems affecting the entire European continent. The debt issue, for example, touched England as it did France, while both Germany and England were subject to American investments. The American film, the assembly line, and other features of mass culture were spreading to the rest of Europe. As in France, these developments generated "a flood of books about America," most of them "violently anti-American."[28] The new literature characteristically denounced the United States as "a gigantic Babbitt warren"—to use the title of a British report—which was oppressed by materialism and conformity.[29] This reaction was also tied to the changes brought about by the war. As one British observer put it, "This War did more to alter British impressions of the quality of American life than did the Civil War."[30] A German counterpart remarked, "The victory in the World War has, for the first time, presented that great land [the United States] to European eyes as an actual personality with a new and individual way."[31] Moreover, in both countries the 1920s image of America survived the depression and World War II.[32]

The similar response to the United States throughout Europe suggests that anti-Americanism in France ought to be treated as part of a European movement rather than as a campaign generated by factors peculiar to France. However, certain differences in tone and emphasis appear to distinguish French anti-Americanism from the two other movements. First, French hostility was intensified ironically by the necessity of repudiating the entente. By comparison,

Anglo-American diplomatic relations were less volatile. During the war, the English could provide no counterpart to Lafayette to appeal to American sentiments. The Anglo-American relationship, however, was based on firmer ethnic ties, which could outlast the wartime entente and restrain anti-Americanism in England during the twenties.

By contrast, German-American relations reached their low point in 1918 and 1919. The Germans, of course, blamed their defeat in the war on the United States. However, this initial hostility also helped to restrain the expression of anti-American feelings in the late twenties, because there was no wartime euphoria to erase as there was in France. Moreover, German observers, like their British counterparts, were somewhat more at ease in America by virtue of the large German-American population in the United States.

One additional factor accentuated French anti-Americanism. Their opposition to mass culture, similar in kind to the response of other Europeans, was intensified by the relative strength of the French commitment to individualism and stability. These two values were, of course, cherished by most Europeans, but nowhere so intensely as in France. It is appropriate, therefore, that a Frenchman, Georges Duhamel, should have acquired the reputation as the most outspoken anti-American in Europe during the interwar period.[33] The popularity of his views in France suggests that his countrymen also reacted to the American threat in a more vitriolic fashion than their fellow Europeans. While both the opposition to the United States and the defense of traditional values were the common concerns of the European elite, the French may be said to have led the way by articulating these positions with a special clarity and vigor.

NOTES

1. In 1946. Guérin published a two-volume study entitled *La lutte de classes sous la première république*; Julien entitled his book on the American labor movement: *L'Amérique en révolution* (Paris, 1956).

2. Julien commented in patronizing fashion: "When he experienced a feeling of nausea while visiting the Chicago stockyards, Georges Duhamel

found his proper position in the chain of tourists who strive for an original way of introducing a country." He added that the United States was "too vast and too diverse to be usefully observed in a few weeks." *Le nouveau nouveau monde* (Paris, 1960), I, 9. Guérin had already denounced *Scènes de la vie future* in 1930, at the time of its publication. *Où va le peuple américain?* (Paris, 1950), II, 11.

3. Nonetheless, sections of *Où va le peuple américain?* were selected and published in Sartre's journal, *Les Temps Modernes* (January-March 1950).

4. *Le nouveau nouveau monde*, II, 268.

5. Guérin cited Berle and Means's 1932 study, *The Modern Corporation and Private Property*, to support his claim of corporate domination in America. *Où va le peuple américain?*, I, 27.

6. *Où va le peuple américain?*, I, 235-236, 192, 207, 264; II, 129, 309. *Le nouveau nouveau monde*, I, 207; II, 9.

7. Raymond Cartier, *Les 48 Amériques* (Paris, 1953); Pierre and Renée Gosset, *L'Amérique aux Américains* (Paris, 1953). Cartier addressed the issue of cultural convergence in the following manner: "The only profound difference between the human condition from one side of the Atlantic to the other is a noticeable inequality in the material welfare of the most numerous classes. For the rest, the foundations of the individual's life are obviously the same in Western Europe and the United States. The study of differences is fascinating but it leads to errors, if it is not understood that they are inconsequential alongside the similarities." *Les 48 Amériques*, 421.

8. De Gaulle's understanding of Franco-British-American relations was summarized as follows: "England is an island, France the head of a continent; America another world." *Mémoires de guerre* (Paris, 1954), I, 112. Later, he remarked, "Franco-British solidarity remained more than ever in conformity with the natural order of things when the United States intervened in the affairs of the Old World." *Ibid.*, II, 66.

9. Etiemble spoke with reverence of "the only statesman who, since the Liberation, dares resist the pretentions of the dollar." *Parlez-vous franglais?* (Paris, 1964), 238.

10. *Ibid.*, 231-232.

11. *Ibid.*, 238, 241.

12. *Ibid.*, 237.

13. *Ibid.*, 237.

14. The concern with American corruption of the French language was, of course, inherited from the anti-American movement of the 1920s. At that point, it took the form of a protest against the introduction of American films in the original version or with French dubbing under American direction. See Part III, chapter 9, p. 149.

15. *Parlez-vous franglais?*, 340-343.

16. *Ibid.*, 328-329, 333.

Although Etiemble makes no acknowledgment of his source, it is likely that the expression "cauchemar climatisée" was drawn from the translated title of Henry Miller's *The Air-Conditioned Nightmare*, which appeared in French in 1954 as *Le cauchemar climatisée*.

The expression "cancer yanqui" may also have been drawn, in part, from an earlier work. It recalls Aron and Dandieu's *Le cancer américain* (1931). Etiemble's use of these pejorative characterizations of American culture shows how close in spirit he is to the anti-Americans of the prewar period. Indeed, even Miller, despite his American origins, might be grouped with the French anti-Americans by virtue of his long residence in France between the wars.

17. *Le défi américain* (Paris, 1967), 55, 218.

18. *Ibid.*, 36-37, 43, 45, 55.

19. *Ibid.*, 219, 292.

20. *Ni Marx ni Jésus; de la seconde révolution américaine à la seconde révolution mondiale* (Paris, 1970), 120, 76, 93, 166-167, 76, 35.

21. *Ibid.*, 57, 141.

22. "L'antiaméricanisme et la révolution américaine." In the chapter, Revel identified clearly the two major sources of anti-Americanism in France in 1970. On the right, Frenchmen were still concerned with the corruption of the French way of life and jealous of American power. On the left, ironically, there was also a nostalgia for the past. Leftists wanted to accomplish a proletarian revolution, although economic gains under the American system had ruled out such a revolution. *Ibid.*, 152, 159-160.

23. Examples of recent French studies of America which have adopted a Marxist approach are: Eric Gaument, *Le mythe américain* (Paris, 1970); and Francois Masnata, *Autopsie d'une Amérique* (Paris, 1973). Both books critique the pro-American views of Servan-Schreiber and Revel, suggesting that the concept of America as a model for French development is by no means universally accepted in France. Masnata, for example, denounces both authors for "presenting the United States as the model which should inspire the old continent, France in particular" (p. 5). For Gaument, Servan-Schreiber has helped to nourish a "myth" about America (p. 7).

24. See the introduction for specific examples of these approaches.

25. "Consistent Misapprehension: European Views of America and Their Logic," *Daedalus* (Fall 1972), 87-88.

26. See, for example, Durand Echeverria, *Mirage in the West* (Princeton, 1957); and René Rémond, *L'Amérique devant l'opinion francaise, 1815-1852*, 2 vols. (Paris, 1962).

27. This response has been studied in David Strauss, "The French Image of America: A Study of French Opinion, 1945-1962" (unpublished master's essay, Columbia University, 1963).

28. Earl R. Beck, *Germany Rediscovers America* (Tallahassee, 1968), 17, x.

29. Cited in Richard Rapson, *Britons View America: Travel Commentary, 1860-1935* (Seattle, 1971), 67. The phrase "Babbitt warren" was used by C. H. Bretherton, *Midas, or, The United States and the Future* (New York, 1926). The journalist C. E. M. Joad also entitled his study of America *The Babbitt Warren* (New York, 1927).

30. Cited in Rapson, *Britons View America*, 54.

31. Cited in Beck, *Germany Rediscovers America*, 17-18.

32. See Beck, *Germany Rediscovers America*, 254-284; and Rapson, *Britons View America*, 54.

33. An assessment of the European dimension of anti-Americanism is offered by the Belgian scholar Victor Bohet, "L'Europe devant l'Amérique," *Equilibres, Cahiers périodiques*, 2ième série, 2-3, 1933. Bohet claims that the anti-American movement reached its climax with Duhamel's work, although he recognizes the contributions of the Germans, Keyserling and Müller-Freienfels; and the British critics, Chesterton and Belloc.

 *Bibliography*

## I. PRIMARY SOURCES

For the travel literature in the period 1776-1932, I have relied heavily on Frank Monaghan, *French Travellers in the United States, 1765-1932* (New York: Antiquarian Press, 1961). Several items which pertain to the period before 1932 and were not listed in Monaghan are contained in the Addendum to Monaghan below. For the period after 1932, I have compiled my own bibliography from *Biblio: Catalogue des ouvrages parus en langue francaise dans le monde entier* (1933-1976), reviews in major journals, and references in the travel volumes themselves. The items pertaining to these years comprise a representative but not a complete list of French travelers in the United States.

### A. Addendum to Monaghan

Chinard, Gilbert. *Le doctrine de l'américanisme des puritains au président Wilson*. Paris: Librairie Hachette, 1919.

Ferri-Pisani, Camille. *Prince Napoleon in America, 1861: Letters from his Aide-de-camp*. Translated by Georges Joyaux. Bloomington: Indiana University Press, 1959.

Tocqueville, Alexis de. *Democracy in America*. 2 vols. Edited by Phillips Bradley. Translated by Henry Reeve. New York: Random House, 1954.

———. *Journey to America*. Edited by J. P. P. Mayer. Translated by George Lawrence. New Haven: Yale University Press, 1959.

B. *Selected List of French Travelers in America: 1933-1976*

Arnavon, Cyrille. *L'américanisme et nous*. Paris: del Duca, 1958.

Beauvoir, Simone de. *L'Amérique au jour le jour*. Paris: Librairie Gallimard, 1954 (1948).

Bonnichon, Louis. *Des aspects sociaux de la "Réforme Roosevelt."* Paris: Librairie du Recueil Sirey, 1934.

Boris, Georges, *La révolution Roosevelt*. Paris: Librairie Gallimard, 1934.

Bost, Jacques-Laurent. *Trois mois aux Etats-Unis*. Paris: Les éditions de minuit, 1946.

Bourcier, Emmanuel. *U.S.A.—33: L'écroulement américain*. Paris: Editions Baudinière, 1934.

Bruckberger, R. L. *Image of America*. Translated by C. G. Paulding and Virgilia Peterson. New York: Viking Press, 1959.

Cartier, Raymond. *Les 48 Amériques*. Paris: Librairie Plon, 1953.

Drujon, François. *L'Amérique et l'avenir*. Paris: Editions Corrêa, 1938.

Dubreuil, Hyacinthe. *Les codes de Roosevelt et le perspective de la vie sociale*. Paris: Bernard Grasset, éditeur, 1934.

Etiemble (René). *Parlez-vous franglais?* Collections idées. Paris: Librairie Gallimard, 1964.

Faÿ, Bernard. *Civilisation américaine*. Paris: Sagittaire, 1939.

————. *Roosevelt et son Amérique*, Paris: Librairie Plon, 1933.

Franck, Louis R. *L'expérience Roosevelt et le milieu social américain*. Paris: Librairie Félix Alcan, 1937.

Gaument, Eric. *Le mythe américain*. Paris: Editions Sociales, 1970.

Gosset, Pierre, and Gosset, Renée. *L'Amérique aux Américains*. 2 vols. Paris: René Julliard, 1953.

Guérin, Daniel. *Où va le peuple américain?* Les Temps Modernes. 2 vols. Paris: René Julliard, 1950.

Jouvenel, Bertrand de. *La crise du capitalisme américain*. Les Documents Bleus. Paris: Librairie Gallimard, 1933.

Julien, Claude. *Le nouveau nouveau monde*. 2 vols. Paris: René Julliard, 1960.

Lefranc, G. *Roosevelt contre la crise*. Paris: Publications de l'institut supérieur ouvrier, 1936.

Lyautey, Pierre. *Révolution américaine*. Paris: Librairie Hachette, 1934.

Maritain, Jacques. *Réflexions sur l'Amérique*. Paris: Librairie Arthème Fayard, 1958.

Marjolin, Robert. *L'évolution du syndicalisme aux Etats-Unis de Washington à Roosevelt*. Paris: Librairie Félix Alcan, 1936.

Masnata, Francois. *Autopsie d'une Amérique*. Paris: Payot, 1973.

Maurois, André. *Chantiers américains*. Paris: Librairie Gallimard, 1933.

———. *Etats-Unis 39: Journal d'un voyage en Amérique*. Paris: Les éditions de France, 1939.

———. *Etudes américaines*. New York: Editions de la Maison Française, 1945.

Milhaud, Darius. *Notes without Music: An Autobiography*. Translated by Donald Evans. New York: Alfred A. Knopf, 1953.

Page, Lucien. *L'expérience Roosevelt: Ses causes—son développement—ses conséquences*. Paris: Les presses modernes, 1934.

Recouly, Raymond. *L'Amérique pauvre*. Paris: Les éditions de France, 1933.

Revel, Jean-Francois. *Ni Marx ni Jésus: de la seconde révolution américaine à la seconde révolution mondiale*. Paris: Editions Robert Laffont, 1970.

Romains, Jules. *Visite aux Américains*. Paris: Ernest Flammarion, éditeur, 1936.

Roy, Claude. *Clefs pour l'Amérique*. Paris: Librairie Gallimard, 1949.

Saint-Jean, Robert de. *La vraie révolution de Roosevelt*. Paris: Bernard Grasset, éditeur, 1934.

Sartre, Jean-Paul. *Situations III*. Paris: Librairie Gallimard, 1949.

Schaeffer, Pierre. *Amérique, nous t'ignorons*. Paris: Editions du Seuil, 1946.

Servan-Schreiber, Emile. *L'Amérique réagit*. Paris: Librairie Plon, 1934.

Servan-Schreiber, Jean-Jacques. *Le défi américain*. Paris: Editions Denoël, 1967.

Siegfried, André. *Etats-Unis, Canada, Mexique: Lettres de voyage écrites au Petit Havre, juin-decembre 1935*. Le Havre: Imprimerie du Journal *le Petit Havre*, 1935.

———. *Qu'est-ce que l'Amérique?* "Directives." Paris: Ernest Flammarion, éditeur, 1937.

Vercors (Jean Bruhlers). *Les pas dans le sable: L'Amérique—La Chine et la France*. Paris: A. Michel, 1954.

## C. The American Empire and the Decline of Europe

Aron, Robert, and Dandieu, Arnaud. *Décadence de la nation française*. Paris: Les éditions Rieder, 1931.

Bonnefon-Craponne, Jean. *Le pénétration économique et financière des capitaux américains en Europe*. Paris: Imprimerie Labor, 1930.

Chastanet, J. L. *L'Oncle Shylock ou l'impérialisme américain à la conquête du monde*. Paris: Ernest Flammarion, éditeur, 1927.

Dahriman, Georges. *Pour les états confédérés d'Europe*. Paris: Editions Argo, 1929.

De Gaulle, Charles. *Mémoires de Guerre*. 3 vols. Paris: Librairie Plon, 1954.

Delaisi, Francis. *Les contradictions du monde moderne*. Paris: Payot, 1925.

Demangeon, A. *Le déclin de l'Europe*. Paris: Payot, 1920.

Duhamel, Georges; Benda, Julien; Benes, Edouard; et al. *Entretiens: L'avenir de l'esprit européen*. Société des Nations, Institut International de Cooperation Intellectuelle. Paris: Librairie Stock, 1934.

Duhamel, Georges; Arguédas, Alcédés; Conéda, E. Diez; et al. *Entretiens: Europe—Amérique Latine*. Société des Nations, Institut International de Cooperation Intellectuelle. Paris: Librairie Stock, 1937.

Duhamel, Georges. *Querelles de famille*. Paris: Mercure de France, 1932.

————. *Le voyage de Moscou*. Paris: Mercure de France, 1927.

Durtain, Luc. *L'autre Europe: Moscou et sa foi*. Paris: Librairie Gallimard, 1928.

————. *Dieux blancs, hommes jaunes*. Paris: Ernest Flammarion, éditeur, 1930.

————. *Le globe sous le bras*. Paris: Ernest Flammarion, éditeur, 1936.

Fabre-Luce, Alfred. *A quoi rêve le monde*. Paris: Bernard Grasset, éditeur, 1931.

————. *Russie 1927*. Paris: Bernard Grasset, éditeur, 1927.

Fourgeaud, André. *La rationalisation: Etats-Unis-Allemagne*. Paris: Payot, 1929.

Gachon, Jean. *La politique étrangère des Etats-Unis: Qui la conduit?* Paris: Librairie Félix Alcan, 1929.

Gillouin, René. *Le destin de l'Occident*. Paris: Editions Prométhée, 1929.

Grousset, René. *Le reveil de l'Asie: L'impérialisme britannique et la revolte des peuples*. Paris: Librairie Plon, 1924.

Guénon, René. *La crise du monde moderne*. Paris: Editions Bossard, 1927.

————. *Orient et Occident*. Paris: Payot, 1924.

Herriot, Edouard. *Europe*. Paris: Les éditions Rieder, 1930.

Homberg, Octave. *La grande injustice (La question des dettes interalliées)*. Paris: Bernard Grasset, éditeur, 1926.

Kadmi-Cohen. *L'abomination américaine: essai politique*. Paris: Ernest Flammarion, éditeur, 1930.

Le Corbusier, and Jeanneret, P. *Oeuvres complètes, 1934-1938*. Zurich: Les éditions d'Architecture, 1964.

Laurent, Pierre. *L'impérialisme économique américain*. Paris: Librairie du Receuil Sirez, 1931.

Massis, Henri. *Défense de l'Occident*. Paris: Librairie Plon, 1927.

Morand, Paul. *A. O. F.: de Paris à Timboucton*. Paris: Ernest Flammarion, éditeur, 1928.

———. *Chronique de XX᷉ siecle: Magie noire*. Paris: Bernard Grasset, éditeur, 1928.

———. *Journal d'un attaché d'ambassade, 1916-1917*. Paris: La Table Ronde, 1947.

———. *Londres*. Paris: Librairie Plon, 1933.

———. *Rien que la terre*. Paris: Bernard Grasset, éditeur, 1926.

Muret, Maurice. *Le crépuscule des nations blancs*. Paris: Payot, 1925.

Picard, Roger, and Hugon, Paul. *Le problème des dettes interalliées: necessité d'une révision*. Paris: Librairie Plon, 1934.

Pomaret, Charles. *L'Amérique à la conquête de l'Europe*. Paris: Librairie Armond Colin, 1931.

Riou, Gaston. *Europe, ma patrie*. Paris: Librairie Valois, 1928.

Rolland, Romains. *I Will Not Rest*. Translated by K. S. Shelvanker. New York: Liveright Publishing Corporation, 1937.

Romier, Lucien. *Explication de notre temps*. Paris: Bernard Grasset, éditeur, 1925.

———. *L'homme nouveau: esquisse des conséquences du progrès*. Paris: Librairie Hachette, 1929.

———. *Nation et civilisation*. Paris: Simon Kra, 1926.

———. *Se le capitalisme disparaissait*. Paris: Librairie Hachette, 1933.

Rougemont, Denis de. *Vingt-huit siècles d'Europe: la conscience européene à travers les textes d'Hesiode à nos jours*. Paris: Payot, 1961.

Siegfried, André. *Amérique Latine*. Paris: Librairie Armand Colin, 1934.

———. *L'âme des peuples*. Paris: Librairie Hachette, 1950.

———. *L'Angleterre d'aujourd'hui: son évolution économique et politique*. Paris: Les Editions G. Crès et Co., 1924.

———. *La crise brittanique du XX᷉ siècle*. Paris: Librairie Armand Colin, 1952 (1931).

———. *La crise de l'Europe*. Paris: Calmann-Lévy, 1935.

———. *Mes souvenirs de la III᷉ République: mon père et son temps: Jules Siegfried, 1836-1922*. Paris: Editions du grand siècle, 1946.

———. *Tableau des partis en France*. Paris: Bernard Grasset, éditeur, 1930.

———. *De la III᷉ à la IV᷉ République*. Paris: Bernard Grasset, éditeur, 1956.

Valéry, Paul. *Regards sur le monde actuel*. Collection idées. Paris: Librairie Gallimard, 1945.

———. *Variété*. Paris: Librairie Gallimard, 1924.

## D. Periodicals

*Arts, Beaux Arts, Littérature, Spectacles*, 1945-1949.
*Cahiers d'Art*, 1945-1962.
*Europe Nouvelle*, 1918-1940.
*L'Express*, 1957-1962.
*France-Amérique*, 1910-1960 (monthly).
*France-Amérique*, 1943-1945 (weekly).
*Jazz Hot*, 1945-1962.
*Mercure de France*, 1918-1940.
*New York Times*, 1917-1945.
*Pour la victoire*, 1942-1945.
*La Revue de Paris*, 1918-1940.
*La Revue des Deux Mondes*, 1918-1942; 1948-1962.
*La Revue Universelle*, 1927-1933.
*La Table Ronde*, 1948-1962.
*View*, 1941-1947.
*XXᵉ Siècle*, 1951-1962.
*VVV*, 1942-1944.

## II. SECONDARY SOURCES

### A. Studies of the French Image of America

Anderson, Emmett Harvey. "Appraisal of American Life by French Travelers, 1860-1914." Unpublished Ph.D. dissertation, University of Virginia, 1953.

Baker, Joseph E. "How the French See America." *Yale Review* (Winter 1958), 239-253.

Benjamin, Mary M. "Fluctuations in the Prestige of the United States in France." Unpublished Ph.D. dissertation, Columbia University, 1959.

Boswell, George Bigler. "Coup d'oeil français sur l'Amérique." Unpublished Ph.D. dissertation, Princeton University, 1952.

Chester, Edward A. "Trends in Recent European Thought on America." Unpublished Ph.D. dissertation, Brown University, 1936.

Cook, Will Mercer. "French Travelers in the United States, 1840-1870." Unpublished Ph.D. dissertation, Brown University, 1936.

Copans, Simon. "French Opinion of American Democracy." Unpublished Ph.D. dissertation, Brown University, 1942.

————. "Tocqueville's Later Years—A Reaffirmation of Faith." *The Romanic Review* (April 1945), 113-121.

Duberman, David. "American Civilization and French Travelers, 1865-1914." Unpublished Ph.D. dissertation, University of Pennsylvania, 1963.

Echeverria, Durand. "L'Amérique devant l'opinion française, 1734-1870: Questions de méthode et d'interpretation." *Revue D'Histoire Moderne et Contemporaine* (1961), 51-62.

————. *Mirage in the West. A History of the French Image of American Society to 1815*. Princeton: Princeton University Press, 1957.

"Les Etats-Unis, les Américains, et la France, 1945-1953." *Sondages: Revue Francaise de l'Opinion Publique* (Paris, 1953).

Gagnon, Paul. "French Views of the Second American Revolution." *French Historical Studies* (Fall 1962), 3-22.

————. "French Views of Postwar America, 1919-1932." Unpublished Ph.D. dissertation, Harvard University, 1960.

Gavronsky, Serge. "American Slavery and French Liberals: An Interpretation of the Role of Slavery in French Politics during the Second Empire." *The Journal of Negro History* (January 1966), 36-52.

————. "The French Liberal Opposition and the American Civil War." Unpublished Ph.D. dissertation, Columbia University, 1965.

Gibson, Delbert L. "French Impressions of American Character and Culture." Unpublished Ph.D. dissertation, University of Wisconsin, 1938.

Gonnaud, Maurice, and Flak, Micheline. "Thoreau in France." In *Twelve Bibliographical Essays*. Edited by Eugene F. Timpe. Hamden, Connecticut: Shoe String Press, 1971.

Hubbard, Genevieve. "French Travelers in America, 1775-1840." Unpublished Ph.D. dissertation, American University, 1936.

Huvos, Kornel. *Cinq mirages américains: Les Etats-Unis dans l'oeuvre de Georges Duhamel, Jules Romains, André Maurois, Jacques Maritain et Simone de Beauvoir*. Paris: Librairie Marcel Didier, 1972.

Jeune, Simon. *De F. T. Graindorge à A. O. Barnabooth: Les types américains dans le roman et le théatre français (1861-1917)*. Paris: Librairie Marcel Didier, 1963.

Keating, L. Clark. "What the French Think of Us." *The Modern Language Journal* (May 1963), 191-194.

Lewis, Michàel. "Les derniers jugements des écrivains francaise sur la civilisation américaine." Unpublished Ph.D. dissertation, University of Poitiers, 1931.

McLellan, David. "The French Image of America: A Study of French Postwar Non-Communist Publications and Polls." Unpublished Ph.D. dissertation, Yale University, 1954.

Noble, George Bernard. *Policies and Opinions at Paris: Wilsonian Diplomacy, the Versailles Peace, and French Public Opinion.* New York: Macmillan, 1935.

Peyre, Henri. "American Literature through French Eyes." *Virginia Quarterly Review* (Spring 1955), 421-438.

Pingeon, Frances M. "French Opinion of Roosevelt and the New Deal." Unpublished master's essay, Columbia University, 1962.

Rémond, René. *Les Etats-Unis devant l'opinion française, 1815-1852.* 2 vols. Paris: Librairie Armand Colin, 1962.

————. "La France regarde les Etats-Unis (1815-1852)." *Bulletin de la Société d'Histoire Moderne.* Douzième série (Juillet 1960), 12-19.

Rodrigue, Elisabeth M. "Les voyageurs français aux Etats-Unis pendant la première moitié du dix-neuvième siècle." Unpublished Ph.D. dissertation, Radcliffe College, 1945.

Simon, J. "L'Amérique telle que l'ont vue les romanciers français (1917-1937)." *Etudes Anglaises* (November 1937), 498-521.

Strauss, David. "The French Image of America: A Study of French Opinion, 1945-1962." Unpublished master's essay, Columbia University, 1963.

Weinberg, Michael. "The Liberal Image of America in France and England, 1789-1890." Unpublished Ph.D. dissertation, Harvard University, 1960.


## B. Other Image Studies

Beck, Earl R. *Germany Rediscovers America.* Tallahassee: Florida State University Press, 1968.

Berger, Max. *The British Traveler in America, 1836-1860.* New York: Columbia University Press, 1943.

Bohet, Victor. "L'Europe en face de l'Amérique." *Equilibres: Cahiers Périodiques.* Deuxième série. Nos. 2-3. 1933.

Boorstin, Daniel. *America and the Image of Europe.* New York: Meridian Books, 1960.

Burnham, James, ed. *What Europe Thinks of America.* New York: John Day, 1953.

Cantril, Hadley, and Buchanan, William. *How Nations See Each Other: A Study in Public Opinion.* Urbana: University of Illinois Press, 1953.

Chiappelli, Fred, ed. *First Images of America: The Impact of the New*

*World on the Old*. 2 vols. Berkeley: University of California Press, 1976.

Commager, Henry Steele, ed. *America in Perspective: The United States through Foreign Eyes*. New York: New American Library, 1947.

Cunliffe, Marcus. "Europe and America." *Encounter* (December 1961), 19-29.

Evans, J. Martin. *America: The View from Europe*. San Francisco: San Francisco Book Company, 1976.

Farrell, John C., and Smith, Asa P. *Image and Reality in World Politics*. New York: Columbia University Press, 1967.

Galantière, Lewis, ed. *America and the Mind of Europe*. London: H. Hamilton, 1951.

Gerbi, Antonello. *The Dispute of the New World: The History of a Polemic, 1750-1900*. Translated by Jerome Moyle. Pittsburgh: University of Pittsburgh Press, 1973.

Halasz, Nicholas. *Roosevelt through Foreign Eyes*. New York: D. Van Nostrand, 1961.

Jones, Howard M. *American and French Culture*. Chapel Hill: University of North Carolina Press, 1927.

———. *O Strange New World—American Culture: The Formative Years*. New York: Viking Press, 1964.

Joseph, Franz M., ed. *As Others See Us: The United States through Foreign Eyes*. Princeton: Princeton University Press, 1959.

Kelman, Herbert C., ed. *International Behavior: A Social-Psychological Analysis*. New York: Holt, Rinehart and Winston, 1965.

Klineberg, Otto. *The Human Dimension in International Relations*. New York: Holt, Rinehart and Winston, 1964.

Koht, Halvdan. *The American Spirit in Europe: A Survey of Transatlantic Influences*. Philadelphia: University of Pennsylvania Press, 1949.

Knoles, George Harmon. *The Jazz Age Revisited: British Criticism of American Civilization during the 1920's*. Stanford: Stanford University Press, 1955.

Kriegel, Annie. "Consistent Misapprehension: European Views of America and Their Logic." *Daedalus* (Fall 1972), 87-102.

Lasky, Melvin J. "America and Europe." *Encounter* (January 1962), 66-78.

Mesick, Louise Jane. *The English Traveller in America, 1795-1835*. New York: Columbia University Press, 1922.

Rangel, Carlos. *The Latin Americans: Their Love-Hate Relationship with the United States*. Translated from the French by Ivan Kats. New York: Harcourt, Brace, Johanovich, 1977.

Rapson, Richard L. *Britons View America: Travel Commentary, 1860-1935*. Seattle: University of Washington Press, 1971.

Skard, Sigmund. *American Studies in Europe: Their History and Present Organization*. 2 vols. Philadelphia: University of Pennsylvania Press, 1958.

————. *The American Myth and the European Mind: American Studies in Europe*. Philadelphia: University of Pennsylvania Press, 1961.

Strout, Cushing. "America, the Menace of the Future: A European Fantasy." *Virginia Quarterly Review* (Autumn 1957), 569-581.

————. *The American Image of the Old World: Reflections on American Thought*. New York: Harper and Row, 1963.

Visson, André. *As Others See Us*. Garden City, New York: Doubleday, 1948.

White, Elizabeth Brett. *American Opinion of France from Lafayette to Poincaré*. New York: Alfred A. Knopf, 1927.

## C. Relevant Studies of French Political and Cultural History

Albonetti, Achille. *Préhistoire des Etats-Unis de l'Europe*. Paris: Editions Sirey, 1963.

Albrecht-Carrié, René. *One Europe: The Historical Background of European Unity*. Garden City, New York: Doubleday, 1945.

Aron, Raymond. *The Opium of the Intellectuals*. Translated by Terence Kilmartin. New York: W. W. Norton, 1962.

Artaud, Denise. "A propos de l'occupation de la Ruhr." *Revue d'Histoire Moderne et Contemporaine* (January-March, 1970), 1-21.

————. "Le gouvernement américain et la question des dettes de guerre (1919-1920)." *Revue d'Histoire Moderne et Contemporaine* (April-June, 1973), 201-229.

————. *La reconstruction de l'Europe, 1919-1929*. Dossiers Clio. Paris: Presses Universitaires de France, 1973.

Barzun, Jacques. *The French Race*. New York: Columbia University Press, 1932.

Bastid, Paul. "L'Idée d'Europe et l'organisation de l'Europe." *L'Europe du XIX<sup>e</sup> et XX<sup>e</sup> siècle (1914-aujourd'hui): Problèmes et interpretations historiques*. Edited by Max Beloff et al. Vol. 1. Milan: Marzorati, éditeur, 1964.

Baumont, Maurice. *La faillite de la paix (1918-1939)*. Vol. XX of *Peuples et Civilisations*. Troisième édition. Paris: Presses Universitaires de France, 1951.

Beach, Sylvia. *Shakespeare and Company*. New York: Harcourt Brace, 1959.

Bidal, M. L. *Les écrivains de l'Abbaye*. Paris: Boivin, 1936.

Binion, Rudolph. *Defeated Leaders: The Political Fate of Caillaux, Jouvenel, and Tardieu*. New York: Columbia University Press, 1959.

Bonnefous, Edouard. *Histoire politique de la Troisième République*. Vols. 4 and 5. Paris: Presses Universitaires de France, 1960-1962.

Bonnet, Pierre. *La commercialisation de la vie française du Premier Empire à nos jours*. Paris: Librairie Plon, 1929.

Brodin, Pierre. *Les écrivains francais de l'entre-deux-guerres*. Montreal: Editions Bernard Valiguette, 1942.

Brugmans, Henri. *L'idée européene, 1918-1965*. Bruges: de Tempel, 1965.

Burnier, Michel-Antoine. *Choice of Action: The French Existentialists on the Political Front Line*. Translated by Bernard Murchland. New York: Random House, 1966.

Caute, David. *Communism and the French Intellectuals, 1914-1960*. New York: Macmillan, 1964.

Chastanet, Jacques. *Histoire de la Troisième République: Les années d'illusions, 1918-1931*. Paris: Librairie Hachette, 1960.

————. *Raymond Poincaré*. Paris: René Julliard, 1948.

Claudel, Paul. "Claudel et l'Amérique." *Cahier Canadien Claudel*. Ottawa: Editions de l'Université d'Ottawa, 1964.

Delevoy, Robert J. *Léger: Etude biographique et critique*. Translated by Stuart Gilbert. Geneva: Skira, 1962.

Duroselle, Jean-Baptiste. *L'idée de l'Europe dans l'histoire*. Paris: Les Editions Denoël, 1965.

Fohlen, Claude. *La France de l'entre-deux-guerres (1917-1939)*. Paris: Casterman, 1966.

Furniss, Edgar S. *France, Troubled Ally: De Gaulle's Heritage and Prospects*. New York: Frederick A. Praeger, 1960.

Gide, André. *The Journals of André Gide*. Translated by Justin O'Brien. 3 vols. New York: Alfred A. Knopf, 1941-1951.

Goguel, Francois. *La politique des partis sous la troisième république*. Paris: Editions du Seuil, 1948 (1946).

Gramont, Sanche de. *The French: Portrait of a People*. New York: G.P. Putnam's Sons, 1969.

Haig, Robert Murray. *The Public Finances of Postwar France*. New York: Columbia University Press, 1929.

Hayes, C. J. H. *France, A Nation of Patriots*. New York: Columbia University Press, 1930.

Hoffman, Stanley et al. *In Search of France*. Cambridge: Harvard University Press, 1963.

Hughes. H. Stuart. *Consciousness and Society: The Reorientation of European Social Thought, 1890-1930*. New York: Alfred A. Knopf, 1961 (1958).

————. *The Obstructed Path: French Social Thought in the Years of Desperation, 1930-1960*. New York: Harper and Row, 1968.

Jaffe, William, and Ogburn, William F. *The Economic Development of Postwar France: A Survey of Production*. New York: Columbia University Press, 1929.

Kindleberger, Charles. *Economic Growth in France and Great Britain, 1851-1950*. A Clarion Book. New York: Simon and Schuster, 1968 (1964).

Landes, David. *The Unbound Prometheus: Technological Change and Industrial Development in Western Europe from 1750 to the Present*. Cambridge, England: Cambridge University Press, 1969.

Larmour, Peter J. *The French Radical Party in the 1930's*. Palo Alto: Stanford University Press, 1964.

Leuthy, Herbert. *France Against Herself: The Past, Politics and Crises of Modern France*. Translated by Eric Mosbacher. New York: Meridian Books, 1955.

Maier, Charles S. *Recasting Bourgeois Europe: Stabilization in France, Germany, and Italy in the Decade after World War I*. Princeton: Princeton University Press, 1975.

Manévy, Raymond. *Histoire de la presse (1914-1939)*. Paris: Editions Corréa, 1945.

Maurois, André. *From Proust to Camus: Profiles of Modern French Writers*. Translated by Carl Morse and Renaud Bruce. New York: Doubleday, 1966.

————. *Mémoires*. Paris: Ernest Flammarion, éditeur, 1970.

Mayer. J. P. *Alexis de Tocqueville: A Biographical Study in Political Science*. New York: Harper and Brothers, 1960 (1939).

Mead, Margaret, and Metraux, Rhoda. *Themes in French Culture: A Preface to a Study of French Community*. Hoover Institute Studies. Palo Alto: Stanford University Press, 1954.

Michaud, Guy. "La crise de la civilisation européene." *L'Europe du XIX^e et du XX^e siècle (1914-aujourd'hui): Problèmes et interpretations historiques*. Vol. 1. Edited by Max Beloff et al. Milan: Marzorati, éditeur, 1964.

Nadeau, Maurice. *The History of Surrealism*. Translated by Richard Howard. New York: Macmillan, 1965.

Noakes, Warren David. "Boris Vian (1920-1959): Témoin d'une époque." Unpublished Ph.D. dissertation, New York University, 1963.

Nourissier, Francois. *The French*. Translated by Adrienne Foulke. New York: Alfred A. Knopf, 1968.

Peyre, Henri. *The Contemporary French Novel*. New York: Oxford University Press, 1955.

Pierson, George Wilson. *Tocqueville in America*. Abridged by Dudley C. Lunt. Garden City, New York: Doubleday, 1959.

Poster, Mark. *Existential Marxism in Postwar France from Sartre to Althusser*. Princeton: Princeton University Press, 1975.

Prévost, Jean. *Histoire de France depuis la guerre*. Paris: Les éditions Rieder, 1932.

Rémond, René. *The Right Wing in France from 1815 to de Gaulle*. Translated by James M. Laux. Philadelphia: University of Pennsylvania Press, 1966.

Shattuck, Roger. *The Banquet Years*. New York: Doubleday, 1961 (1958).

Suarez, Georges. *Briand: sa vie—son oeuvre avec son journal et de nombreux documents inédits*. Vols. 5 and 6. Paris: Librairie Plon, 1952.

Tarr, Francis de. *The French Radical Party from Herriot to Mendes-France*. London: Oxford University Press, 1961.

Thibaudet, Albert. *La république des professeurs*. Paris: Bernard Grasset, éditeur, 1927.

Voyenne, Bernard. *Histoire de l'idée européene*. Petite Bibliothèque Payot. Paris: Payot, 1964 (1952).

Zeldin, Theodore. *France, 1848-1945*. Vol. II. *Intellect, Taste and Anxiety*. Oxford: Oxford University Press, 1977.

## D. Studies of Franco-American Relations

Archimbaud, Léon. *La Conférence de Washington (12 novembre 1921-6 février 1922)*. Paris: Payot, 1923.

Bailey, Thomas. *A Diplomatic History of the American People*. Eighth edition. New York: Appleton-Century-Crofts, 1968.

Blumenthal, Henry A. *A Reappraisal of Franco-American Relations, 1830-1871*. Chapel Hill: University of North Carolina Press, 1959.

———. *American and French Culture, 1800-1900: Interchanges in Art, Science, Literature, and Society*. Baton Rouge: Louisiana State University Press, 1975.

———. *France and the United States: Their Diplomatic Relations, 1789-1914*. Chapel Hill: University of North Carolina Press, 1970.

Brinton, Crane. *The Americans and the French*. Cambridge: Harvard University Press, 1968.

Buckley, Thomas H. *The United States and the Washington Conference, 1921-1922*. Knoxville: University of Tennessee Press, 1970.

Carroll, Daniel B. *Henri Mercier and the American Civil War*. Princeton: Princeton University Press, 1971.

Carter, John. *Conquest: America's Painless Imperialism*. New York: Harcourt, Brace, 1928.

Case, Lynn M., and Spencer, Warren F. *The United States and France: Civil War Diplomacy*. Philadelphia: University of Pennsylvania Press, 1970.

Castigliola, Frank. "The Other Side of Isolationism: The Establishment of the First World Bank, 1929-1930." *Journal of American History* (December 1972).

Crokaert, Jacques. *La Méditerranée américaine: l'expansion des Etats-Unis dans la mer des Antilles*. Paris: Payot, 1927.

Duboscq, André. *Le problème du Pacifique*. Paris: Librairie Delagrave, 1927.

Duroselle, Jean-Baptiste. *From Wilson to Roosevelt: Foreign Policy of the United States, 1913-1945*. Translated by Nancy Lyman Roelker. New York: Harper and Row, 1968 (1960).

Feis, Herbert. *The Diplomacy of the Dollar: First Era, 1919-1932*. Baltimore: The Johns Hopkins Press, 1950.

Ferrell, Robert. *American Diplomacy in the Great Depression: Hoover-Stimson Foreign Policy, 1929-1933*. New Haven: Yale University Press, 1957.

————. *Peace in Their Time: The Origins of the Kellogg-Briand Pact*. New Haven: Yale University Press, 1952.

Jordan, W. M. *Great Britain, France, and the German Problem, 1918-1939*. London: Oxford University Press, 1943.

McKay, Donald C. *The United States and France*. Cambridge: Harvard University Press, 1951.

Motherwell, Hiram. *The Imperial Dollar*. New York: Brentano's, 1929.

Mott, T. Bentley. *Myron T. Herrick, Friend of France*. Garden City, New York: Doubleday, 1929.

Moulton, Harold G., and Lewis, Cleona. *The French Debt Problem*. New York: Macmillan, 1925.

Moulton, Harold G., and Pasvolsky, Leo. *War Debts and World Prosperity*. Washington, D.C.: Brookings Institution, 1932.

Mowrer, Edgar A. *The American World*. New York: J. H. Sears, 1928.

O'Connor, Raymond G. *Perilous Equilibrium: The United States and the*

*London Naval Conference of 1930*. Lawrence: University of Kansas Press, 1962.

Parrini, Carl B. *Heir to Empire: United States Economic Diplomacy, 1916-1923*. Pittsburgh: University of Pittsburgh Press, 1969.

Pusey, Merlo. *Charles Evans Hughes*. Vol. 2. New York: Macmillan, 1951.

Schuker, Stephen A. *The End of French Predominance in Europe: The Financial Crisis of 1924 and the Adoption of the Dawes Plan*. Chapel Hill: University of North Carolina Press, 1976.

Simonds, Frank H. *Can Americans Stay at Home?* New York: Harper and Brothers, 1932.

Sklar, Robert. *Movie-Made America*. New York: Random House, 1975.

Southard, Frank A., Jr. *American Industry in Europe*. Boston: Houghton Mifflin, 1931.

Sprout, Harold, and Sprout, Margaret. *Toward a New Order of Sea Power: American Naval Policy and the World Scene, 1918-1922*. Princeton: Princeton University Press, 1940.

Susman, Warren I. "The Expatriate Image." In Cushing Strout, ed., *Intellectual History in America: From Darwin to Niebuhr*. Vol. 2. New York: Harper and Row, 1968.

Tate, Merze. *The United States and Armaments*. Cambridge: Harvard University Press, 1948.

Viallate, Achille. *Economic Imperialism and International Relations during the Last Fifty Years*. New York: Macmillan, 1923.

————. *Les Finances américains, 1789-1922*. Paris: Société d'études et d'informations économiques, 1923.

————. *Le monde économique, 1918-1927*. Paris: Marcel Rivière, 1928.

Viorst, Milton. *Hostile Allies: F. D. R. and Charles de Gaulle*. New York: Macmillan, 1965.

Wilkins, Mira. *The Maturing of Multinational Enterprises: American Business Abroad from 1914 to 1970*. Cambridge: Harvard University Press, 1974.

Williams, Benjamin H. *Economic Foreign Policy of the United States*. New York: McGraw-Hill, 1929.

Williams, Francis. *The American Invasion*. New York: Crown, 1962.

Wilson, Joan Hoff. *American Business and Foreign Policy, 1920-1933*. Lexington: University Press of Kentucky, 1971.

Wolfers, Arnold. *Britain and France between Two Wars: Conflicting Strategies of Peace from Versailles to World War II*. New York: W. W. Norton, 1966 (1940).

Zahniser, Martin. *Uncertain Friendship: American-French Diplomatic Relations Through the Cold War*. New York: Wiley, 1975.

# Index

## ABOUT THE AUTHOR

**David Strauss** teaches in the Department of History at Kalamazoo College, Kalamazoo, Michigan. He was Fulbright Visiting Professor at the University of Lyon in 1970-71, and has published in the *American Quarterly*, the *American Studies Journal*, and the *Journal of Popular Culture*.